Y0-BVN-344

Socially Responsible IT Management

Socially Responsible IT Management

Michael Erbschloe

HD
60
.E73
2003
West

Digital Press

An imprint of Elsevier Science
Amsterdam • Boston • London • New York • Oxford • Paris • San Diego
San Francisco • Singapore • Sydney • Tokyo

Digital Press is an imprint of Elsevier Science.

Copyright © 2003 by Elsevier Science (USA). All rights reserved.

No part of this publication may be reproduced, stored in a retrieval system, or transmitted in any form or by any means, electronic, mechanical, photocopying, recording, or otherwise, without the prior written permission of the publisher.

 Recognizing the importance of preserving what has been written, Elsevier Science prints its books on acid-free paper whenever possible.

Library of Congress Cataloging-in-Publication Data

ISBN 1-55558-290-7

British Library Cataloguing-in-Publication Data

A catalogue record for this book is available from the British Library.

The publisher offers special discounts on bulk orders of this book.
For information, please contact:

Manager of Special Sales
Elsevier Science
200 Wheeler Road
Burlington, MA 01803
Tel: 781-313-4700
Fax: 781-313-4882

For information on all Digital Press publications available, contact our World Wide Web home page at: http://www.digitalpress.com or http://www.bh.com/digitalpress

10   9   8   7   6   5   4   3   2   1

Printed in the United States of America

To my mother
To High-Tech Tonya

Contents

12 Organizing for Socially Responsible Information Technology Management   **321**

13 The Future of Socially Responsible Information Technology Management   **333**

Index   **343**

Foreword

There are many interest groups that tout their perspectives on the social impact of information technology. Some claim that the end of privacy has come. Others fear the government's use of computers to control the population and the economy. Addressing issues of social responsibility in information technology has been a long and complicated process. The one thing that we can count on for sure is that computers are here to stay. What we need to address is a varied and complex group of issues to mitigate, as much as possible, negative consequences for people, organizations, and the environment.

The interest groups of the world will battle endlessly to convince legislators, managers, and voters that their cause is the most important. This book brings balance to the many perspectives on social responsibility and information technology and identifies ten principles, which, if applied, can help meet some very critical responsibilities.

Another problem when dealing with the issue of social responsibility in any realm of life is how to achieve it. Just how can individuals and organizations meet their social responsibilities? In practical terms this book shows how to get organized and what specific steps can be taken to apply the ten principles of socially responsible information technology management. These steps are not complicated, and most organizations will not find it difficult to move rapidly ahead in applying the principles.

A large obstacle to achieving any type of social responsibility is the need to convince people and organizations that they can actually benefit from their actions. So many causes are advanced in terms of nobility alone and thus become actions that make people feel good about themselves. This book shows, in economic terms, how people and organizations can benefit from applying the ten principles.

The combination of practicality, ease of implementation, and positive return on investment is what makes this book work so well. The easy-to-implement action steps make dealing with these ten social responsibilities something that is almost as easy as buckling your seat belt when you get into an automobile.

—Brandon L. Harris

Preface

Information technology is pervasive in most industrial nations, and it is quickly taking hold around the world. The rapid growth of technology usage has been fueled by the expansion of the Internet, which, in a few short years, has added hundreds of thousands of newcomers to the computer-using population. This has made the challenge of managing information technology go far beyond the physical act of acquiring equipment and software and making a computer operate.

This book addresses issues that did not exist in the 1950s, when computers first started making their way into organizations. These new issues are rooted in organizational dynamics, social processes, personal beliefs, and environmental consequences. As with the emergence of industrial manufacturing and petroleum-powered transportation, computers have become so widely used that they are starting to impact entire societies and nations.

Regulation and social responsibility came slowly to industry and transportation. It took well over 100 years to begin to address the environmental blight and pollution that industrial manufacturing causes. A global solution to the negative impact of industrialization is still far off in the future. The regulation of automobiles and the establishment of product liability for them was a hard-fought struggle, starting in the 1950s. It took nearly four decades of advocacy to achieve safer, less polluting automobiles, and fuel efficiency is still elusive.

Governments have been very lax when it comes to regulating information technology manufacturers. This is partially because computers are the new technology and regulators are uncertain how to go about determining the negative impact of the technology, let alone devising ways to mitigate that impact. In addition, many people believe that information technology is one of the major driving forces behind economic growth, and under current economic conditions no government wants to stand in the way of economic growth.

Unlike industrialization and transportation, the execution of social responsibility in the management of information technology will rest largely on the owners and users of the technology and not the manufacturers. The producers of computers and related equipment do face some social responsibility, including creating ergonomic designs, making systems that are easily recycled, and addressing energy efficiency. But these manufacturers have been slow to respond.

Addressing the issues of privacy, system and data security, virus protection, staffing, training users, intellectual property management, assuring ergonomic environments for users, and recycling old equipment have, for the most part, been deemed the user's responsibility.

The purpose of this book is to help managers in all sizes of businesses become aware of how information technology is negatively impacting societies and to provide practical steps to mitigate those impacts. Socially responsible information technology management is quickly becoming a requirement rather than just a noble option.

Acknowledgments

The Digital Press team that worked on this book provided outstanding comments and input on the book. They did a great job.

I also want to acknowledge my associates at Computer Economics for their support. Peter Daley, president of Computer Economics supported the project and the process of socially responsible information technology management. Peter also gave permission to use the Computer Economics research to illustrate the value of the socially responsible information technology management process. Anne Zalatan, vice president of Computer Economics, should be acknowledged for her ongoing support of my research and various endeavors.

In addition, I want to acknowledge my professional and personal associates for their never-ending input and support, starting with Brandon L. Harris, a true philosopher of technology, who has contributed to much of my work over the years. Brandon always manages to look at things from a unique perspective. Tonya Heartfield is an extreme computer geek who anonymously wanders the corridors of cyberspace and always brings me back something interesting. Tonya, like myself, started programming computers at a young age and grew to understand the technical, social, political, and economic aspects of information technology from a variety of perspectives. Brandon and Tonya have helped to bring out my best thoughts and analyses.

Finally, I want to acknowledge my professional associates in the High Tech Crime Investigators Association, who have supported the process of socially responsible information technology management and helped to solidify the analyses that led to the writing of this book.

Introduction

This book analyzes the need for and the process of implementing ten principles of socially responsible information technology management. The author has analyzed the impact of technology on society as well as social trends that impact technology development for more than 30 years. The ten principles of socially responsible information technology management can be summarized as the following actions:

- Appropriately staff IT departments
- Fairly compensate IT workers
- Adequately train computer users
- Provide ergonomic user environments
- Maintain secure and virus-free computer systems
- Safeguard the privacy of information
- Ethically manage intellectual property
- Utilize energy-efficient technology
- Properly recycle used computer equipment
- Support efforts to reduce the digital divide

Throughout this book the principles of socially responsible information technology management are explained, along with ways to achieve goals, justify expenditures, and show how implementing the principles can result in cost avoidance and reduce exposure to liability.

An overview of how the ten principles were formulated and why they are important is provided in Chapter 1. Each principle is then explored in Chapters 2 through 11. The background of each principle is examined, and supporting information as to the importance of each principle is provided, along with methods to analyze the economic benefits that can be gained by adhering to the principle. Practical, actionable steps are provided in each chapter to help managers develop their own approaches to developing needed solutions.

It is critical to establish policies and to set up an organizational assignment of responsibility for implementing the procedures. In many cases several departments in an organization will play a role in implementing the different principles. Chapter 12 provides a high-level view of how to organize and assign responsibilities to achieve goals in each area of social responsibility. Chapter 12 shows which department is best equipped to handle which tasks and recommends a division of labor for achieving socially responsible information technology management. The importance of internal and external public relations is also explored, along with the role of senior managers.

Chapter 13 discusses the type of actions on the part of government and manufacturers needed to address socially responsible information technology management and when those actions will occur. Chapter 13 also examines forces that drive change, and major events that have led to improving socially responsible management of information technology.

Future events that drive home the need for socially responsible information technology management are easily predictable. But predictions do not always prompt social action. On the other hand, once bitten—or sometimes two or three times—societies do respond. This is fortunate in some ways; it is better to respond late than never to respond at all.

How long it will take to achieve socially responsible information technology management is not predictable. However, the need for socially responsible information technology management is undeniable at this point. Hopefully the events that prompt action will not take an extremely high human toll.

A look at what future events may occur and the expected impact of these events is also provided in Chapter 13.

Questions or comments about the book should be directed to the author, Michael Erbschloe, at michael@compecon.com.

An Overview of Socially Responsible Information Technology Management

I do not fear computers. I fear lack of them.

—Isaac Asimov

The rapid growth in the numbers of organizations and people using computers, combined with global connectivity, brought with it many new information technology management challenges. Many people feel that information technology (IT) has gotten out of control; and in some ways they may be right. However, most organizations in the world now depend on information technology, and that dependency will only increase in the future. The central proposition of this book is that exercising greater social responsibility can help control the potential negative impact of information technology on society and help organizations avoid the many potential liabilities that are emerging as we move further into the digital age.

1.1   How did we get where we are?

Electronic computing was first launched in the early 1950s, making the industry and the practice about 50 years old. What we view as end-user or personal computing got off the drawing board in the late 1970s and by the middle 1980s was in full swing, making it about 25 years old. Networked computing started becoming popular in the late 1980s and by the middle of the 1990s was standard in most organizations, making it about 15 years old. The Internet, although in limited use since the early 1970s, boomed in the middle 1990s with the creation of the browser and by 2000 was a global phenomenon, making it less than ten years old. These events all represented major shifts in computing practices and brought with them a new and unique set of problems.

To overcome these problems will require far more socially responsible behavior on the part of technology producers, governments, and computer users. This chapter summarizes the ten principles of socially responsible information technology. Subsequent chapters provide in-depth analysis of the principles and recommend specific action steps that can help address specific problems.

1.2   The ten principles of socially responsible IT management

There is no magic involved in identifying the issues that individuals, organizations, and societies face as a result of the rapid growth of information technology. The ten principles of socially responsible information technology management are as follows:

- Appropriately staff IT departments
- Fairly compensate IT workers
- Adequately train computer users
- Provide ergonomic user environments
- Maintain secure and virus-free computer systems
- Safeguard the privacy of information
- Ethically manage intellectual property
- Utilize energy-efficient technology
- Properly recycle used computer equipment
- Support efforts to reduce the digital divide

The ten principles of socially responsible IT management proposed in this book will not satisfy every critic, and they are not meant to. The ten principles are designed to help mitigate the negative impacts of information technology. The principles, along with action steps needed to apply the principles, were derived through the following process.

1.2.1   Step one: Establishing a mindset

In formulating the ten principles the first and most basic step was to establish a mindset. Acceptance that computers and the Internet are here to stay and that deliberate social action would be required to mitigate negative impacts is essential. In addition, the manufacturers of IT products will only do so much to help you address the problems that are inherent in IT. Unlike the automobile and pharmaceutical industries, for example, the IT industry is unregulated and is relatively free of product liability.

1.2.2   Step two: Identify and categorize problems

The next step was to identify and categorize the problems that individuals, organizations, and societies face and group them into areas that are addressable through existing management structures.

1.2.3   Step three: Formulate basic principles

The principles had to be easy to communicate and easy to understand. They also had to be intuitive within the context of contemporary society.

1.2.4   Step four: Problem grouping

The fourth step was to group problems and issues that can be addressed by applying each of the ten principles.

1.2.5   Step five: Develop actionable methods

The final step was to provide actionable and workable methods that individuals with a wide range of skills could readily employ.

1.3   Principle one: Appropriately staff IT departments

If IT departments and functions are not appropriately staffed, an organization puts itself at risk in many ways. These include greater vulnerability to security breaches, poorly functioning equipment, improper intellectual property management, and inadequately performing applications. Regardless of how well an organization assigns job functions or trains individual employees, failure remains imminent unless the workload of IT workers is well balanced and humane. Burnout and boredom are two of the most frequent social psychological diseases suffered by IT workers.

Burnout comes from long hours, excessive overtime, and stress. Keeping an IT worker in the same job too long and not having enough workers to adequately cover tasks and meet job or service level-requirements will burn out IT workers very quickly. Boredom comes from repetition of work or performing tasks that do not challenge the intellectual and development desires of an individual employee.

Both burnout and boredom lead to more frequent mistakes and reduced tolerance of coworkers and end users; they can also eventually result in depression. All of these conditions have their effect on the performance of an individual. If such conditions are widespread in an IT department, the performance of the entire department will deteriorate. A balanced working life also requires a large dose of humanity. It is humanity that gives social meaning to work.

In addition, adequate staffing can eliminate single points of failure, which can occur when there are not enough IT staff trained to maintain mission-critical systems. When, for example, there is only one person who totally understands an application, network, or system configuration, an organization becomes more vulnerable to failures or outages when that person is ill, on vacation, or leaves the organization.

Chapter 2 examines several significant challenges that managers face when recruiting and retaining IT professionals, including the following:

- Developing a professional work environment
- Hiring the right people for a workplace
- Aligning job responsibilities with IT worker skills
- Evaluating and mentoring IT workers
- Professional development of IT workers
- Balancing the workload of IT workers
- Evaluating staffing needs

1.4   Principle two: Fairly compensate IT workers

Establishing a fair compensation plan for IT employees can mitigate turnover and the loss of key personnel. A 20-percent reduction in turnover in an IT department can save hundreds of thousands of dollars in recruitment cost. Reduced turnover can also help keep projects on schedule, because work will not be disrupted when staff leaves and replacements must be recruited and brought up to speed on a project. Fairly compensated workers are also more highly motivated and will work more diligently to address security, privacy, and performance issues facing all organizations.

Compensation plans are not easy for many IT departments to develop. There are often corporate policies or procedures set by the human resources department that prove to be obstacles. Large IT departments often have human resources specialists to assist in developing compensation plans.

However, the vast majority of IT departments have less than 100 people and usually do not have such internal support.

One issue in compensation planning is how to pay IT professionals for on-call time. Computer Economics, an independent research organization based in Carlsbad, California, which focuses on helping IT executives control and manage their IT costs, has studied service-level requirements for several years and found that data centers are providing longer service periods and many face 7/24 uptime requirements. Although night shifts and weekends may not require full staffing levels, networks and applications still need to be available to a growing workforce of telecommuters and flex-time workers outside the IT department.

Even when IT professionals do not have to respond to incidents when they are on call, the revolving responsibility for on-call sharing does impact their personal and family lives. Many organizations ignore this point. However, extensive on-call requirements and the resulting disruption of social life will contribute to burnout and to turnover rates. Thus, adequately compensating for on-call time may very well not cost as much as recruiting and training new staff because of high turnover rates.

Chapter 3 analyzes several significant challenges that managers face when establishing fair compensation plans for IT professionals, including the following:

- Developing competitive compensation plans

- Assuring equal pay regardless of gender

- Providing adequate compensation for overtime and holiday hours

- Adequately compensating employees for on-call time

- Appropriately linking compensation to performance

1.5   Principle three: Adequately train computer users

Companies are now spending more on employee training, and e-learning has reached its highest level since 1997, according to the 2002 State of the Industry Report from the American Society for Training and Development (ASTD). Training expenditures for many organizations did not decline with the economic downturn; in fact, companies expected spending on training to grow a healthy 10 percent between 2000 and 2001.

Training computer users is an important step in assuring that an organization gets the best return on investment from its information technology. Chapter 4 analyzes many of the positive results achieved from adequately training users. These include the following:

- Users feel more confident and will try new approaches to completing tasks.

- Users have a better understanding of what information technology can do for the organization.

- Help-desk calls for simple problem solving decline, allowing support staff to spend time on more critical issues.

- Coworkers are not coerced into providing support to undertrained users and will be able to accomplish more on their jobs.

- Accidental security breaches can be reduced.

- Incidents of viruses entering a corporate network can be reduced when users are trained on basic prevention skills.

1.6   Principle four: Provide ergonomic user environments

Even though the current Republican Congress dismantled federal ergonomic requirements established by the Democrats when Bill Clinton was in office, ergonomics remains a critical issue. Furthermore, problems are likely to mount in the future. Within two decades the negative impact of poorly designed office furniture and poorly conceived information technology will result in considerable economic impact on individuals, corporations, the government, and ultimately the taxpayer.

The threat of litigation and the filing of widespread worker's compensation claims are forcing companies to find remedies for the poor ergonomics of standardized off-the-shelf IT products. We estimate that end-user companies will spend over $3.5 billion by 2005 in addressing IT ergonomic issues. To determine how large corporations are dealing with this problem, Computer Economics conducted a focus group of 16 companies that reported that they had remedies in place.

All focus group participants reported that they have had worker's compensation claims filed as a result of IT ergonomics issues. Each of the focus group companies have had on-demand ergonomic assistance for their employees in place for at least two years.

The on-demand approach provides employees with assistance in evaluating their needs and selecting appropriate products to ease the strain they experience when using IT equipment. The group reported a wide variety of methods for providing on-demand services. These included telephone hotlines, e-mail request systems, and walk-in showcase centers where employees can test-drive IT products designed to provide more comfort and to help minimize IT-related worker injuries.

Chapter 5 analyzes how organizations are addressing ergonomic issues.

1.7   Principle five: Maintain secure and virus-free computer systems

All IT managers would agree that protecting their IT resources against security breaches is a necessity, but many are not willing to commit to the continual effort required. Without adequate security, the organization is open to a variety of risks, all of which are detrimental to the bottom line.

Based on Computer Economics' projections, the likelihood that an organization will be hit with a security attack is growing. Computer crime will grow by an estimated 230 percent during 2002. Similar trends are expected with Internet fraud, which will grow over 100 percent, and viruses, which will increase by 22 percent during the same period. These statistics are even more disturbing than they first appear, because the data used as the basis for these projections are probably underreported. According to government and industry sources, only about 20 percent of computer security violations are actually reported.

A firm foundation is required to develop satisfactory security protection, and that foundation is an organizational security policy that covers all the necessary contingencies. Among those contingencies are procedures for installing applications, e-mail and Internet practices, IT user policies, password protection, downloading data considerations, and network monitoring. The policy must provide a plan for responding to security attacks, and that plan must be rehearsed through dry runs and other simulation methods.

Virus and other malicious code attacks are growing in number and so is the cost incurred by companies, government organizations, and private individuals to clean up systems and get them back into working order. In 2001 it cost computer users $13.2 billion in lost productivity to clean up after virus attacks. Incidents such as the "I Love You" virus outbreak shut down systems around the world and had an estimated economic impact of $8.75 billion.

In a highly connected world, computers are more vulnerable to attacks and hacks. In addition, having computers connected to the Internet requires social responsibility similar to that required when operating a vehicle on the city streets, including meeting safety and pollution guidelines.

Chapter 6 analyzes the process of improving security and better protecting your systems from virus infections.

1.8 Principle six: Safeguard the privacy of information

Maintaining the privacy of enterprise information is a meticulous process, one that requires coordination across all departments and functions within an organization. It is important that everyone on the privacy management team understand the basic issues and concepts of privacy management as well as enterprise policies and procedures. An understanding of the basic issues and concepts will help managers make operational decisions about privacy during the day-to-day course of events. It also enables them to more fully participate in formulating policies and procedures.

Unfortunately, the definition of privacy is not straightforward. There are cultural, societal, political, legal, and national viewpoints as to what privacy is and what constitutes a violation of privacy. Thus, it is important to establish an operational definition of privacy in an enterprise. A strong definition of privacy will help prevent inadequate interpretations of policies and procedures as well as poor decisions regarding the privacy of information when there is a lack of specific procedures covering specific incidents or information elements.

When organizations exchange information to help facilitate business processes, the importance of privacy has been fairly well established and has become customary. An organization wants its information kept confidential to prevent damage that may occur if the information was obtained by competitors or other parties that could use the information to negatively impact the competitive position or the well-being of the information-providing company. The provider of the information has a public image to protect, and the misuse of confidential information could result in bad publicity. In the case of publicly held companies, improper dissemination of proprietary information could negatively impact stock value.

Individuals who provide information to businesses or government organizations can also be negatively impacted by the misuse of information. Such misuse may impact their jobs, career choices, and lifetime earnings.

An individual who is gay or lesbian may choose to keep this information private in order to avoid having to deal with potential social or financial negative consequences. People who are making investment decisions, who are considering changing jobs, or who have decided to divorce may suffer damages from the release of information related to their lives or their plans.

The common thread linking the privacy of proprietary corporate information and personal data provided by individuals is that the improper dissemination and use of such information can cause damage. In some cases the damage could be financial, whereas in other cases it could damage reputations.

Chapter 7 analyzes why companies need to be concerned about privacy, potential privacy problems in different sectors, and how to take steps to protect privacy.

1.9   Principle seven: Ethically manage intellectual property

The challenge that businesses face in managing intellectual property has greatly increased during the past decade. Some companies have been caught deliberately violating copyright laws. There have been many cases in which management was unaware that laws were being broken. Cases of carelessness or independent, unauthorized acts by employees can put an organization in jeopardy.

The Software and Information Industry Association (SIIA) and KPMG LLP released a report in November 2001 entitled "Doesn't Everybody Do It? Internet Piracy Attitudes and Behaviors." The survey, conducted to examine the acquisition and use of software and digital content via the Internet, found that nearly 30 percent of business people could be described as pirating software through a variety of electronic methods.

Of the 1,004 business people surveyed, more than half said that they were unaware of corporate policies governing intellectual property that may be in place. According to the study, 54 percent of business users indicated that they do not know whether it is permissible to redistribute information from on-line sites they subscribe to, while 23 percent said that they believe it is permitted.

According to the study, most users of Internet content and software products said they were unaware of the proper legal use of such products, yet roughly seven out of ten (69.5 percent) reported that they used the

Internet to acquire software and 22 percent subscribe to business information services.

Chapter 8 analyzes processes to help organizations better manage intellectual property and reduce their exposure to potential litigation.

1.10   Principle eight: Utilize energy-efficient technology

ENERGY STAR was introduced by the U.S. Environmental Protection Agency (EPA) in 1992 as a voluntary labeling program designed to identify and promote energy-efficient products, in order to reduce carbon dioxide emissions. The EPA partnered with the U.S. Department of Energy in 1996 to promote the ENERGY STAR label, with each agency taking responsibility for particular product categories. ENERGY STAR has expanded to cover new homes, most of the buildings sector, residential heating and cooling equipment, major appliances, office equipment, lighting, and consumer electronics.

If all consumers, businesses, and organizations in the United States made their product choices and building improvement decisions with ENERGY STAR during the next decade, the national annual energy bill would be reduced by about $200 billion. With that would come a sizable contribution to reducing air pollution and protecting the global climate.

A business can save from $7 to $52 per year on utility bills by using ENERGY STAR–labeled computers. ENERGY STAR–labeled computers automatically power down to 15 watts or less when not in use and may actually last longer than conventional products because they spend a large portion of time in a low-power sleep mode. ENERGY STAR–labeled computers also generate less heat than conventional models. Upgrading your existing equipment to ENERGY STAR can lead to reduced cooling costs.

Chapter 9 explains how to go about the process of purchasing and managing IT equipment to reduce energy costs and ease the strain on the environment.

1.11   Principle nine: Properly recycle used computer equipment

As the glut of high-tech junk accumulates, businesses are facing increasing pressure to properly dispose of obsolete computer hardware. In addition to compromising the environment, improper disposal of obsolete computer hardware can result in leakage of proprietary company information and violation of new federal privacy laws that ban the disclosure of nonpublic financial and medical information about employees and customers.

Chapter 10, explains how to develop and maintain a proper disposal program for old technology equipment. Alternatives include recycling, destruction of equipment, and contributions to charity.

1.12   Principle ten: Support efforts to reduce the digital divide

There are numerous compelling reasons why IT managers and companies that are dependent on IT should support efforts to decrease the digital divide. First and foremost, full participation in life in the information age requires computer literacy and Internet access. Computer-literate people are more likely to:

- Have an interest in IT-related careers

- Require less on-the-job training

- Contribute higher value to their employers

- Shop on-line

- Participate in e-government

- Raise computer-literate children

In February 2002, the U.S. Department of Commerce released a report entitled "A NATION ONLINE: How Americans Are Expanding Their Use of the Internet." IT professionals need to be concerned about the digital divide, because this division will likely reduce the number of people who will be interested in IT careers. Businesses that are now or are planning in the future to market or sell on-line need to be concerned about the digital divide because it narrows their potential customer base.

The study determined that there is a sizable segment of the U.S. population (as of September 2001, 46.1 percent of persons and 49.5 percent of households) that does not use the Internet. This illustrates just how big the digital divide is and could serve as a prediction of how many people will grow up with little interest in entering the IT workforce.

Chapter 11 analyzes the need for addressing the digital divide, what IT professionals have done in the past, and new opportunities they may have in the future.

1.13 How the ten principles interlock

The independent treatment of the ten principles in this book allows for an easy understanding of the related issues and the actions required to mitigate the potentially negative consequences of not taking action. However, there are many ways that the ten principles are interrelated.

- Principles one and two—appropriately staff IT departments and fairly compensate IT workers—are interrelated. It will be difficult to appropriately staff IT departments if IT staff are not fairly compensated. In addition, the viewpoint of IT staff toward fairness in compensation will be impacted by their workload and how well IT departments are staffed.

- Appropriately staffed IT departments are also necessary to maintain secure and virus-free computer systems, safeguard the privacy of information, and ethically manage intellectual property. All of these require time, resources, and talent.

- A lack of adequate training for computer users (principle three) in an organization impacts the workload of the IT department because help-desk inquiries in organizations in which training is lacking are more numerous and more frustrating.

- The proper recycling of used computer equipment helps to reduce problems in security, privacy, and intellectual property management.

- Ergonomic user environments can reduce stress and result in greater productivity from a workforce. Reduced stress also improves the viewpoint of employees toward the organization they work for and their level of compensation.

The interrelationships can be compiled numerous ways. The key thing to remember is that adhering to some of the principles will improve operations or reduce potential liability. However, taking a more holistic approach and adhering to as many of the ten principles as possible will yield far greater results, because each of the principles helps to reduce vulnerabilities that may ultimately erode progress made in one area.

1.14   The awareness of socially responsible IT management will continue to evolve

When dealing with a new technology, industrial process, or business practice, it is often the case that organizations first look at the benefits and eventually become aware of the unanticipated problems that inevitably surface.

The industrial revolution resulted in massive pollution and often unsafe working conditions. Both were addressed by legislation over a long period of time. We are just beginning to understand some of the social and legal problems that are inherent in information technology. There has already been considerable legislation to address some of the problems, and subsequent legislation will address them in a more thorough and satisfactory manner.

For the time being, however, applying social responsibility to information technology is largely a personal and organizational decision. This book does not just preach social responsibility. It specifies action steps that can be taken by managers and shows how those steps may end up saving money or avoiding future costs.

2

Principle One: Appropriately Staff IT Departments

The military machine—the army and everything related to it—is basically very simple and therefore seems easy to manage. But we should bear in mind that none of its components is of one piece; each piece is composed of individuals, every one of whom retains his potential of friction. . . . A battalion is made up of individuals, the least important of whom may chance to delay things or somehow make them go wrong.

—Karl von Clausewitz

2.1 Coping with the IT staffing challenge

Since 1990 Computer Economics has conducted an annual benchmarking study, which includes an analysis of IT staffing patterns and trends. Using this analysis Computer Economics has worked with client organizations around the world to address staffing issues and to plan appropriate IT staffing levels. During the course of this work Computer Economics has helped managers deal with many complex IT human resources issues.

Personnel is generally the highest expense item in an IT department's budget, comprising about 40 percent of the average budget. Recruiting costs for new, highly skilled staff can readily exceed $25,000 per person. The turnover rate for a CIO is about 25 percent per year; for other IT positions it can range from 5 percent to 15 percent per year. It is clear that personnel management in IT departments deserves attention and can be the focus of cost control efforts.

Computer Economics has identified several significant challenges that managers face when recruiting and retaining IT professionals, including the following:

- Developing a professional work environment
- Hiring the right people for a workplace
- Aligning job responsibilities with IT worker skills
- Evaluating and mentoring IT workers
- Professional development of IT workers
- Balancing the workload of IT workers
- Evaluate staffing needs

Many CIOs have participated in Computer Economics' surveys and focus groups over the last decade. Personnel management, though not an exciting topic, is an area that CIOs have always expressed considerable frustration about.

In a 1997 focus group a CIO from a Midwest manufacturing company said, "The technology we can figure out, we even manage to eventually determine what the enduser wants, but nailing down what it takes to retain and keep our people happy has been a constantly moving target."

In a 2001 focus group a CIO from an East Coast wholesaler said, "Anybody who thinks that it is hard to keep up with the speed of change in technology has never had the experience of managing an IT staff; people and what they want are constantly changing."

2.1.1 Developing a professional work environment

IT departments and IT workers suffer from most of the same workplace trials and tribulations that other types of employees face. Hiring freezes, downsizing, outsourcing, layoffs, extensive overtime, stress, depression, and alienation are all part of the IT professional's working life. IT managers can in no way control the economy and in most cases cannot mitigate irrational business decisions made by corporate managers. This, however, does not leave an IT department a helpless victim in the cosmic flow of economic disorder or the onslaught of organizational derailments or meltdowns.

Developing a professional work environment for IT professionals starts with a basic philosophy that recognizes both their needs and the goals of the organization. This philosophy and the axioms that guide the management of an IT department should be embodied in a mission statement that publicly declares the expectations of employees as well as the responsibilities of the department in maintaining professional standards.

Such philosophies and mission statements are not a remnant of bleeding-heart liberalism. They are a practical necessity in an organization's effort to recruit and retain professionals in a social and economic environment that is underproducing a much-needed workforce and skill base. Study after study has shown that there is a shortage of IT workers and warns that this shortage is not going to decline over the next decade.

It is thus socially logical that an organization should develop a professional environment for IT staff to work, learn, and grow. The logical consequence of not doing so will likely be felt by those organizations that fail to do so. IT is not going away, nor will it be less widely used. Organizations that can successfully deploy this technology will succeed, while those who do not will likely perish. The practical consequence of a well-thought philosophy and mission statement is that it will help to facilitate recruiting and retaining staff and set the foundation to appropriately staffing an IT department.

2.1.2　Hiring the right people for a workplace

Hiring the right people in any type of organization is a fundamental human resource challenge. When hiring IT professionals, there are several elements to be considered. However, skill set is most often considered the highest priority in staff selection. It is certainly practical to consider skill sets, but there are also other factors that will influence whether or not a new hire will be successful in an organization. When hiring, the following questions should be addressed:

- Does the candidate adhere to the basic philosophies and mission statement of the IT department?

- Is the candidate willing to work in a team-oriented environment?

- Does the candidate have a strong understanding of IT fundamentals?

- Can the candidate complement the skill sets of existing employees?

- Is the candidate willing to be trained in new technologies?

- Will the candidate learn and grow with the department?

- Can the candidate sustain an interest in IT over a long period of time?

- Does the candidate really want to work for the organization?

2.1.3   Aligning job responsibilities with IT worker skills

It is a challenge to manage people and it is even more of a challenge to manage talented and intelligent people who are always pushing themselves to learn more and to accomplish more. It is still important to assure that IT workers are assigned job responsibilities that they are clearly capable of accomplishing. This may very well put managers in a position where they are viewed as holding people back. It is a delicate but critical balance.

Many projects have fallen behind because the IT staff assigned to the project did not have adequate skills or appropriate motivation. In other cases, because of turnover or staff shortages, IT staff have been rapidly promoted into areas of responsibility for which they were not prepared. Real-world pressures of resource management can often result in less than optimal staff assignments.

To properly assign staff to positions requires that a position is thoroughly documented and that the skill set necessary to accomplish required tasks be clearly understood. This may appear to add an unwanted element of bureaucracy to an IT department. But the balance between skills and desire must be maintained. This takes us back to establishing a basic philosophy of how an IT department is managed. If rules are clear about staff assignments, then there will less confusion and fewer people with hurt feelings and bruised egos when staff assignments are made.

During the last five years, for example, conflict over which staff would work on new ecommerce applications was commonplace in IT departments. This conflict was often splattered across an organization. Fortunately, things have settled down on this front. It is clear that the IT department will play a key role in ecommerce, and skill sets of employees have significantly evolved. We have seen repeats of this dynamic as each new technology rolls out. However, we should not forget the lessons of the past as we move into the future.

2.1.4   Evaluating and mentoring IT workers

To facilitate aligning job responsibilities with IT worker skills it is essential that there be strong performance evaluation and assessment processes in place. One of the most serious problems in establishing strong evaluation processes is that many managers, supervisors, and project leaders are not properly trained to conduct performance evaluations. This is a back-to-basics issue that must be addressed.

Without strong performance evaluations, skill sets cannot be adequately determined. When skill sets are not adequately determined, the chances of inappropriate job assignments are higher. This in turn can spiral into the unnecessary frustration of employees as well as managers, supervisors, and project leaders. The following steps are recommended to help establish strong performance evaluation processes:

- All managers, supervisors, and project leaders should be trained in performance evaluation.

- Employees should be trained on how the performance evaluation process works.

- Evaluations should realistically address performance and be very specific about the employee's strengths and weaknesses.

- Required action steps to improve employee performance should be documented.

- Prior evaluations should be reviewed to determine how well both the employee and the organization have followed the action steps to improve performance.

- Performance evaluation should be an ongoing process and not happen just once per year.

- IT staff should be assigned mentors to help them develop skills and improve performance.

2.1.5   Professional development of IT workers

There are several important elements of the professional development process for IT workers. First, the professional development of IT workers should be approached from both the perspective of the organization and that of the individual. Second, professional development should also be tied to the performance evaluations of individual employees. Third, professional development needs to be an organized and ongoing process that is managed by a mentor.

The needs of the organization must be addressed over a long period of time. If new hires met the criteria previously outlined, then they will be interested in pursuing professional development and view it as an opportunity as well as a natural aspect of their employment. This means that as the IT products and applications of an organization evolve, IT workers will be trained in new areas and evolve along with the needs of the organization.

It is important to blend the needs of the individual and the organization. This can best be managed through the mentoring process, in which a senior staff person works with IT staff to determine development issues that must be addressed to improve performance. The basis of this determination is the ongoing performance evaluation of employee strengths and weaknesses.

It is also important to establish effective development approaches. In some cases, on-the-job training under an experienced staff person is the best approach to meet development goals. In other cases, computer-based training, in-house seminars and training sessions, college courses, or conference attendance will help meet development goals.

Many organizations have hired training managers to help to coordinate development efforts. However, training managers cannot take the place of a seasoned mentor. In cases where there are training managers, they should work in conjunction with mentors to help formulate an effective and well-directed training agenda for each employee.

In addition to helping to meet organization objectives and improve individual performance, ongoing professional development can improve morale and reduce turnover in IT staff.

All too often development is viewed as just a perk, especially in the case of conference attendance. That is a very narrow view of professional development and will eventually lead to conflict among staff. Professional development is not only an action, it is an inherent part of a philosophy and mission. IT workers will be the first to know when an organization is taking professional development seriously. Wisdom dictates both prudence and sincerity.

2.1.6   Balancing the workload of IT workers

Regardless of how well an organization selects new hires, conducts performance evaluations, assigns job functions, or develops individual employees, failure remains imminent unless the workload of IT workers is well balanced and humane. Burnout and boredom are two of the most frequent social psychological diseases suffered by IT workers.

A balanced working life also requires a large dose of humanity. It is humanity that gives social meaning to work. Individuals need to have their accomplishments celebrated. Teams need to be rewarded for their achievements. The entire IT department needs to be recognized for its contribution to the organization.

Again, wisdom dictates both prudence and sincerity. A balanced work-load and humane management is not an add-on when IT workers reach the burnout stage. It is fundamental in the philosophy and mission of the IT department or it will be viewed as a shallow attempt to appease the work-force and will be resented.

2.2   How to evaluate staffing needs

Appropriate staffing of IT departments is one of the ten principles of socially responsible IT management and is fundamental to organization success. Socially responsible IT management starts the first thing every morning and is practiced throughout the day. It is not something that is pulled off the shelf and applied when the going gets rough or when IT workers get upset.

One key action that helps in maintaining minimum staffing abilities is to compile an in-house knowledge base to serve as a catalog of skills needed and skills available in-house. This should be comprehensive and cover every skill area as well as the various skills of every IT employee. When there is a shortage of skilled employees to cover critical tasks, more employees should be cross-trained in the areas of the greatest weakness.

The knowledge base should also contain a history of all systems and applications. It usually contains fixes and resolutions to prior problems and events. If kept current, it can be a very productive source of information. It can also be very helpful in eliminating some of the problems that can occur when a key employee or support person leaves the organization.

Computer Economics has conducted annual studies of IT staffing and spending trends since 1990. The studies provide a benchmarking approach for organizations to compare their operations, staffing, and spending trends with other organizations. The following benchmarks are helpful in compar-ing your organization's staffing patterns and trends with those of other orga-nizations. When you find considerable variance from these numbers, you should do further investigation and always collect qualitative data from your staff through an interview process.

2.2.1   Sizing up your organization

The first step in dealing with adequate staffing is to determine, in general terms, how information technology intensive your organization may be when considering trends in your sector. The Information Technology

Intensity Index is a proprietary index established by Computer Economics to illustrate the relative importance of information technology among industry sectors. Factors considered in the Information Technology Intensity Index and an explanation of their importance are as follows:

- Computing power trends: Those sectors and organizations that are increasing their consumption of mainframe, midrange, and server power rank higher on the Information Technology Intensity Index, while those that are either decreasing their consumption or not increasing their consumption as rapidly as other organizations rank lower on the Index.

- IS budget changes: Those sectors and organizations that are increasing their IS spending on information technology rank higher on the Information Technology Intensity Index, while those that are either decreasing their spending or holding their spending steady relative to other organizations rank lower on the Index.

- Centralization of IT spending: Those organizationS that centralize spending and control of information technology assets rank higher on the Information Technology Intensity Index, while those that do not track or centralize 75 percent or more of their IT spending rank lower on the Index.

- Central IS budgets as a percent of revenue: Those organizations that spend larger amounts of their revenue on information technology rank higher on the Information Technology Intensity Index, while those that spend less rank lower on the Index.

- Central IS spending per employee: Those organizations that spend more per employee to provide IS support rank higher on the Information Technology Intensity Index, while those that spend less per employee rank lower on the Index.

- IS staffing mix: Those organizations that have a higher percentage of IT specialists and highly skilled technical people on their IS departmental staff rank higher on the Information Technology Intensity Index. This includes programmers, systems analysts and engineers, network engineers, e-commerce developers, and database specialists. Organizations with lower percentages of IT specialists on staff rank lower on the Index.

- IS staffing trends: Those organizations that are expanding their IS staff rank higher on the Information Technology Intensity Index, while those that are not expanding or are decreasing IS staff rank lower on the Index.

■ Technology acquisition plans: Those organizations that have buying plans for a range of technologies, including processors, networking equipment, and application and e-commerce software, rank higher on the Information Technology Intensity Index, while those that are not acquiring new products rank lower on the index.

■ Technology implementation status and e-business practices: Those organizations that are implementing or have in place Internet and e-commerce applications, telecommuting capabilities, and enterprise resource management or planning applications rank higher on the Information Technology Intensity Index, while those that are not implementing such applications rank lower on the index.

For 2002 the four top-ranked information technology–intensive sectors are insurance, banking and financial, retail distribution, and discrete manufacturing. The four lowest-ranked information technology–intensive sectors in 2002 are health care, state and local government, professional services, and utilities. It is important to note that the prevailing trend in all sectors is

Table 2.1   *Information Technology Intensity Index*

Industry Sector	2002 Intensity Score	2002 Ranking
Banking and Finance	84.9	2
Discrete Manufacturing	55.6	4
Health Care	10.4	12
Insurance	100.0	1
Process manufacturing	38.5	8
Professional services	14.2	10
Retail distribution	60.8	3
State and local government	13.9	11
Trade services	50.3	6
Transportation	51.2	5
Utilities	29.6	9
Wholesale distribution	40.8	7

Source: Computer Economics 2002 Information Systems and E-Business Spending Report

toward more computer use and more e-commerce use. Rankings in the Information Technology Intensity Index will change from year to year and are tied heavily to economic conditions and the momentum within an industry to adopt new technologies. Table 2.1 shows the relative information technology intensity of various sectors.

If your organization is in a sector that ranks high on the Information Technology Intensity Index, your situation may be more critical, but it is also likely that IT efforts are being managed better since the dependency on technology is so obvious. If your organization ranks lower, it does not mean that there are no problems to address. In fact, in organizations where the dependency on information technology is not so obvious awareness of staffing needs is often lower.

2.2.2 Evaluating the number of workers supported per IS employee

An applicable benchmark from the Computer Economics annual studies is the Workers Supported per IS Employee InfoTechMark. Table 2.2 presents the number of workers within the entire organization that each IS employee supports. This InfoTechMark serves as another measure of IS productivity. It is popular among IS managers because fluctuations in the total budget do not impact this measurement as much as they affect the IS spending as a percentage of the total budget InfoTechMark.

The lower quartile, median, and upper quartile are presented. The lower quartile (25th percentile) presents the lowest 25 percent of workers supported in all of the organizations, where 25 percent supported less than that amount. The median (50th percentile) is the level at which half of the organizations supported less and the remainder supported more. The upper quartile (75th percentile) presents the highest 25 percent of workers sup-

Table 2.2 *Workers Supported per IS Employee*

All Sectors	AnnuMark 2002	TriMark 1999 to 2001
25th percentile	7.0	5.3
Median	15.5	14.0
75th percentile	35.1	37.7

Source: Computer Economics 2002 Information Systems and E-Business Spending Report

ported in all of the organizations, where 25 percent supported more than that amount. Trends in the number of workers supported per IS employee in 2002 are:

■ The number of workers supported per IT employee is relatively stable compared with the prior three-year period. However, these trends vary considerably by industry sector.

■ At the 25th percentile 7.0 employees are supported by each IS staff person, which is an increase from 5.3 employees for the prior three-year period. Median companies have experienced the least dramatic shift and now have 15.5 employees supported per IS employee compared with 14.0 during the prior three-year period.

■ At the 75th percentile 35.1 workers are supported by each IS staff person in 2002 compared with 37.7 workers during the prior three-year period. We expect that the number of workers supported per IS employee will continue to bounce around because of shifts in the workforce.

2.2.3   Evaluating the IS staffing mix

Another important benchmark is the IS staffing mix InfoTechMark. Table 2.3 provides a breakdown by percentage for each major IS labor category. Results are presented for all sectors. The IS labor categories are top IS managers; e-commerce staff; network administrators (including intranets and the Internet); system operators (including job scheduler and supervisor); application programmers and system analysts (including project leader and supervisor); system engineers and technical specialists; system programmers (including leader and supervisor); database administrators (including supervisor); end-user support, training, and help-desk staff; documentation specialists (including supervisor); quality assurance/control staff (including supervisor); clerical support; PC technical support; data entry (including supervisor) staff; and other personnel. Trends in IS staffing mix in 2002 are:

■ Shifts in IT staffing are reflective of changes in technology and how technology is used to support business goals. Thus, there have been rather dramatic shifts over the last decade in the staffing patterns of IT organizations.

■ In 2002, e-commerce staff comprise 6.5 percent of the IT workers in an organization compared with 4.2 percent for the prior three-year period and significantly higher than the prior decade when very few organizations had e-commerce staff until 1998.

Table 2.3   *IS Staffing Mix InfoTechMark*

Job Function	AnnuMark 2002	TriMark 1999 to 2001
Data entry	1.4%	2.5%
Systems operators	9.5%	9.0%
Network administrators	9.7%	7.9%
PC technical support	6.3%	6.5%
Help desk	9.5%	8.4%
Systems engineering	4.8%	4.4%
Systems programmers	4.3%	4.7%
Database administration	3.4%	4.1%
Applications programmers	24.9%	30.6%
Documentation specialists	1.5%	1.7%
Quality assurance	2.5%	1.8%
E-commerce staff	6.5%	4.2%
IS managers/administrators	9.3%	6.9%
Clerical support	3.2%	3.5%
Other	3.5%	4.0%

Source: Computer Economics 2002 Information Systems and E-Business Spending Report

- The number of IT managers has risen over the last decade and now comprises only 9.3 percent of the IT staff compared with 6.9 percent for the prior three-year period.

- Applications programmers have also declined; they make up 24.9 percent of the IT staff in 2002 compared with 30.6 for the prior three-year period.

2.2.4   Evaluating the use of contractor/temporary personnel

It is also helpful to examine the use of contractor/temporary personnel as a percentage of total IS staff. Table 2.4 compares the number of contractor and temporary staff with the total staff in the information systems department.

Table 2.4   *Use of Contractor/Temporary Personnel as a Percentage of*
Total IS staff InfoTechMark

All Sectors	AnnuMark 2002	TriMark 1999 to 2001
25th percentile	0.5%	3.0%
Median	3.9%	10.6%
75th percentile	16.4%	20.3%

Source: Computer Economics 2002 Information Systems and
E-Business Spending Report

The results are provided for all sectors. The data are presented for the lower quartile, median, and upper quartile. The lower quartile (25th percentile) presents the lowest 25 percent of contractor/temporary personnel used by all of the organizations, where 25 percent used less than that amount. The median (50th percentile) is the level at which half of the organizations used less and the remainder used more. The upper quartile (75th percentile) presents the highest 25 percent of contractor/temporary personnel used by all of the organizations, where 25 percent used more than that amount.

The use of contractor and temporary IS personnel as a percentage of all IT workers in an organization has plummeted with the economic downturn. At all percentiles, the percent of contractor and temporary employees has fallen dramatically compared with prior periods.

2.2.5   Getting the viewpoints of your employees

Benchmarks are a good starting point in evaluating your staffing needs and patterns. However, it is very important that IS employees have an opportunity to state their viewpoints. Your primary concern should be to identify trouble spots or weak points. Discussing staffing needs with supervisors is a good start, but it is advisable to get as many viewpoints as possible. Special attention should be given to areas where there is high turnover or where recruitment has been difficult.

Informal conversations are a good way to start the process. If you identify a trouble spot, you should request that the supervisor document his or her viewpoints on staffing needs. In addition, supervisors should be asked their viewpoints on adequate staffing for specific functions and provide any supporting evidence possible to justify the shift in staffing or increased headcount.

2.3   Making the case for adequate staffing

When dealing with upper management to justify headcount increases, the benchmarks are often compelling because they were derived through a structured study process conducted by an independent, unbiased organization. However, it is advisable to support the benchmarks with results from your own study and interviews to show that you took the extra steps necessary to evaluate staffing needs.

Other chapters of this book also provide compelling support to address staffing needs. The sections on security, privacy, intellectual property protection, and equipment disposal provide supporting arguments for staffing needs. The bottom line is the critical mission of the IS department, combined with new challenges

3

Principle Two: Fairly Compensate IT Workers

Appraisals are where you get together with your team leader and agree what an outstanding member of the team you are, how much your contribution has been valued, what massive potential you have, and, in recognition of all this, would you mind having your salary halved.

—Theodore Roosevelt

3.1   The hurdles to fair compensation

Establishing a fair compensation plan for IT employees can mitigate turnover and the loss of key personnel. A 20 percent reduction in turnover in an IT department can save as much as $200,000 in recruitment costs. Reduced turnover can also help keep projects on schedule, because work will not be disrupted when a staff member leaves and replacements must be recruited and brought up to speed on a project.

Computer Economics has identified several significant challenges that managers face when establishing fair compensation plans for IT professionals, including the following:

- Assuring equal pay regardless of gender
- Providing adequate compensation for overtime and holiday hours
- Adequately compensating employees for on-call time
- Appropriately linking compensation to performance
- Developing competitive compensation plans

3.1.1   Assuring equal pay regardless of gender

Unfortunately, there seems to be a disparity in compensation of IT professionals because of their gender. Even more unfortunate is the fact that there remains disparity in compensation between men and women in many professions. Over the long term, IT departments may gain more than they think they save by compensating women equally with men. Consider these points:

- Women generally hold positions longer than men.

- Women can turn into long-term employees even if they have children and take extended leaves of absence.

- When women return to the workplace after their children become teenagers or go to college, they are often looking for long-term employment.

- Postchild-rearing women are typically mature and patient and have experience managing multiple projects simultaneously.

Given the ongoing need for experienced IT professionals, it may very well benefit IT departments not only to examine their compensation plans but also to expend more effort recruiting women. Many people argue that women don't make good geeks because they are not inherently fascinated by gadgetry. In balance, however, how many documentation-resisting, gadget-fascinated geeks who scare end users to death do you really need running around your IT department?

3.1.2   Providing adequate compensation for overtime and holiday hours

IT professionals are generally overworked. This is particularly true of those who work in areas of server management, network administration, security, and virus protection. These areas suffer from more ongoing crisis conditions than most other IT functions, and they are often grossly understaffed, which drives the need for overtime. Excessive overtime leads to burnout and can contribute to myriad personal and family problems.

It is important to manage overtime so it does not become a destructive force. It is also equally important to adequately compensate IT professionals for the overtime that they do work. This compensation will help build higher levels of morale and reduce turnover.

3.1.3   Adequately compensating employees for on-call time

Another issue in compensation planning is how to pay IT professionals for on-call time. Computer Economics has studied service-level requirements for several years and has found that data centers are providing longer service periods and that many face 7/24 uptime requirements. Although night shifts and weekends may not require full staffing levels, networks and applications still need to be available to a growing workforce of telecommuters and flex-time workers outside the IT department.

Even when IT professionals do not have to respond to incidents when they are on call, the revolving responsibility for on-call sharing has its effect on their personal and family lives. Many organizations ignore this point. However, extensive on-call requirements and the resulting disruption of social life will contribute to burnout and to turnover rates. Thus, adequately compensating for on-call time may very well not cost as much as recruiting and training new staff because of high turnover rates.

Establishing a standard for compensating staff for on-call time can be difficult. If the employee is call-in or works remotely to solve problems, then compensation should be equal to the employee's hourly rate. If the work occurs on overtime status, then the rate should match the overtime pay that the employee would receive. If there are no calls that the employee needs to respond to during his or her on-call time, then compensation can be set lower and equal 35 percent to 50 percent of normal compensation. The 35 percent may be acceptable for nonholiday time, while the 50 percent would better compensate the employee during holidays.

3.1.4   Appropriately linking compensation to performance

As was discussed in the analysis of adequate IT staffing, it is beneficial to both the employee and the IT department to conduct structured performance evaluations. It is also an issue of fairness that compensation be tied to top performance and contribution. Giving equal annual pay increases to all staff regardless of their performance is not only ridiculous, it will likely cause considerable backlash. This can come in the form of declining morale, disgruntlement, and eventually higher turnover.

3.1.5   Developing competitive compensation plans

Compensation plans are not easy for many IT departments to develop. There are often corporate policies or procedures set by the human resources department that prove to be obstacles. Large IT departments often have human resources specialists to assist in developing compensation plans. However, the vast majority of IT departments comprise less than 100 people and usually do not have such internal support.

Regardless of the size of the IT department, the process of developing a competitive compensation plan has several phases, including:

■ Evaluation of talent mix needed immediately and what will be needed over the next several years

■ Assessment of the local market and availability of IT professionals within a 50-mile radius of the work location

■ Assessment of the regional market and availability of IT professionals within a 150-mile radius of the work location

■ Determining how other companies in the local and regional markets are compensating IT staff

■ Developing an organization profile to determine whether there are inherent benefits offered because of brand, reputation, or the status of an organization

Once these tasks are accomplished, IT managers should be able to determine what salary levels should be for various positions. This documentation is the basis for making a case to management to adjust salary levels.

Computer Economics has conducted salary analysis of IT positions for over 15 years. The figures listed in Table 3.1 through Table 3.21 show salaries for 40 IT functions and positions by region and city. Salaries are provided for IT staff with more than eight years' experience, four to seven years' experience, and up to three years' experience. To make comparison easier, the basic job descriptions go with each position listed in the salary tables are specified in the following subsections.

Application programmer/systems analyst

Application programmers and systems analysts design, develop, and modify computer systems; produce requirements documents and design specifications; develop and debug software; and design, conduct, and report software tests. Because application programmers and systems analysts are evaluated in terms of how well they meet system requirements and schedule deadlines, programmers often work in a high-stress environment. Managers are frequently responsible for satisfying budgetary targets. Application programmers and systems analysts coordinate with other technical staff members, managers, and end users.

AS/400 manager

AS/400 managers are responsible for formulating, directing, and evaluating the design, development, test, and deployment of AS/400 systems. Managers recommend, establish, and review organizational policies for the selection, procurement, installation, use, and disposal of information systems. Duties are often varied and dynamic. Managers are often also responsible for satisfying budgetary targets, coordinating with other managers, technical staff members, and end users.

AS/400 programmer

AS/400 programmers design, develop, and modify AS/400 systems; produce requirements documents and design specifications; develop and debug software; and design, conduct, and report software tests. AS/400 programmers coordinate with other technical staff members, managers, and end users.

C++ programmer

C++ programmers design, develop, and modify business applications; produce requirements documents and design specifications; develop and debug software; and design, conduct, and report software tests. C++ programmers are evaluated in terms of how well they meet system requirements and schedule deadlines, so programmers often work in a high-stress environment. Managers are often also responsible for satisfying budgetary targets. C++ programmers coordinate with other technical staff members, managers, and end users.

Certified Novell engineer

Certified Novell engineers (CNEs) support an enterprise computing environment with multiple servers that have a wide variety of sophisticated applications. CNEs plan server configuration and deployment, support networked services and applications, perform troubleshooting, and work on systems security.

Chief information officer

The duties of chief information officers (CIOs) are often varied and tailored to the specific needs of the organization. CIOs often define their own jobs, which are frequently dynamic and fluid, in conjunction with other senior executives. Most CIOs are responsible for overall organizational IT and tele-communications strategies. Solutions are aimed at long-term needs of the organization, including hardware and software selection, procurement, development, and staffing. CIOs are the spokespeople for the IT function—often presenting a vision of the future needs of the organization and the path for reaching those goals. CIOs coordinate with senior executives, their subordinate managers, and their contemporaries in other organizations.

Cisco systems engineer

Cisco certification as an internetwork expert requires passing the qualification exam and the CCIE lab exam. Networking personnel have a choice of the following three CCIE certifications: Routing and Switching, ISP DIAL, and WAN Switching. Successful certification often depends on several factors, including depth and breadth of hands-on internetworking experience as well as theoretical and practical industry knowledge. All three certifications require general experience in information systems technology and Cisco product experience. Cisco-certified experts must be recertified every two years. Each of the three CCIE exam tracks follow the same basic structure—a preliminary written test followed by a two-day, hands-on laboratory exam. The lab exam emphasizes Cisco equipment command knowledge and network troubleshooting skills.

Database administrator

Database administration personnel design, develop, and maintain databases; establish and administer data dictionaries; and ensure that organization database policies are followed. Database administrators are evaluated in terms of how well they meet system requirements and schedule deadlines, so they often work in a high-stress environment. Managers are frequently responsible for satisfying budgetary targets. Database administrators coordinate with other technical staff members, managers, and end users.

Data entry clerk

Data entry personnel input data to computer systems by means of terminals or desktop PCs. Ability is judged by a combination of the accuracy and volume of data entered.

Data warehouse administrator

Data warehouse administrators design, develop, and maintain data warehouses; establish and administer data dictionaries; and ensure that organization data warehouse policies are followed. Data warehouse administrators are evaluated in terms of how well they meet system requirements and schedule deadlines, so it can be a high-stress position. Managers are often also responsible for satisfying budgetary targets. Data warehouse administrators coordinate with other technical staff members, managers, and end users.

EDI application developer

EDI application developers are responsible for creating and implementing EDI applications to facilitate business functions such as order processing, inventory control, and supply chain or distribution channel management. They work with business unit managers to determine business requirements and with e-commerce managers to evaluate and select EDI products that are appropriate to meet corporate needs. They also do a considerable amount of work with suppliers, maintain data integrity, and provide adequate security to protect corporate information.

EDP auditor

EDP auditors design, develop, and maintain methods to assure corporate applications adequately control and track financial functions. EDP auditors are evaluated in terms of how well they meet financial audit requirements and protect corporate assets from fraud and abuse.

Electronic commerce manager

Electronic commerce managers are responsible for developing corporate e-commerce strategies for a wide variety of business goals, including revenue generation, customer services, business-to-business applications, and business process streamlining. They must work with multiple electronic business approaches, including EDI, the Internet, and enterprise resource planning tools. E-commerce managers are also responsible for developing corporate-wide e-commerce plans, recruiting and managing staff, implementing e-commerce methods, and working across departments to align technology with business goals. We found considerable variation in job descriptions for e-commerce managers and have synthesized several positions to develop our description. We also found that responsibilities varied by organization size and the Internet intensity of an organization.

End-user support and help-desk personnel

End-user support and help desk-personnel are often viewed as a lifeline by nontechnical computer users. These support staff members often work in direct contact with end users, by phone, e-mail, or on-site. Duties include answering questions, educating end users on features of specific applications, and recording problems for repair by technicians and programmers. Excellent "people skills" coupled with intimate knowledge of each application are essential requirements.

Information security specialist

Information security specialists design, develop, and maintain methods to assure that corporate applications and systems are safe from internal and external threats. They administer, select, and implement appropriate software; establish and administer password programs; and test systems for security risks.

Internet strategy director

Internet strategy directors are responsible for developing, implementing, and coordinating how an organization will use Web technology to facilitate business functions such as sales, marketing, customer support, and information dissemination.

IT purchasing specialist

IT purchasing and acquisition management (ITPAM) staff support the product and services acquisition needs of IT departments and other departments in an organization that purchases equipment, software, and services from centralized contacts or through special request-for-bid or request-for-proposal processes. ITPAM staff convey standards and requirements to vendors; receive bids and proposals; analyze and compare purchasing options; and negotiate discounts on equipment, software, and services. They also develop and negotiate multiyear service and support contracts. It is important to note that titles for ITPAM staff vary considerably across organizations.

IT training specialist

IT training specialists plan, prepare, present, and evaluate training programs covering a variety of computer and telecommunications topics. Training specialists recommend whether specific content is best learned through such techniques as classroom instruction, self-paced instruction, on-line courses, or training manuals.

Java programmer

Java programmers are joining the ranks of many IT shops across the country. Our analysis shows that salaries in end-user organizations are lower than those paid by software developers. We have also found that there is a lack of consistency in age and education for Java programmers compared with the traditional applications programmer position.

Lotus Notes administrator/developer

Lotus Notes developers design, develop, and modify business applications; produce requirements documents and design specifications; develop and debug software; and design, conduct, and report software tests. Because Lotus Notes developers are evaluated in terms of how well they meet system requirements and schedule deadlines, this can be a high-stress position. Managers are often responsible for satisfying budgetary targets. Lotus Notes developers coordinate with other technical staff members, managers, and end users.

MIS director

IS managers serve in a variety of staff and line positions. Managers are responsible for formulating, directing, and evaluating the design, development, test, and deployment for IS and telecommunications systems. Managers recommend, establish, and review organizational policies for the selection, procurement, installation, use, and disposal of information systems. Duties are often varied and dynamic. Managers are often also responsible for satisfying budgetary targets. IS managers coordinate with other managers, technical staff members, and end users.

Network administrator

Network administrators plan, monitor, modify, and direct repairs of organization networks. Administrators ensure application of proper security techniques, establish that only valid users are provided with access, and account for organizational resources dedicated to network infrastructures. Timely problem resolution is required in the event of a network crash or serious malfunction. Managers are often also responsible for satisfying budgetary targets. Network administrators coordinate with other technical staff members, managers, and end users.

NT administrator

Windows NT administrators support an enterprise computing environment with multiple servers and multiple domains that have a wide variety of sophisticated server applications. NT administrators plan the implementation of a directory services architecture and choose a protocol for various situations, including TCP/IP, TCP/IP with DHCP and WINS, NWLink

IPX/SPX Compatible Transport Protocol, Data Link Control (DLC), and AppleTalk. They install Windows NT servers, configure protocols and protocol bindings, and configure server services. They configure hard disks and printers, manage user and group accounts, and create and manage policies and profiles for local and remote users. They also administer remote servers from various types of client computers; configure NT servers for interoperability with various gateways and multiprotocol routing functions; and monitor performance of processors, memory, disks, and networks.

On-line editor

On-line editors are responsible for editing and preparing textual and graphic material for on-line delivery over the Web, intranets, or extranets. Editing functions include developmental editing, style development, copyediting, and working with contributing writers or product managers who are tasked with presenting their material in an on-line environment. On-line editors also work with site designers and Web site administrators to develop techniques that facilitate electronic publishing, and evaluate and select appropriate software to edit and present textual and illustrated material in an on-line environment.

On-line marketer

On-line marketers are responsible for developing Web-based marketing strategies and programs. They work with business units and product managers to develop requirements and select appropriate on-line marketing methods. They also work with Web site designers and Web administrators to implement, monitor, and evaluate on-line marketing approaches.

Oracle database developer

Oracle database developers design, develop, and modify business applications; produce requirements documents and design specifications; develop and debug software; and design, conduct, and report software tests. Because Oracle database developers are evaluated in terms of how well they meet system requirements and schedule deadlines, database development can be a high-stress environment. Managers are often also responsible for satisfying budgetary targets. Oracle database developers coordinate with other technical staff members, managers, and end users.

PC technical support personnel

PC technical support personnel plan, install, repair, and upgrade PC system hardware and software. PC technical support personnel may conduct their duties by remote administration and testing or at end users' sites. Managers are often also responsible for satisfying budgetary targets and establishing or recommending organizational PC policies and procedures. PC technical support personnel coordinate with other technical staff members, managers, and end users.

PowerBuilder programmer

PowerBuilder programmers design, develop, and modify business applications; produce requirements documents and design specifications; develop and debug software; and design, conduct, and report software tests. They are evaluated on how well they meet system requirements and schedule deadlines. Managers are often also responsible for satisfying budgetary targets. PowerBuilder programmers coordinate with other technical staff, managers, and end users. As you evaluate salaries for programmers, keep in mind both the complexity of their programming tasks as well as the training required for specific tools. PowerBuilder, like many fourth-generation (4GL) tools, requires training beyond basic coding skills. This usually results in higher salaries. Our research also shows that once proficiency has been achieved with one set of 4GL tools, programmers can learn how to use similar tools with greater ease. Training can also be very expensive and take several months.

Quality assurance/control personnel

Quality assurance/control personnel are responsible for evaluating the degree to which IT systems meet established standards and specifications. Quality assurance/control personnel plan and execute methods for system evaluation, maintain system quality records, verify and validate system performance, and oversee the use of quality control identification markings. Managers are often also responsible for satisfying budgetary targets. Quality assurance/control personnel coordinate with other technical staff members, managers, and end users.

SAP programmer

Growth in enterprise resource planning software has created a demand for highly talented programmers to develop applications based on complex business rules. This need, combined with SAP A.G.'s growth, has dramatically impacted salaries. SAP programmers design, develop, and produce requirements documents and design specifications; develop and debug software; and design, conduct, and report software tests for the SAP environment. They are evaluated on how well they meet business requirements and schedule deadlines. Managers often must satisfy budgetary targets. SAP programmers coordinate with other technical staff, managers, and end users.

SQL developer

SQL developers design, develop, and modify business applications; produce requirements documents and design specifications; develop and debug software; and design, conduct, and report software tests. Because SQL developers are evaluated in terms of how well they meet system requirements and schedule deadlines, this can be a high-stress position. Managers are often responsible for satisfying budgetary targets. SQL developers coordinate with other technical staff members, managers, and end users.

System programmer

System programmers design, develop, repair, and test operating system software. Programming at this level requires extensive training and knowledge of total system implications of any system software changes. Because system programmers are evaluated in terms of how well they meet system requirements and schedule deadlines, they often work in a high-stress environment. Managers are frequently also responsible for satisfying budgetary targets. System programmers coordinate with other technical staff members, managers, and end users.

System/computer operator

System/computer operators perform all of the activities in the computer center, including operating, scheduling, and controlling hardware and software; monitoring operations; detecting and correcting faults; and maintaining records.

Technical writer

Technical writers produce documentation required for developing and maintaining corporate applications. They interact with programmers, systems analysts, and end users to determine system functioning and documentation requirements. Technical writers are proficient in flow charting, diagramming system functioning, and writing descriptions of how applications work.

Telecommunications administrator

Telecommunications administrators plan, monitor, modify, and direct repairs of telecommunications networks. Administrators ensure application of proper security techniques, establish that only valid users are provided with access, and account for organizational resources dedicated to telecommunications infrastructures. Timely problem resolution is required in the event of a telecommunications crash or serious malfunction. Managers are often also responsible for satisfying budgetary targets. Telecommunications administrators coordinate with other technical staff members, managers, and end users.

UNIX system administrator

UNIX system administrators are responsible for supporting an enterprise computing environment with multiple servers and multiple domains that have a wide variety of sophisticated server applications. UNIX system administrators plan and implement a directory services architecture and choose a protocol for various situations, including TCP/IP, TCP/IP with DHCP and WINS, NWLink IPX/SPX Compatible Transport Protocol, Data Link Control (DLC), and AppleTalk. They install server software, configure protocols and protocol bindings, and configure server services. They configure hard disks and printers, manage user and group accounts, and create and manage policies and profiles for local and remote users. They also administer remote servers from various types of client computers; configure servers for interoperability with various gateways and multiprotocol routing functions; and monitor performance of processors, memory, disks, and networks.

Visual BASIC programmer

Visual BASIC programmers design, develop, and modify business applications; produce requirements documents and design specifications; develop and debug software; and design, conduct, and report software tests. Because Visual BASIC programmers are evaluated in terms of how well they meet system requirements and schedule deadlines, they often work in a high-stress environment. Managers are frequently also responsible for satisfying budgetary targets. Visual BASIC programmers coordinate with other technical staff members, managers, and end users.

Web graphic artists

Web graphic artists are responsible for designing and creating a wide variety of graphic elements for Web sites. They work with on-line marketers, Web site designers, and Web administrators to select and implement appropriate graphics to support Web-based functions such as marketing, sales, and customer relations. The position requires extensive computer graphics skills and the ability to work with current graphics software packages and technologies.

Web site administrator

Web administrators are responsible for managing the technology, personnel, and connectivity to develop and maintain a corporate Web site. Experience is required in HTML, computer operating systems, and Internet communications and connectivity, as well as Web site management software. Web administrators must also be able to hire and supervise technical staff and work with other departments in the company to bring content to a Web site.

Web site designer

Web site designers are responsible for directing the overall design, layout, and functionality of Web sites. They direct the work of graphics artists, programmers, and database administrators. They also coordinate requirements analysis among various corporate departments that are using Web technology to support activities such as sales, marketing, and customer relations.

Table 3.1   *2002 Salaries for IT Staff with More Than Eight Years' Experience—*
By Regions

	Region			
Salaries across All Sectors	**East ($)**	**Central ($)**	**Mountain ($)**	**Pacific ($)**
Application Programmer/Systems Analyst	69,235	65,081	61,619	72,004
AS/400 Manager	96,850	91,039	86,197	100,724
AS/400 Programmer	77,950	73,273	69,376	81,068
C++ Programmer	87,550	82,297	77,920	91,052
Certified Novell Engineer	79,940	75,144	71,147	83,138
Chief Information Officer	274,500	258,030	244,305	285,480
Cisco Systems Engineer	102,680	96,519	91,385	106,787
Database Administrator	81,785	76,878	72,789	85,056
Data Entry Clerk	28,650	26,931	25,499	29,796
Data Warehouse Administrator	147,650	138,791	131,409	153,556
EDI Application Developer	84,700	79,618	75,383	88,088
EDP Auditor	64,450	60,583	57,361	67,028
Electronic Commerce Manager	138,350	130,049	123,132	143,884
End-User Support and Help-Desk Personnel	73,960	69,522	65,824	76,918
Information Security Specialist	105,900	99,546	94,251	110,136
Internet Strategy Director	94,375	88,713	83,994	98,150
IT Purchasing Specialist	94,850	89,159	84,417	98,644
IT Training Specialist	51,435	48,349	45,777	53,492
Java Programmer	92,475	86,927	82,303	96,174
Lotus Notes Administrator/Developer	98,685	92,764	87,830	102,632
MIS Director	176,295	165,717	156,903	183,347
Network Administrator	95,345	89,624	84,857	99,159
NT Administrator	75,285	70,768	67,004	78,296
On-line Editor	51,575	48,481	45,902	53,638
On-line Marketer	72,765	68,399	64,761	75,676

Table 3.1   *2002 Salaries for IT Staff with More Than Eight Years' Experience—*
By Regions (continued)

Salaries across All Sectors	Region			
	East ($)	Central ($)	Mountain ($)	Pacific ($)
Oracle Database Developer	85,690	80,549	76,264	89,118
PC Technical Support Personnel	74,835	70,345	66,603	77,828
PowerBuilder Programmer	91,400	85,916	81,346	95,056
Quality Assurance/Control Personnel	79,360	74,598	70,630	82,534
SAP Programmer	114,295	107,437	101,723	118,867
SQL Developer	71,350	67,069	63,502	74,204
System Programmer	102,315	96,176	91,060	106,408
System/Computer Operator	89,335	83,975	79,508	92,908
Technical Writer	52,775	49,609	46,970	54,886
Telecommunications Administrator	82,825	77,856	73,714	86,138
UNIX System Administrator	82,500	77,550	73,425	85,800
Visual BASIC Programmer	72,300	67,962	64,347	75,192
Web Graphic Artists	46,385	43,602	41,283	48,240
Web Site Administrator	58,950	55,413	52,466	61,308
Web Site Designer	55,580	52,245	49,466	57,803

Source: Computer Economics

Table 3.2   *2002 Salaries for IT Staff with Four to Seven Years' Experience—
By Regions*

Salaries across All Sectors	Region			
	East ($)	Central ($)	Mountain ($)	Pacific ($)
Application Programmer/Systems Analyst	53,657	50,438	47,755	55,803
AS/400 Manager	75,059	70,555	66,802	78,061
AS/400 Programmer	60,411	56,787	53,766	62,828
C++ Programmer	67,851	63,780	60,388	70,565
Certified Novell Engineer	61,954	58,236	55,139	64,432
Chief Information Officer	212,738	199,973	189,336	221,247
Cisco Systems Engineer	79,577	74,802	70,824	82,760
Database Administrator	63,383	59,580	56,411	65,919
Data Entry Clerk	22,204	20,872	19,761	23,092
Data Warehouse Administrator	114,429	107,563	101,842	119,006
EDI Application Developer	65,643	61,704	58,422	68,268
EDP Auditor	49,949	46,952	44,454	51,947
Electronic Commerce Manager	107,221	100,788	95,427	111,510
End-User Support and Help-Desk Personnel	57,319	53,880	51,014	59,612
Information Security Specialist	82,073	77,148	73,045	85,355
Internet Strategy Director	73,141	68,752	65,095	76,066
IT Purchasing Specialist	73,509	69,098	65,423	76,449
IT Training Specialist	39,862	37,470	35,477	41,457
Java Programmer	71,668	67,368	63,785	74,535
Lotus Notes Administrator/Developer	76,481	71,892	68,068	79,540
MIS Director	136,629	128,431	121,599	142,094
Network Administrator	73,892	69,459	65,764	76,848
NT Administrator	58,346	54,845	51,928	60,680
On-line Editor	39,971	37,572	35,574	41,569
On-line Marketer	56,393	53,009	50,190	58,649

Table 3.2   *2002 Salaries for IT Staff with Four to Seven Years' Experience—*
By Regions (continued)

Salaries across All Sectors	Region			
	East ($)	Central ($)	Mountain ($)	Pacific ($)
Oracle Database Developer	66,410	62,425	59,105	69,066
PC Technical Support Personnel	57,997	54,517	51,617	60,317
PowerBuilder Programmer	70,835	66,585	63,043	73,668
Quality Assurance/Control Personnel	61,504	57,814	54,739	63,964
SAP Programmer	88,579	83,264	78,835	92,122
SQL Developer	55,296	51,978	49,214	57,508
System Programmer	79,294	74,536	70,572	82,466
System/Computer Operator	69,235	65,081	61,619	72,004
Technical Writer	40,901	38,447	36,402	42,537
Telecommunications Administrator	64,189	60,338	57,129	66,757
UNIX System Administrator	63,938	60,101	56,904	66,495
Visual BASIC Programmer	56,033	52,671	49,869	58,274
Web Graphic Artists	35,948	33,791	31,994	37,386
Web Site Administrator	45,686	42,945	40,661	47,514
Web Site Designer	43,075	40,490	38,336	44,797

Source: Computer Economics

Table 3.3   *2002 Salaries for IT Staff with One to Three Years' Experience—*
By Regions

Salaries across All Sectors	Region			
	East ($)	Central ($)	Mountain ($)	Pacific ($)
Application Programmer/Systems Analyst	39,810	37,422	35,431	41,403
AS/400 Manager	56,173	52,803	49,994	58,420
AS/400 Programmer	45,211	42,498	40,238	47,019
C++ Programmer	50,779	47,732	45,193	52,810
Certified Novell Engineer	46,365	43,583	41,265	48,220
Chief Information Officer	159,210	149,657	141,697	165,578
Cisco Systems Engineer	59,554	55,981	53,003	61,937
Database Administrator	47,435	44,589	42,217	49,333
Data Entry Clerk	16,617	15,620	14,789	17,282
Data Warehouse Administrator	85,637	80,499	76,217	89,062
EDI Application Developer	49,126	46,178	43,722	51,091
EDP Auditor	37,381	35,138	33,269	38,876
Electronic Commerce Manager	80,243	75,428	71,416	83,453
End-User Support and Help-Desk Personnel	42,897	40,323	38,178	44,613
Information Security Specialist	61,422	57,737	54,666	63,879
Internet Strategy Director	54,738	51,453	48,716	56,927
IT Purchasing Specialist	55,013	51,712	48,962	57,214
IT Training Specialist	29,832	28,042	26,551	31,026
Java Programmer	53,636	50,417	47,736	55,781
Lotus Notes Administrator/Developer	57,237	53,803	50,941	59,527
MIS Director	102,251	96,116	91,003	106,341
Network Administrator	55,300	51,982	49,217	57,512
NT Administrator	43,665	41,045	38,862	45,412
On-line Editor	29,914	28,119	26,623	31,110
On-ine Marketer	42,204	39,671	37,561	43,892

Table 3.3   *2002 Salaries for IT Staff with One to Three Years' Experience—*
By Regions (continued)

Salaries across All Sectors	Region			
	East ($)	Central ($)	Mountain ($)	Pacific ($)
Oracle Database Developer	49,700	46,718	44,233	51,688
PC Technical Support Personnel	43,404	40,800	38,630	45,140
PowerBuilder Programmer	53,012	49,831	47,181	55,132
Quality Assurance/Control Personnel	46,029	43,267	40,966	47,870
SAP Programmer	66,291	62,314	58,999	68,943
SQL Developer	41,383	38,900	36,831	43,038
System Programmer	59,343	55,782	52,815	61,716
System/Computer Operator	51,814	48,705	46,115	53,887
Technical Writer	30,610	28,773	27,242	31,834
Telecommunications Administrator	48,039	45,156	42,754	49,960
UNIX System Administrator	47,850	44,979	42,587	49,764
Visual BASIC Programmer	41,934	39,418	37,321	43,611
Web Graphic Artists	26,903	25,289	23,944	27,979
Web Site Administrator	34,191	32,140	30,430	35,559
Web Site Designer	32,236	30,302	28,690	33,526

Source: Computer Economics

Table 3.4   *2002 Salaries for IT Staff with More Than Eight Years' Experience—Atlanta, Austin, Baltimore, and Boston Metro*

| Salaries across All Sectors | Cities | | | |
	Atlanta ($)	Austin ($)	Baltimore ($)	Boston Metro ($)
Application Programmer/Systems Analyst	70,468	66,382	65,779	70,870
AS/400 Manager	98,575	92,859	92,016	99,137
AS/400 Programmer	79,338	74,738	74,059	79,791
C++ Programmer	89,109	83,942	83,180	89,617
Certified Novell Engineer	81,364	76,646	75,950	81,828
Chief Information Officer	279,389	263,189	260,798	280,982
Cisco Systems Engineer	104,509	98,449	97,555	105,105
Database Administrator	83,242	78,415	77,703	83,716
Data Entry Clerk	29,160	27,469	27,220	29,327
Data Warehouse Administrator	150,280	141,566	140,280	151,137
EDI Application Developer	86,209	81,210	80,472	86,700
EDP Auditor	65,598	61,794	61,233	65,972
Electronic Commerce Manager	140,814	132,649	131,444	141,617
End-User Support and Help-Desk Personnel	75,277	70,912	70,268	75,707
Information Security Specialist	107,786	101,536	100,614	108,401
Internet Strategy Director	96,056	90,486	89,664	96,604
IT Purchasing Specialist	96,539	90,941	90,116	97,090
IT Training Specialist	52,351	49,315	48,868	52,650
Java Programmer	94,122	88,664	87,859	94,659
Lotus Notes Administrator/Developer	100,443	94,618	93,759	101,015
MIS Director	179,435	169,030	167,495	180,458
Network Administrator	97,043	91,416	90,586	97,597
NT Administrator	76,626	72,183	71,527	77,063
On-line Editor	52,494	49,450	49,001	52,793
On-line Marketer	74,061	69,767	69,133	74,483

Table 3.4   *2002 Salaries for IT Staff with More Than Eight Years' Experience—Atlanta, Austin, Baltimore, and Boston Metro (continued)*

	Cities			
Salaries across All Sectors	**Atlanta ($)**	**Austin ($)**	**Baltimore ($)**	**Boston Metro ($)**
Oracle Database Developer	87,216	82,159	81,413	87,714
PC Technical Support Personnel	76,168	71,751	71,100	76,602
PowerBuilder Programmer	93,028	87,634	86,838	93,558
Quality Assurance/Control Personnel	80,773	76,090	75,399	81,234
SAP Programmer	116,331	109,585	108,590	116,994
SQL Developer	72,621	68,410	67,789	73,035
System Programmer	104,137	98,099	97,208	104,731
System/Computer Operator	90,926	85,654	84,876	91,445
Technical Writer	53,715	50,600	50,141	54,021
Telecommunications Administrator	84,300	79,412	78,691	84,781
UNIX System Administrator	83,969	79,100	78,382	84,448
Visual BASIC Programmer	73,588	69,321	68,691	74,007
Web Graphic Artists	47,211	44,474	44,070	47,480
Web Site Administrator	60,000	56,521	56,008	60,342
Web Site Designer	56,570	53,290	52,806	56,893

Source: Computer Economics

Table 3.5   *2002 Salaries for IT Staff with Four to Seven Years' Experience—Atlanta, Austin, Baltimore, and Boston Metro*

	Cities			
Salaries across All Sectors	Atlanta ($)	Austin ($)	Baltimore ($)	Boston Metro ($)
Application Programmer/Systems Analyst	54,613	51,446	50,979	54,924
AS/400 Manager	76,396	71,966	71,312	76,831
AS/400 Programmer	61,487	57,922	57,396	61,838
C++ Programmer	69,060	65,055	64,464	69,454
Certified Novell Engineer	63,057	59,401	58,861	63,417
Chief Information Officer	216,526	203,971	202,119	217,761
Cisco Systems Engineer	80,994	76,298	75,605	81,456
Database Administrator	64,512	60,772	60,220	64,880
Data Entry Clerk	22,599	21,289	21,095	22,728
Data Warehouse Administrator	116,467	109,713	108,717	117,131
EDI Application Developer	66,812	62,938	62,366	67,193
EDP Auditor	50,838	47,890	47,456	51,128
Electronic Commerce Manager	109,131	102,803	101,869	109,753
End-User Support and Help-Desk Personnel	58,340	54,957	54,458	58,673
Information Security Specialist	83,534	78,690	77,976	84,011
Internet Strategy Director	74,443	70,127	69,490	74,868
IT Purchasing Specialist	74,818	70,480	69,840	75,245
IT Training Specialist	40,572	38,220	37,872	40,803
Java Programmer	72,945	68,715	68,091	73,361
Lotus Notes Administrator/Developer	77,843	73,329	72,663	78,287
MIS Director	139,062	130,999	129,809	139,855
Network Administrator	75,208	70,847	70,204	75,637
NT Administrator	59,385	55,942	55,434	59,724
On-line Editor	40,683	38,324	37,975	40,915
On-line Marketer	57,397	54,069	53,578	57,725

Table 3.5   *2002 Salaries for IT Staff with Four to Seven Years' Experience—Atlanta, Austin, Baltimore, and Boston Metro (continued)*

	Cities			
Salaries across All Sectors	Atlanta ($)	Austin ($)	Baltimore ($)	Boston Metro ($)
Oracle Database Developer	67,593	63,673	63,095	67,978
PC Technical Support Personnel	59,030	55,607	55,102	59,367
PowerBuilder Programmer	72,097	67,916	67,299	72,508
Quality Assurance/Control Personnel	62,599	58,970	58,434	62,956
SAP Programmer	90,156	84,929	84,157	90,670
SQL Developer	56,281	53,018	52,536	56,602
System Programmer	80,706	76,027	75,336	81,167
System/Computer Operator	70,468	66,382	65,779	70,870
Technical Writer	41,629	39,215	38,859	41,866
Telecommunications Administrator	65,333	61,544	60,985	65,705
UNIX System Administrator	65,076	61,303	60,746	65,447
Visual BASIC Programmer	57,030	53,724	53,236	57,356
Web Graphic Artists	36,589	34,467	34,154	36,797
Web Site Administrator	46,500	43,804	43,406	46,765
Web Site Designer	43,842	41,300	40,924	44,092

Source: Computer Economics

Table 3.6   *2002 Salaries for IT Staff with One to Three Years' Experience—Atlanta, Austin, Baltimore, and Boston Metro*

	Cities			
Salaries across All Sectors	Atlanta ($)	Austin ($)	Baltimore ($)	Boston Metro ($)
Application Programmer/Systems Analyst	40,519	38,170	37,823	40,750
AS/400 Manager	57,173	53,858	53,369	57,500
AS/400 Programmer	46,016	43,348	42,954	46,279
C++ Programmer	51,683	48,687	48,244	51,978
Certified Novell Engineer	47,191	44,455	44,051	47,460
Chief Information Officer	162,046	152,649	151,263	162,970
Cisco Systems Engineer	60,615	57,100	56,582	60,961
Database Administrator	48,280	45,481	45,068	48,555
Data Entry Clerk	16,913	15,932	15,788	17,009
Data Warehouse Administrator	87,162	82,108	81,362	87,659
EDI Application Developer	50,001	47,102	46,674	50,286
EDP Auditor	38,047	35,841	35,515	38,264
Electronic Commerce Manager	81,672	76,936	76,238	82,138
End-User Support and Help-Desk Personnel	43,661	41,129	40,756	43,910
Information Security Specialist	62,516	58,891	58,356	62,872
Internet Strategy Director	55,712	52,482	52,005	56,030
IT Purchasing Specialist	55,993	52,746	52,267	56,312
IT Training Specialist	30,364	28,603	28,343	30,537
Java Programmer	54,591	51,425	50,958	54,902
Lotus Notes Administrator/Developer	58,257	54,879	54,380	58,589
MIS Director	104,072	98,038	97,147	104,666
Network Administrator	56,285	53,021	52,540	56,606
NT Administrator	44,443	41,866	41,486	44,696
On-line Editor	30,446	28,681	28,420	30,620
On-line Marketer	42,955	40,465	40,097	43,200

Table 3.6   *2002 Salaries for IT Staff with One to Three Years' Experience—Atlanta, Austin, Baltimore, and Boston Metro (continued)*

	Cities			
Salaries across All Sectors	**Atlanta ($)**	**Austin ($)**	**Baltimore ($)**	**Boston Metro ($)**
Oracle Database Developer	50,585	47,652	47,219	50,874
PC Technical Support Personnel	44,177	41,616	41,238	44,429
PowerBuilder Programmer	53,956	50,828	50,366	54,264
Quality Assurance/Control Personnel	46,849	44,132	43,731	47,116
SAP Programmer	67,472	63,559	62,982	67,857
SQL Developer	42,120	39,678	39,317	42,360
System Programmer	60,400	56,897	56,381	60,744
System/Computer Operator	52,737	49,679	49,228	53,038
Technical Writer	31,155	29,348	29,082	31,332
Telecommunications Administrator	48,894	46,059	45,641	49,173
UNIX System Administrator	48,702	45,878	45,462	48,980
Visual BASIC Programmer	42,681	40,206	39,841	42,924
Web Graphic Artists	27,382	25,795	25,560	27,539
Web Site Administrator	34,800	32,782	32,484	34,998
Web Site Designer	32,811	30,908	30,627	32,998

Source: Computer Economics

Table 3.7   *2002 Salaries for IT Staff with More Than Eight Years' Experience—Chicago Metro; Cleveland; Dallas and Fort Worth; and Denver, Boulder, and Greeley*

Salaries across All Sectors	Chicago Metro ($)	Cleveland ($)	Dallas & Fort Worth ($)	Denver, Boulder, Greeley ($)
Application Programmer/Systems Analyst	69,999	67,789	69,865	66,717
AS/400 Manager	97,919	94,827	97,732	93,328
AS/400 Programmer	78,810	76,322	78,660	75,115
C++ Programmer	88,516	85,721	88,347	84,366
Certified Novell Engineer	80,822	78,270	80,668	77,033
Chief Information Officer	277,530	268,766	276,999	264,516
Cisco Systems Engineer	103,813	100,535	103,615	98,946
Database Administrator	82,688	80,077	82,529	78,810
Data Entry Clerk	28,966	28,052	28,911	27,608
Data Warehouse Administrator	149,280	144,566	148,994	142,280
EDI Application Developer	85,635	82,931	85,471	81,619
EDP Auditor	65,161	63,104	65,037	62,106
Electronic Commerce Manager	139,877	135,460	139,609	133,318
End-User Support and Help-Desk Personnel	74,776	72,415	74,633	71,270
Information Security Specialist	107,069	103,688	106,864	102,048
Internet Strategy Director	95,417	92,404	95,234	90,943
IT Purchasing Specialist	95,897	92,869	95,713	91,400
IT Training Specialist	52,003	50,361	51,903	49,564
Java Programmer	93,496	90,543	93,317	89,112
Lotus Notes Administrator/Developer	99,774	96,623	99,583	95,096
MIS Director	178,241	172,612	177,900	169,883
Network Administrator	96,397	93,353	96,213	91,877
NT Administrator	76,116	73,712	75,970	72,547
On-line Editor	52,144	50,498	52,044	49,699

Table 3.7   *2002 Salaries for IT Staff with More Than Eight Years' Experience—Chicago Metro; Cleveland; Dallas and Fort Worth; and Denver, Boulder, and Greeley (continued)*

Salaries across All Sectors	Cities			
	Chicago Metro ($)	Cleveland ($)	Dallas & Fort Worth ($)	Denver, Boulder, Greeley ($)
On-line Marketer	73,568	71,245	73,427	70,119
Oracle Database Developer	86,636	83,900	86,470	82,573
PC Technical Support Personnel	75,661	73,272	75,516	72,113
PowerBuilder Programmer	92,409	89,491	92,232	88,076
Quality Assurance/Control Personnel	80,236	77,702	80,082	76,474
SAP Programmer	115,557	111,907	115,335	110,138
SQL Developer	72,138	69,859	71,999	68,755
System Programmer	103,444	100,178	103,246	98,594
System/Computer Operator	90,321	87,469	90,148	86,086
Technical Writer	53,358	51,673	53,255	50,856
Telecommunications Administrator	83,739	81,095	83,579	79,813
UNIX System Administrator	83,411	80,777	83,251	79,499
Visual BASIC Programmer	73,098	70,790	72,958	69,670
Web Graphic Artists	46,897	45,416	46,807	44,698
Web Site Administrator	59,601	57,719	59,487	56,806
Web Site Designer	56,193	54,419	56,086	53,559

Source: Computer Economics

Table 3.8   *2002 Salaries for IT Staff with Four to Seven Years' Experience—Chicago Metro; Cleveland; Dallas and Fort Worth; and Denver, Boulder, and Greeley*

Salaries across All Sectors	Cities			
	Chicago Metro ($)	Cleveland ($)	Dallas & Fort Worth ($)	Denver, Boulder, Greeley ($)
Application Programmer/Systems Analyst	54,249	52,536	54,146	51,706
AS/400 Manager	75,887	73,491	75,742	72,329
AS/400 Programmer	61,078	59,149	60,961	58,214
C++ Programmer	68,600	66,434	68,469	65,384
Certified Novell Engineer	62,637	60,659	62,517	59,700
Chief Information Officer	215,086	208,293	214,674	205,000
Cisco Systems Engineer	80,455	77,915	80,301	76,683
Database Administrator	64,083	62,059	63,960	61,078
Data Entry Clerk	22,449	21,740	22,406	21,396
Data Warehouse Administrator	115,692	112,038	115,470	110,267
EDI Application Developer	66,367	64,271	66,240	63,255
EDP Auditor	50,500	48,905	50,403	48,132
Electronic Commerce Manager	108,405	104,981	108,197	103,322
End-User Support and Help-Desk Personnel	57,952	56,122	57,841	55,234
Information Security Specialist	82,978	80,358	82,820	79,088
Internet Strategy Director	73,948	71,613	73,806	70,481
IT Purchasing Specialist	74,320	71,973	74,178	70,835
IT Training Specialist	40,302	39,029	40,225	38,412
Java Programmer	72,459	70,171	72,320	69,062
Lotus Notes Administrator/Developer	77,325	74,883	77,177	73,699
MIS Director	138,137	133,774	137,872	131,659
Network Administrator	74,708	72,349	74,565	71,205
NT Administrator	58,990	57,127	58,877	56,224
On-line Editor	40,412	39,136	40,334	38,517

Table 3.8   *2002 Salaries for IT Staff with Four to Seven Years' Experience—Chicago Metro;*
Cleveland; Dallas and Fort Worth; and Denver, Boulder, and Greeley (continued)

	Cities			
Salaries across All Sectors	Chicago Metro ($)	Cleveland ($)	Dallas & Fort Worth ($)	Denver, Boulder, Greeley ($)
Onl-ine Marketer	57,015	55,215	56,906	54,342
Oracle Database Developer	67,143	65,022	67,014	63,994
PC Technical Support Personnel	58,637	56,786	58,525	55,888
PowerBuilder Programmer	71,617	69,355	71,480	68,259
Quality Assurance/Control Personnel	62,183	60,219	62,064	59,267
SAP Programmer	89,556	86,728	89,385	85,357
SQL Developer	55,907	54,141	55,800	53,285
System Programmer	80,169	77,638	80,016	76,410
System/Computer Operator	69,999	67,788	69,865	66,717
Technical Writer	41,352	40,046	41,273	39,413
Telecommunications Administrator	64,898	62,848	64,774	61,855
UNIX System Administrator	64,643	62,602	64,519	61,612
Visual BASIC Programmer	56,651	54,862	56,543	53,995
Web Graphic Artists	36,345	35,197	36,276	34,641
Web Site Administrator	46,191	44,732	46,102	44,025
Web Site Designer	43,550	42,175	43,467	41,508

Source: Computer Economics

Table 3.9   *2002 Salaries for IT Staff with One to Three Years' Experience—Chicago Metro; Cleveland; Dallas and Fort Worth; and Denver, Boulder, and Greeley*

Salaries across All Sectors	Cities			
	Chicago Metro ($)	Cleveland ($)	Dallas & Fort Worth ($)	Denver, Boulder, Greeley ($)
Application Programmer/Systems Analyst	40,250	38,978	40,172	38,362
AS/400 Manager	56,793	55,000	56,684	54,130
AS/400 Programmer	45,710	44,267	45,623	43,567
C++ Programmer	51,339	49,718	51,241	48,932
Certified Novell Engineer	46,877	45,397	46,787	44,679
Chief Information Officer	160,967	155,884	160,659	153,420
Cisco Systems Engineer	60,212	58,310	60,096	57,388
Database Administrator	47,959	46,444	47,867	45,710
Data Entry Clerk	16,800	16,270	16,768	16,013
Data Warehouse Administrator	86,582	83,848	86,417	82,522
EDI Application Developer	49,668	48,100	49,573	47,339
EDP Auditor	37,794	36,600	37,721	36,021
Electronic Commerce Manager	81,129	78,567	80,973	77,325
End-User Support and Help-Desk Personnel	43,370	42,001	43,287	41,337
Information Security Specialist	62,100	60,139	61,981	59,188
Internet Strategy Director	55,342	53,594	55,236	52,747
IT Purchasing Specialist	55,620	53,864	55,514	53,012
IT Training Specialist	30,162	29,209	30,104	28,747
Java Programmer	54,228	52,515	54,124	51,685
Lotus Notes Administrator/Developer	57,869	56,042	57,758	55,156
MIS Director	103,380	100,115	103,182	98,532
Network Administrator	55,910	54,145	55,803	53,289
NT Administrator	44,147	42,753	44,063	42,077
On-line Editor	30,244	29,289	30,186	28,826

Table 3.9   *2002 Salaries for IT Staff with One to Three Years' Experience—Chicago Metro; Cleveland; Dallas and Fort Worth; and Denver, Boulder, and Greeley (continued)*

	Cities			
Salaries across All Sectors	**Chicago Metro ($)**	**Cleveland ($)**	**Dallas & Fort Worth ($)**	**Denver, Boulder, Greeley ($)**
On-line Marketer	42,670	41,322	42,588	40,669
Oracle Database Developer	50,249	48,662	50,153	47,893
PC Technical Support Personnel	43,883	42,498	43,799	41,826
PowerBuilder Programmer	53,597	51,905	53,495	51,084
Quality Assurance/Control Personnel	46,537	45,067	46,448	44,355
SAP Programmer	67,023	64,906	66,895	63,880
SQL Developer	41,840	40,519	41,760	39,878
System Programmer	59,998	58,103	59,883	57,184
System/Computer Operator	52,386	50,732	52,286	49,930
Technical Writer	30,947	29,970	30,888	29,496
Telecommunications Administrator	48,569	47,035	48,476	46,291
UNIX System Administrator	48,378	46,850	48,286	46,110
Visual BASIC Programmer	42,397	41,058	42,316	40,409
Web Graphic Artists	27,200	26,341	27,148	25,925
Web Site Administrator	34,568	33,477	34,502	32,947
Web Site Designer	32,592	31,563	32,530	31,064

Source: Computer Economics

Table 3.10   *2002 Salaries for IT Staff with More Than Eight Years' Experience— Detroit, Ann Arbor, and Flint; Houston; Kansas City; and Los Angeles and Riverside*

Salaries across All Sectors	Cities			
	Detroit, Ann Arbor, Flint ($)	Houston ($)	Kansas City ($)	Los Angeles & Riverside ($)
Application Programmer/Systems Analyst	69,530	66,449	65,109	79,444
AS/400 Manager	97,263	92,953	91,079	111,131
AS/400 Programmer	78,282	74,813	73,305	89,444
C++ Programmer	87,923	84,027	82,333	100,460
Certified Novell Engineer	80,281	76,723	75,176	91,728
Chief Information Officer	275,671	263,454	258,143	314,976
Cisco Systems Engineer	103,118	98,548	96,561	117,821
Database Administrator	82,134	78,494	76,911	93,845
Data Entry Clerk	28,772	27,497	26,943	32,875
Data Warehouse Administrator	148,280	141,709	138,852	169,422
EDI Application Developer	85,061	81,292	79,653	97,189
EDP Auditor	64,725	61,857	60,609	73,953
Electronic Commerce Manager	138,940	132,783	130,106	158,750
End-User Support and Help-Desk Personnel	74,275	70,984	69,553	84,866
Information Security Specialist	106,352	101,639	99,589	121,515
Internet Strategy Director	94,778	90,577	88,751	108,291
IT Purchasing Specialist	95,255	91,033	89,198	108,836
IT Training Specialist	51,654	49,365	48,370	59,019
Java Programmer	92,869	88,754	86,964	106,111
Lotus Notes Administrator/Developer	99,106	94,714	92,804	113,237
MIS Director	177,047	169,201	165,790	202,291
Network Administrator	95,752	91,508	89,663	109,404
NT Administrator	75,606	72,256	70,799	86,386
On-line Editor	51,795	49,500	48,502	59,180

Table 3.10   *2002 Salaries for IT Staff with More Than Eight Years' Experience— Detroit, Ann Arbor, and Flint; Houston; Kansas City; and Los Angeles and Riverside (continued)*

Salaries across All Sectors	Detroit, Ann Arbor, Flint ($)	Houston ($)	Kansas City ($)	Los Angeles & Riverside ($)
On-line Marketer	73,075	69,837	68,429	83,495
Oracle Database Developer	86,055	82,242	80,584	98,325
PC Technical Support Personnel	75,154	71,824	70,376	85,870
PowerBuilder Programmer	91,790	87,722	85,953	104,877
Quality Assurance/Control Personnel	79,698	76,167	74,631	91,062
SAP Programmer	114,782	109,696	107,484	131,148
SQL Developer	71,654	68,479	67,098	81,871
System Programmer	102,751	98,198	96,218	117,402
System/Computer Operator	89,716	85,740	84,012	102,508
Technical Writer	53,000	50,651	49,630	60,557
Telecommunications Administrator	83,178	79,492	77,889	95,038
UNIX System Administrator	82,852	79,180	77,584	94,665
Visual BASIC Programmer	72,608	69,391	67,992	82,961
Web Graphic Artists	46,583	44,518	43,621	53,225
Web Site Administrator	59,201	56,578	55,437	67,642
Web Site Designer	55,817	53,343	52,268	63,776

Source: Computer Economics

Table 3.11   *2002 Salaries for IT Staff with Four to Seven Years' Experience—Detroit, Ann Arbor, and Flint; Houston; Kansas City; and Los Angeles and Riverside*

Salaries across All Sectors	Cities			
	Detroit, Ann Arbor, Flint ($)	Houston ($)	Kansas City ($)	Los Angeles & Riverside ($)
Application Programmer/Systems Analyst	53,886	51,498	50,460	61,569
AS/400 Manager	75,379	72,038	70,586	86,127
AS/400 Programmer	60,669	57,980	56,811	69,319
C++ Programmer	68,141	65,121	63,808	77,856
Certified Novell Engineer	62,218	59,460	58,262	71,089
Chief Information Officer	213,645	204,177	200,060	244,107
Cisco Systems Engineer	79,916	76,375	74,835	91,311
Database Administrator	63,654	60,833	59,606	72,730
Data Entry Clerk	22,298	21,310	20,881	25,478
Data Warehouse Administrator	114,917	109,824	107,610	131,302
EDI Application Developer	65,922	63,001	61,731	75,322
EDP Auditor	50,162	47,939	46,972	57,314
Electronic Commerce Manager	107,679	102,907	100,832	123,032
End-User Support and Help-Desk Personnel	57,563	55,012	53,903	65,771
Information Security Specialist	82,423	78,770	77,182	94,175
Internet Strategy Director	73,453	70,197	68,782	83,926
IT Purchasing Specialist	73,822	70,551	69,128	84,348
IT Training Specialist	40,032	38,258	37,487	45,740
Java Programmer	71,974	68,784	67,397	82,236
Lotus Notes Administrator/Developer	76,807	73,403	71,923	87,758
MIS Director	137,211	131,131	128,487	156,775
Network Administrator	74,208	70,919	69,489	84,788
NT Administrator	58,595	55,998	54,869	66,949
On-line Editor	40,141	38,362	37,589	45,864

Table 3.11   *2002 Salaries for IT Staff with Four to Seven Years' Experience—Detroit, Ann Arbor, and Flint; Houston; Kansas City; and Los Angeles and Riverside (continued)*

	Cities			
Salaries across All Sectors	Detroit, Ann Arbor, Flint ($)	Houston ($)	Kansas City ($)	Los Angeles & Riverside ($)
On-line Marketer	56,633	54,124	53,032	64,708
Oracle Database Developer	66,693	63,737	62,452	76,202
PC Technical Support Personnel	58,244	55,663	54,541	66,549
PowerBuilder Programmer	71,137	67,985	66,614	81,280
Quality Assurance/Control Personnel	61,766	59,029	57,839	70,573
SAP Programmer	88,956	85,014	83,300	101,640
SQL Developer	55,532	53,071	52,001	63,450
System Programmer	79,632	76,103	74,569	90,986
System/Computer Operator	69,530	66,449	65,109	79,444
Technical Writer	41,075	39,255	38,463	46,932
Telecommunications Administrator	64,463	61,606	60,364	73,654
UNIX System Administrator	64,210	61,365	60,127	73,365
Visual BASIC Programmer	56,271	53,778	52,694	64,295
Web Graphic Artists	36,102	34,502	33,806	41,249
Web Site Administrator	45,881	43,848	42,964	52,423
Web Site Designer	43,258	41,341	40,508	49,426

Source: Computer Economics

Table 3.12   *2002 Salaries for IT Staff with One to Three Years' Experience—Detroit, Ann Arbor, and Flint; Houston; Kansas City; and Los Angeles and Riverside*

	Cities			
Salaries across All Sectors	Detroit, Ann Arbor, Flint ($)	Houston ($)	Kansas City ($)	Los Angeles & Riverside ($)
Application Programmer/Systems Analyst	39,980	38,208	37,438	45,680
AS/400 Manager	56,413	53,913	52,826	64,456
AS/400 Programmer	45,404	43,392	42,517	51,878
C++ Programmer	50,996	48,736	47,753	58,267
Certified Novell Engineer	46,563	44,499	43,602	53,202
Chief Information Officer	159,889	152,803	149,723	182,686
Cisco Systems Engineer	59,808	57,158	56,006	68,336
Database Administrator	47,638	45,527	44,609	54,430
Data Entry Clerk	16,688	15,948	15,627	19,067
Data Warehouse Administrator	86,002	82,191	80,534	98,265
EDI Application Developer	49,336	47,149	46,199	56,370
EDP Auditor	37,540	35,877	35,153	42,893
Electronic Commerce Manager	80,585	77,014	75,461	92,075
End-User Support and Help-Desk Personnel	43,080	41,171	40,341	49,222
Information Security Specialist	61,684	58,950	57,762	70,479
Internet Strategy Director	54,971	52,535	51,476	62,809
IT Purchasing Specialist	55,248	52,799	51,735	63,125
IT Training Specialist	29,960	28,632	28,055	34,231
Java Programmer	53,864	51,477	50,439	61,544
Lotus Notes Administrator/Developer	57,481	54,934	53,827	65,677
MIS Director	102,687	98,137	96,158	117,329
Network Administrator	55,536	53,075	52,005	63,454
NT Administrator	43,852	41,908	41,063	50,104
On-line Editor	30,041	28,710	28,131	34,324

Table 3.12 *2002 Salaries for IT Staff with One to Three Years' Experience—Detroit, Ann Arbor, and Flint; Houston; Kansas City; and Los Angeles and Riverside (continued)*

	Cities			
Salaries across All Sectors	**Detroit, Ann Arbor, Flint ($)**	**Houston ($)**	**Kansas City ($)**	**Los Angeles & Riverside ($)**
On-line Marketer	42,384	40,505	39,689	48,427
Oracle Database Developer	49,912	47,700	46,739	57,029
PC Technical Support Personnel	43,589	41,658	40,818	49,804
PowerBuilder Programmer	53,238	50,879	49,853	60,829
Quality Assurance/Control Personnel	46,225	44,177	43,286	52,816
SAP Programmer	66,574	63,624	62,341	76,066
SQL Developer	41,559	39,718	38,917	47,485
System Programmer	59,596	56,955	55,806	68,093
System/Computer Operator	52,035	49,729	48,727	59,455
Technical Writer	30,740	29,378	28,785	35,123
Telecommunications Administrator	48,243	46,105	45,176	55,122
UNIX System Administrator	48,054	45,925	44,999	54,906
Visual BASIC Programmer	42,113	40,247	39,435	48,117
Web Graphic Artists	27,018	25,821	25,300	30,870
Web Site Administrator	34,337	32,815	32,154	39,233
Web Site Designer	32,374	30,939	30,315	36,990

Source: Computer Economics

Table 3.13   *2002 Salaries for IT Staff with More Than Eight Years' Experience—Miami, Minneapolis and St. Paul, New York and Northern New Jersey, and Oakland*

Salaries across All Sectors	Miami ($)	Minneapolis & St. Paul ($)	New York & Northern NJ ($)	Oakland ($)
Application Programmer/Systems Analyst	68,860	68,392	81,387	69,597
AS/400 Manager	96,326	95,670	113,848	97,357
AS/400 Programmer	77,528	77,000	91,631	78,358
C++ Programmer	87,076	86,483	102,916	88,008
Certified Novell Engineer	79,508	78,966	93,970	80,358
Chief Information Officer	273,015	271,156	322,678	275,936
Cisco Systems Engineer	102,125	101,429	120,702	103,217
Database Administrator	81,343	80,789	96,139	82,213
Data Entry Clerk	28,495	28,301	33,678	28,800
Data Warehouse Administrator	146,851	145,851	173,564	148,423
EDI Application Developer	84,242	83,668	99,566	85,143
EDP Auditor	64,101	63,665	75,762	64,787
Electronic Commerce Manager	137,602	136,665	162,632	139,074
End-User Support and Help-Desk Personnel	73,560	73,059	86,941	74,347
Information Security Specialist	105,327	104,610	124,487	106,454
Internet Strategy Director	93,864	93,225	110,939	94,869
IT Purchasing Specialist	94,337	93,694	111,497	95,346
IT Training Specialist	51,157	50,808	60,462	51,704
Java Programmer	91,975	91,348	108,706	92,959
Lotus Notes Administrator/Developer	98,151	97,483	116,005	99,201
MIS Director	175,341	174,147	207,237	177,217
Network Administrator	94,829	94,183	112,079	95,844
NT Administrator	74,878	74,368	88,498	75,679
On-line Editor	51,296	50,947	60,627	51,845
On-line Marketer	72,371	71,879	85,536	73,146

Table 3.13   *2002 Salaries for IT Staff with More Than Eight Years' Experience—Miami,*
Minneapolis and St. Paul, New York and Northern New Jersey, and Oakland (continued)

		Cities		
Salaries across All Sectors	**Miami ($)**	**Minneapolis & St. Paul ($)**	**New York & Northern NJ ($)**	**Oakland ($)**
Oracle Database Developer	85,226	84,646	100,730	86,138
PC Technical Support Personnel	74,430	73,923	87,969	75,227
PowerBuilder Programmer	90,906	90,287	107,442	91,878
Quality Assurance/Control Personnel	78,931	78,393	93,289	79,775
SAP Programmer	113,677	112,903	134,355	114,893
SQL Developer	70,964	70,481	83,873	71,723
System Programmer	101,761	101,069	120,273	102,850
System/Computer Operator	88,852	88,247	105,014	89,802
Technical Writer	52,489	52,132	62,038	53,051
Telecommunications Administrator	82,377	81,816	97,362	83,258
UNIX System Administrator	82,054	81,495	96,980	82,932
Visual BASIC Programmer	71,909	71,419	84,990	72,678
Web Graphic Artists	46,134	45,820	54,526	46,628
Web Site Administrator	58,631	58,232	69,296	59,258
Web Site Designer	55,279	54,903	65,335	55,871

Source: Computer Economics

Table 3.14   *2002 Salaries for IT Staff with Four to Seven Years' Experience—Miami, Minneapolis and St. Paul, New York and Northern New Jersey, and Oakland*

Salaries across All Sectors	Cities			
	Miami ($)	Minneapolis & St. Paul ($)	New York & Northern NJ ($)	Oakland ($)
Application Programmer/Systems Analyst	$53,367	$53,003	$63,075	$53,938
AS/400 Manager	74,653	74,144	88,232	75,451
AS/400 Programmer	60,084	59,675	71,014	60,727
C++ Programmer	67,484	67,025	79,760	68,206
Certified Novell Engineer	61,618	61,199	72,827	62,278
Chief Information Officer	211,587	210,146	250,076	213,851
Cisco Systems Engineer	79,146	78,608	93,544	79,993
Database Administrator	63,040	62,611	74,508	63,715
Data Entry Clerk	22,084	21,933	26,101	22,320
Data Warehouse Administrator	113,810	113,035	134,512	115,027
EDI Application Developer	65,287	64,843	77,164	65,986
EDP Auditor	49,679	49,340	58,715	50,210
Electronic Commerce Manager	106,641	105,915	126,040	107,782
End-User Support and Help-Desk Personnel	57,009	56,621	67,379	57,619
Information Security Specialist	81,628	81,073	96,477	82,502
Internet Strategy Director	72,745	72,250	85,978	73,523
IT Purchasing Specialist	73,111	72,613	86,410	73,893
IT Training Specialist	39,646	39,377	46,858	40,071
Java Programmer	71,280	70,795	84,247	72,043
Lotus Notes Administrator/Developer	76,067	75,549	89,904	76,881
MIS Director	135,889	134,964	160,609	137,344
Network Administrator	73,493	72,992	86,861	74,279
NT Administrator	58,030	57,635	68,586	58,651
On-line Editor	39,754	39,484	46,986	40,180
On-line Marketer	56,088	55,706	66,291	56,688

Table 3.14   *2002 Salaries for IT Staff with Four to Seven Years' Experience—Miami, Minneapolis and St. Paul, New York and Northern New Jersey, and Oakland (continued)*

	Cities			
Salaries across All Sectors	Miami ($)	Minneapolis & St. Paul ($)	New York & Northern NJ ($)	Oakland ($)
Oracle Database Developer	66,050	65,601	78,065	66,757
PC Technical Support Personnel	57,683	57,291	68,176	58,301
PowerBuilder Programmer	70,452	69,972	83,267	71,206
Quality Assurance/Control Personnel	61,171	60,755	72,299	61,826
SAP Programmer	88,099	87,500	104,125	89,042
SQL Developer	54,997	54,623	65,001	55,586
System Programmer	78,865	78,328	93,211	79,709
System/Computer Operator	68,860	68,391	81,386	69,597
Technical Writer	40,679	40,402	48,079	41,115
Telecommunications Administrator	63,842	63,407	75,455	64,525
UNIX System Administrator	63,592	63,159	75,159	64,272
Visual BASIC Programmer	55,729	55,350	65,867	56,326
Web Graphic Artists	35,754	35,510	42,258	36,136
Web Site Administrator	45,439	45,130	53,705	45,925
Web Site Designer	42,841	42,550	50,635	43,300

Source: Computer Economics

Table 3.15   *2002 Salaries for IT Staff with One to Three Years' Experience—Miami, Minneapolis and St. Paul, New York and Northern New Jersey, and Oakland*

	Cities			
Salaries across All Sectors	Miami ($)	Minneapolis & St. Paul ($)	New York & Northern NJ ($)	Oakland ($)
Application Programmer/Systems Analyst	39,595	39,325	46,797	40,018
AS/400 Manager	55,869	55,489	66,032	56,467
AS/400 Programmer	44,966	44,660	53,146	45,448
C++ Programmer	50,504	50,160	59,691	51,045
Certified Novell Engineer	46,114	45,800	54,503	46,608
Chief Information Officer	158,349	157,270	187,153	160,043
Cisco Systems Engineer	59,232	58,829	70,007	59,866
Database Administrator	47,179	46,857	55,761	47,684
Data Entry Clerk	16,527	16,415	19,533	16,704
Data Warehouse Administrator	85,174	84,594	100,667	86,085
EDI Application Developer	48,860	48,528	57,748	49,383
EDP Auditor	37,179	36,926	43,942	37,577
Electronic Commerce Manager	79,809	79,265	94,327	80,663
End-User Support and Help-Desk Personnel	42,665	42,374	50,426	43,121
Information Security Specialist	61,090	60,674	72,202	61,743
Internet Strategy Director	54,441	54,071	64,345	55,024
IT Purchasing Specialist	54,715	54,343	64,668	55,301
IT Training Specialist	29,671	29,469	35,068	29,988
Java Programmer	53,345	52,982	63,049	53,916
Lotus Notes Administrator/Developer	56,928	56,540	67,283	57,537
MIS Director	101,698	101,005	120,197	102,786
Network Administrator	55,001	54,626	65,006	55,589
NT Administrator	43,429	43,133	51,329	43,894
On-line Editor	29,752	29,549	35,164	30,070
On-line Marketer	41,975	41,690	49,611	42,425

Table 3.15   *2002 Salaries for IT Staff with One to Three Years' Experience—Miami, Minneapolis and St. Paul, New York and Northern New Jersey, and Oakland (continued)*

Salaries across All Sectors	Miami ($)	Minneapolis & St. Paul ($)	New York & Northern NJ ($)	Oakland ($)
			Cities	
Oracle Database Developer	49,431	49,095	58,423	49,960
PC Technical Support Personnel	43,169	42,876	51,022	43,631
PowerBuilder Programmer	52,725	52,366	62,316	53,289
Quality Assurance/Control Personnel	45,780	45,468	54,107	46,270
SAP Programmer	65,932	65,484	77,926	66,638
SQL Developer	41,159	40,879	48,646	41,600
System Programmer	59,022	58,620	69,758	59,653
System/Computer Operator	51,534	51,183	60,908	52,085
Technical Writer	30,444	30,237	35,982	30,770
Telecommunications Administrator	47,779	47,453	56,470	48,290
UNIX System Administrator	47,591	47,267	56,248	48,100
Visual BASIC Programmer	41,707	41,423	49,294	42,153
Web Graphic Artists	26,758	26,576	31,625	27,044
Web Site Administrator	34,006	33,774	40,192	34,370
Web Site Designer	32,062	31,844	37,894	32,405

Source: Computer Economics

Table 3.16   *2002 Salaries for IT Staff with More Than Eight Years' Experience—Philadelphia, Phoenix, Pittsburgh, and San Diego*

	Cities			
Salaries across All Sectors	**Philadelphia ($)**	**Phoenix ($)**	**Pittsburgh ($)**	**San Diego ($)**
Application Programmer/Systems Analyst	68,459	64,372	61,827	64,640
AS/400 Manager	95,764	90,048	86,487	90,423
AS/400 Programmer	77,076	72,475	69,610	72,777
C++ Programmer	86,568	81,401	78,182	81,740
Certified Novell Engineer	79,043	74,326	71,387	74,635
Chief Information Officer	271,421	255,221	245,129	256,283
Cisco Systems Engineer	101,528	95,469	91,693	95,866
Database Administrator	80,868	76,041	73,034	76,358
Data Entry Clerk	28,329	26,638	25,585	26,749
Data Warehouse Administrator	145,994	137,280	131,852	137,852
EDI Application Developer	83,750	78,751	75,637	79,079
EDP Auditor	63,727	59,924	57,554	60,173
Electronic Commerce Manager	136,798	128,633	123,547	129,169
End-User Support and Help-Desk Personnel	73,131	68,766	66,046	69,052
Information Security Specialist	104,712	98,462	94,569	98,872
Internet Strategy Director	93,317	87,747	84,277	88,112
IT Purchasing Specialist	93,786	88,188	84,701	88,556
IT Training Specialist	50,858	47,823	45,932	48,022
Java Programmer	91,438	85,980	82,580	86,338
Lotus Notes Administrator/Developer	97,578	91,754	88,126	92,136
MIS Director	174,318	163,913	157,432	164,596
Network Administrator	94,276	88,649	85,143	89,018
NT Administrator	74,441	69,998	67,230	70,289
On-line Editor	50,997	47,953	46,057	48,152
On-line Marketer	71,949	67,655	64,979	67,936

Table 3.16   *2002 Salaries for IT Staff with More Than Eight Years' Experience—Philadelphia, Phoenix, Pittsburgh, and San Diego (continued)*

Salaries across All Sectors	Cities			
	Philadelphia ($)	Phoenix ($)	Pittsburgh ($)	San Diego ($)
Oracle Database Developer	84,729	79,672	76,521	80,003
PC Technical Support Personnel	73,996	69,579	66,828	69,869
PowerBuilder Programmer	90,375	84,981	81,620	85,334
Quality Assurance/Control Personnel	78,470	73,786	70,869	74,093
SAP Programmer	113,013	106,268	102,066	106,710
SQL Developer	70,550	66,339	63,716	66,615
System Programmer	101,168	95,129	91,368	95,525
System/Computer Operator	88,333	83,061	79,776	83,407
Technical Writer	52,183	49,068	47,128	49,273
Telecommunications Administrator	81,896	77,008	73,963	77,329
UNIX System Administrator	81,575	76,706	73,673	77,025
Visual BASIC Programmer	71,489	67,222	64,564	67,502
Web Graphic Artists	45,865	43,127	41,422	43,307
Web Site Administrator	58,289	54,810	52,642	55,038
Web Site Designer	54,957	51,676	49,633	51,892

Source: Computer Economics

Table 3.17   *2002 Salaries for IT Staff with Four to Seven Years' Experience—Philadelphia, Phoenix, Pittsburgh, and San Diego*

Salaries across All Sectors	Cities			
	Philadelphia ($)	Phoenix ($)	Pittsburgh ($)	San Diego ($)
Application Programmer/Systems Analyst	53,055	49,889	47,916	50,096
AS/400 Manager	74,217	69,787	67,028	70,078
AS/400 Programmer	59,734	56,168	53,947	56,402
C++ Programmer	67,090	63,086	60,591	63,348
Certified Novell Engineer	61,259	57,602	55,325	57,842
Chief Information Officer	210,352	197,796	189,975	198,620
Cisco Systems Engineer	78,685	73,988	71,062	74,296
Database Administrator	62,673	58,932	56,602	59,177
Data Entry Clerk	21,955	20,644	19,828	20,730
Data Warehouse Administrator	113,145	106,392	102,185	106,835
EDI Application Developer	64,906	61,032	58,619	61,286
EDP Auditor	49,389	46,441	44,604	46,634
Electronic Commerce Manager	106,019	99,691	95,749	100,106
End-User Support and Help-Desk Personnel	56,676	53,293	51,186	53,515
Information Security Specialist	81,152	76,308	73,291	76,626
Internet Strategy Director	72,320	68,004	65,315	68,287
IT Purchasing Specialist	72,684	68,346	65,643	68,631
IT Training Specialist	39,415	37,063	35,597	37,217
Java Programmer	70,864	66,635	64,000	66,912
Lotus Notes Administrator/Developer	75,623	71,109	68,298	71,405
MIS Director	135,096	127,033	122,010	127,562
Network Administrator	73,064	68,703	65,986	68,989
NT Administrator	57,692	54,248	52,103	54,474
On-line Editor	39,522	37,163	35,694	37,318
On-line Marketer	55,760	52,432	50,359	52,651

Table 3.17   *2002 Salaries for IT Staff with Four to Seven Years' Experience—Philadelphia, Phoenix, Pittsburgh, and San Diego (continued)*

	Cities			
Salaries across All Sectors	**Philadelphia ($)**	**Phoenix ($)**	**Pittsburgh ($)**	**San Diego ($)**
Oracle Database Developer	65,665	61,746	59,304	62,003
PC Technical Support Personnel	57,347	53,924	51,792	54,148
PowerBuilder Programmer	70,041	65,860	63,256	66,134
Quality Assurance/Control Personnel	60,814	57,184	54,923	57,422
SAP Programmer	87,585	82,358	79,101	82,700
SQL Developer	54,676	51,413	49,380	51,627
System Programmer	78,405	73,725	70,810	74,032
System/Computer Operator	68,458	64,372	61,827	64,640
Technical Writer	40,442	38,028	36,524	38,186
Telecommunications Administrator	63,469	59,681	57,321	59,930
UNIX System Administrator	63,220	59,447	57,096	59,694
Visual BASIC Programmer	55,404	52,097	50,037	52,314
Web Graphic Artists	35,545	33,424	32,102	33,563
Web Site Administrator	45,174	42,478	40,798	42,654
Web Site Designer	42,591	40,049	38,466	40,216

Source: Computer Economics

Table 3.18   *2002 Salaries for IT Staff with One to Three Years' Experience—Philadelphia, Phoenix, Pittsburgh, and San Diego*

Salaries across All Sectors	Cities			
	Philadelphia ($)	Phoenix ($)	Pittsburgh ($)	San Diego ($)
Application Programmer/Systems Analyst	$39,364	$37,014	$35,551	$37,168
AS/400 Manager	55,543	52,228	50,163	52,445
AS/400 Programmer	44,704	42,036	40,374	42,211
C++ Programmer	50,210	47,213	45,346	47,409
Certified Novell Engineer	45,845	43,109	41,404	43,288
Chief Information Officer	157,424	148,028	142,175	148,644
Cisco Systems Engineer	58,886	55,372	53,182	55,602
Database Administrator	46,903	44,104	42,360	44,287
Data Entry Clerk	16,431	15,450	14,839	15,514
Data Warehouse Administrator	84,677	79,622	76,474	79,954
EDI Application Developer	48,575	45,676	43,870	45,866
EDP Auditor	36,962	34,756	33,381	34,900
Electronic Commerce Manager	79,343	74,607	71,657	74,918
End-User Support and Help-Desk Personnel	42,416	39,884	38,307	40,050
Information Security Specialist	60,733	57,108	54,850	57,346
Internet Strategy Director	54,124	50,893	48,881	51,105
IT Purchasing Specialist	54,396	51,149	49,127	51,362
IT Training Specialist	29,498	27,737	26,640	27,853
Java Programmer	53,034	49,869	47,897	50,076
Lotus Notes Administrator/Developer	56,595	53,217	51,113	53,439
MIS Director	101,104	95,070	91,310	95,465
Network Administrator	54,680	51,416	49,383	51,630
NT Administrator	43,176	40,599	38,993	40,768
On-line Editor	29,578	27,813	26,713	27,928
On-line Marketer	41,730	39,240	37,688	39,403

Table 3.18   *2002 Salaries for IT Staff with One to Three Years' Experience—Philadelphia, Phoenix, Pittsburgh, and San Diego (continued)*

	Cities			
Salaries across All Sectors	**Philadelphia ($)**	**Phoenix ($)**	**Pittsburgh ($)**	**San Diego ($)**
Oracle Database Developer	49,143	46,210	44,382	46,402
PC Technical Support Personnel	42,918	40,356	38,760	40,524
PowerBuilder Programmer	52,417	49,289	47,340	49,494
Quality Assurance/Control Personnel	45,513	42,796	41,104	42,974
SAP Programmer	65,548	61,635	59,198	61,892
SQL Developer	40,919	38,477	36,955	38,637
System Programmer	58,677	55,175	52,993	55,405
System/Computer Operator	51,233	48,175	46,270	48,376
Technical Writer	30,266	28,460	27,334	28,578
Telecommunications Administrator	47,500	44,665	42,899	44,851
UNIX System Administrator	47,313	44,489	42,730	44,675
Visual BASIC Programmer	41,464	38,989	37,447	39,151
Web Graphic Artists	26,602	25,014	24,025	25,118
Web Site Administrator	33,808	31,790	30,533	31,922
Web Site Designer	31,875	29,972	28,787	30,097

Source: Computer Economics

Table 3.19   *2002 Salaries for IT Staff with More Than Eight Years' Experience—San Francisco, San Jose, Seattle and Tacoma, and Washington DC Metro*

| Salaries across All Sectors | Cities | | | |
	San Francisco ($)	San Jose ($)	Seattle & Tacoma ($)	Washington DC Metro ($)
Application Programmer/Systems Analyst	78,707	90,698	63,301	69,798
AS/400 Manager	110,100	126,873	88,549	97,638
AS/400 Programmer	88,615	102,114	71,269	78,584
C++ Programmer	99,528	114,690	80,046	88,262
Certified Novell Engineer	90,877	104,721	73,088	80,590
Chief Information Officer	312,055	359,594	250,972	276,733
Cisco Systems Engineer	116,728	134,510	93,879	103,515
Database Administrator	92,974	107,138	74,775	82,450
Data Entry Clerk	32,570	37,531	26,194	28,883
Data Warehouse Administrator	167,850	193,421	134,995	148,851
EDI Application Developer	96,288	110,957	77,440	85,389
EDP Auditor	73,268	84,429	58,926	64,974
Electronic Commerce Manager	157,278	181,238	126,492	139,475
End-User Support and Help-Desk Personnel	84,079	96,887	67,621	74,562
Information Security Specialist	120,388	138,728	96,823	106,761
Internet Strategy Director	107,287	123,631	86,286	95,143
IT Purchasing Specialist	107,827	124,253	86,720	95,622
IT Training Specialist	58,472	67,380	47,026	51,853
Java Programmer	105,127	121,142	84,549	93,227
Lotus Notes Administrator/Developer	112,186	129,277	90,226	99,488
MIS Director	200,414	230,946	161,184	177,729
Network Administrator	108,389	124,901	87,173	96,121
NT Administrator	85,585	98,623	68,832	75,897
On-line Editor	58,631	67,563	47,154	51,995
On-line Marketer	82,720	95,322	66,528	73,357

Table 3.19   *2002 Salaries for IT Staff with More Than Eight Years' Experience—San Francisco, San Jose, Seattle and Tacoma, and Washington DC Metro (continued)*

Salaries across All Sectors	San Francisco ($)	San Jose ($)	Seattle & Tacoma ($)	Washington DC Metro ($)
Oracle Database Developer	97,413	112,253	78,345	86,387
PC Technical Support Personnel	85,073	98,033	68,421	75,444
PowerBuilder Programmer	103,905	119,734	83,566	92,144
Quality Assurance/Control Personnel	90,217	103,961	72,558	80,006
SAP Programmer	129,932	149,726	104,498	115,225
SQL Developer	81,112	93,468	65,234	71,930
System Programmer	116,313	134,032	93,545	103,147
System/Computer Operator	101,557	117,028	81,678	90,062
Technical Writer	59,995	69,135	48,252	53,204
Telecommunications Administrator	94,156	108,500	75,726	83,499
UNIX System Administrator	93,787	108,075	75,429	83,171
Visual BASIC Programmer	82,192	94,713	66,103	72,888
Web Graphic Artists	52,731	60,764	42,409	46,762
Web Site Administrator	67,015	77,224	53,897	59,430
Web Site Designer	63,184	72,810	50,816	56,032

Source: Computer Economics

Table 3.20   *2002 Salaries for IT Staff with Four to Seven Years' Experience—San Francisco, San Jose, Seattle and Tacoma, and Washington DC Metro*

Salaries across All Sectors	Cities			
	San Francisco ($)	San Jose ($)	Seattle & Tacoma ($)	Washington DC Metro ($)
Application Programmer/Systems Analyst	60,998	70,291	49,058	54,094
AS/400 Manager	85,328	98,327	68,625	75,669
AS/400 Programmer	68,676	79,138	55,233	60,903
C++ Programmer	77,134	88,885	62,036	68,403
Certified Novell Engineer	70,430	81,159	56,643	62,457
Chief Information Officer	241,843	278,685	194,503	214,468
Cisco Systems Engineer	90,464	104,245	72,756	80,224
Database Administrator	72,055	83,032	57,951	63,899
Data Entry Clerk	25,242	29,087	20,301	22,384
Data Warehouse Administrator	130,084	149,901	104,621	115,360
EDI Application Developer	74,623	85,991	60,016	66,177
EDP Auditor	56,782	65,433	45,668	50,355
Electronic Commerce Manager	121,890	140,459	98,031	108,093
End-User Support and Help- Desk Personnel	65,161	75,088	52,406	57,785
Information Security Specialist	93,301	107,515	75,038	82,740
Internet Strategy Director	83,147	95,814	66,872	73,736
IT Purchasing Specialist	83,566	96,296	67,208	74,107
IT Training Specialist	45,316	52,219	36,445	40,186
Java Programmer	81,473	93,885	65,525	72,251
Lotus Notes Administrator/Developer	86,944	100,190	69,926	77,103
MIS Director	155,321	178,983	124,918	137,740
Network Administrator	84,002	96,799	67,559	74,493
NT Administrator	66,328	76,433	53,345	58,821
On-line Editor	45,439	52,361	36,545	40,296
On-line Marketer	64,108	73,874	51,559	56,852

Table 3.20   *2002 Salaries for IT Staff with Four to Seven Years' Experience—San Francisco, San Jose, Seattle and Tacoma, and Washington DC Metro (continued)*

	Cities			
Salaries across All Sectors	San Francisco ($)	San Jose ($)	Seattle & Tacoma ($)	Washington DC Metro ($)
Oracle Database Developer	75,495	86,996	60,718	66,950
PC Technical Support Personnel	65,932	75,976	53,026	58,469
PowerBuilder Programmer	80,526	92,793	64,764	71,411
Quality Assurance/Control Personnel	69,919	80,570	56,232	62,004
SAP Programmer	100,697	116,038	80,986	89,299
SQL Developer	62,861	72,438	50,557	55,746
System Programmer	90,143	103,875	72,498	79,939
System/Computer Operator	78,707	90,697	63,300	69,798
Technical Writer	46,496	53,580	37,395	41,233
Telecommunications Administrator	72,971	84,088	58,688	64,712
UNIX System Administrator	72,685	83,758	58,457	64,458
Visual BASIC Programmer	63,698	73,402	51,230	56,488
Web Graphic Artists	40,867	47,092	32,867	36,241
Web Site Administrator	51,937	59,849	41,770	46,058
Web Site Designer	48,968	56,427	39,382	43,425

Source: Computer Economics

Table 3.21   *2002 Salaries for IT Staff with One to Three Years' Experience—San Francisco, San Jose, Seattle and Tacoma, and Washington DC Metro*

Salaries across All Sectors	Cities			
	San Francisco ($)	San Jose ($)	Seattle & Tacoma ($)	Washington DC Metro ($)
Application Programmer/Systems Analyst	45,257	52,151	36,398	40,134
AS/400 Manager	63,858	73,586	51,358	56,630
AS/400 Programmer	51,396	59,226	41,336	45,579
C++ Programmer	57,726	66,520	46,427	51,192
Certified Novell Engineer	52,709	60,738	42,391	46,742
Chief Information Officer	180,992	208,564	145,564	160,505
Cisco Systems Engineer	67,702	78,016	54,450	60,039
Database Administrator	53,925	62,140	43,370	47,821
Data Entry Clerk	18,890	21,768	15,193	16,752
Data Warehouse Administrator	97,353	112,184	78,297	86,334
EDI Application Developer	55,847	64,355	44,915	49,526
EDP Auditor	42,495	48,969	34,177	37,685
Electronic Commerce Manager	91,221	105,118	73,365	80,896
End-User Support and Help-Desk Personnel	48,766	56,195	39,220	43,246
Information Security Specialist	69,825	80,463	56,157	61,922
Internet Strategy Director	62,226	71,706	50,046	55,183
IT Purchasing Specialist	62,539	72,067	50,298	55,461
IT Training Specialist	33,914	39,080	27,275	30,075
Java Programmer	60,974	70,262	49,038	54,072
Lotus Notes Administrator/Developer	65,068	74,981	52,331	57,703
MIS Director	116,240	133,948	93,487	103,083
Network Administrator	62,866	72,443	50,560	55,750
NT Administrator	49,639	57,201	39,923	44,021
On-line Editor	34,006	39,187	27,350	30,157
On-line Marketer	47,978	55,287	38,586	42,547

Table 3.21   *2002 Salaries for IT Staff with One to Three Years' Experience—San Francisco,*
San Jose, Seattle and Tacoma, and Washington DC Metro (continued)

Salaries across All Sectors	Cities			
	San Francisco ($)	San Jose ($)	Seattle & Tacoma ($)	Washington DC Metro ($)
Oracle Database Developer	56,500	65,107	45,440	50,105
PC Technical Support Personnel	49,343	56,859	39,684	43,757
PowerBuilder Programmer	60,265	69,445	48,468	53,443
Quality Assurance/Control Personnel	52,326	60,297	42,084	46,403
SAP Programmer	75,361	86,841	60,609	66,830
SQL Developer	47,045	54,212	37,836	41,720
System Programmer	67,462	77,739	54,256	59,825
System/Computer Operator	58,903	67,876	47,373	52,236
Technical Writer	34,797	40,098	27,986	30,859
Telecommunications Administrator	54,611	62,930	43,921	48,429
UNIX System Administrator	54,396	62,683	43,749	48,239
Visual BASIC Programmer	47,671	54,933	38,340	42,275
Web Graphic Artists	30,584	35,243	24,597	27,122
Web Site Administrator	38,869	44,790	31,260	34,469
Web Site Designer	36,647	42,230	29,473	32,499

Source: Computer Economics

Principle Three: Adequately Train Computer Users

> *The commander must be at constant pains to keep his troops abreast of all the latest tactical experience and developments, and must insist on their practical application. He must see to it that his subordinates are trained in accordance with the latest requirements. The best form of welfare for the troops is first-class training, for this saves unnecessary casualties.*
>
> —Erwin Rommel

4.1 The positive outcomes of training

Training computer users is an important step in assuring that an organization gets the best return on investment from its information technology. There are many positive results achieved from adequately training users, including the following:

- Users feel more confident and will try new approaches to completing tasks.

- Users have a better understanding of what information technology can do for the organization.

- Help-desk calls for simple problem solving decline, allowing support staff to spend time on more critical issues.

- Coworkers are not coerced into providing support to the under-trained user and will be able to accomplish more on their jobs.

- Accidental security breaches can be reduced.

- The incidents of viruses entering a corporate network can be reduced when users are trained on basic prevention skills.

4.1.1   Spending for training

Central IS budget allocations for training have traditionally ranged from 1 percent to 3 percent. The IS Budget Allocations TriMark compares the average spending in major budget categories for the years from 1999 to 2001. The IS Budget Allocations TriMark process is designed to provide IT executives with a strategic comparison of budget allocations over an entire decade of IT spending. The central IS budget allocations for training by organization revenue levels for the period 1999 to 2001 are shown in Table 4.1.

The IS Budget Allocations DeciMark compares the average spending in major budget categories for the years from 1992 to 2002. The IS Budget Allocations DeciMark process is designed to provide IT executives with a strategic comparison of budget allocations over an entire decade of IT spending. The central IS budget allocation for training by industry sector for the period 1991 to 2000 is shown in Table 4.2.

4.1.2   Return on investment for training

Companies are spending more on employee training, and e-learning has reached its highest level since 1997, according to the 2002 ASTD "State of the Industry Report" from the American Society for Training & Development (ASTD). Training expenditures for many organizations did not decline with the recent economic downturn; in fact, companies expected spending on training to grow a healthy 10 percent between 2000 and 2001. Additional key findings of the study include the following:

- Total training expenditures increased both on a per-employee basis ($677 in 1999 to $704 in 2000) and as a percentage of annual payroll (1.8 percent in 1999 to 2.0 percent in 2000). Training expenditures are projected to increase in both 2001 and 2002.

- Companies that made a dedicated commitment in 2000 to developing the knowledge, skills, and abilities of their employees spent an average of $1,574 on training per employee, more than double what the average company spent.

- Industry sectors spending the most on training as a percentage of payroll in 2000 included finance, insurance, and real estate (2.8 percent); transportation and public utilities (2.7 percent); and technology (2.5 percent).

Table 4.1   *IS Budget Allocations for Training by Organization Revenue*

Annual Revenue	Percent of IS Budget Allocated for Training 1999 to 2001
Over $500 million	2.2%
$200–$500 million	2.1%
Under $200 million	2.7%

Source: Computer Economics 2002 Information Systems and E-Business Spending Report

Table 4.2   *IS Budget Allocations for Training by Industry Sector*

Sector	Percent of IS Budget Allocated for Training 1991 to 2000
All sectors	2.1%
Banking and finance	2.1%
Discrete manufacturing	2.3%
Federal government	2.3%
Health care	1.1%
Insurance	2.3%
Process Manufacturing	2.7%
Professional Services	1.9%
Retail Distribution	2.1%
State and Local	2.2%
Trade Services	1.8%
Transportation	2.1%
Utilities	1.4%
Wholesale Distribution	2.1%

Source: Computer Economics 2002 Information Systems and E-Business Spending Report

- E-learning reached new heights as firms began using learning technologies to deliver more training (8.8 percent in 2000). Despite a leveling off of e-learning during past years, most firms indicated that they have made significant investments in e-learning systems and courseware and that their e-learning expenditures would continue to grow into 2001 and beyond.

- Outsourcing increased as firms spent a larger percentage of training expenditures on outside providers (19.9 percent in 1999 to 22.2 percent in 2000). Preliminary indications suggested that this percentage would rise in 2001.

- Firms spent the largest share of training expenditures on training in technical processes and procedures and information technology (IT) skills (13.5 percent and 11 percent, respectively). Training in managerial/supervisory skills, occupational safety, and product knowledge all gained 9 percent of the typical firm's training expenditures.

Additional findings from the report include a look at the major trends shaping the workplace learning and performance industry. Practitioners and experts from various sectors, including business, nonprofit, and academia, from around the world identified the top ten trends affecting the future of training and the workplace learning and performance field. The top three trends identified include:

- Money. Increasing pressure from shareholders for short-term profits means that there is a greater pressure on employees to produce results and on training to show a return on investment.

- Diversity. The growing cultural diversity of organizations means a greater need for people with different backgrounds to work together and find better ways of balancing the local with the global.

- Time. The increasing expectation for just-in-time products and services is resulting in shorter time frames for learning, often facilitated through technology.

The 2002 ASTD "State of the Industry Report" includes findings from 367 U.S. organizations that participated in the Benchmarking Service during 2001 and provided sufficient amounts of valid data on their training activities during 2000 and the latter part of 2001. The Benchmarking Service is free, and participation is open to all organizations.

4.2   **Where the future workforce received training**

In a survey of high school seniors, Computer Economics found that most teens say that they acquired their existing computer and Internet skills on their own. However, despite their previous independence, the majority of the same teens say they expect their schools and employers to provide them with training to build on these skills in the future.

These findings send a strong message to employers and college-level academic programs that the coming generation of employees and students will be depending on them to expand their computer knowledge. The survey also suggests that, for institutions and companies willing to provide the training these students will require, different approaches for men and women will be appropriate because of the different ways male and female students say they had acquired and will acquire their computer skills.

Over three-quarters of the male students learned their existing computer skills on their own. In contrast, just under half of the female students had learned their skills independently. The women tended to rely on friends and family (24.3 percent) at a much higher rate than the male students did (13.6 percent).

Another 21.6 percent of the female students gained their Internet and computer skills from computer classes at school, school-related assignments, or training at work. Only about 5 percent of males said they learned their computer skills in classes at school, and none of them said they gained their skills from school-related assignments or training at work. Very few students of either gender said they acquired their computing skills as a result of work-related assignments.

Compared with the 63 percent of students who learned their existing computer and Internet skills on their own, about 20 percent fewer students believe they will continue to do so in the future. Many more students anticipate that they will be acquiring these future skills through computer classes at school. At over 18 percent, males are more likely than females (13.5 percent) to believe they will utilize this opportunity.

Women are much more likely to believe their continued Internet and computer knowledge will come from formal training at work, with nearly one-quarter of women thinking this way, compared with only about 9 percent of men. In terms of school-related assignments, just under one-quarter of women anticipate that this will be the most significant source of computer knowledge for them, whereas only another 9 percent of men believe so. None of the students thinks they will continue to depend on friends and family to help them with computer skills in the future.

4.3   The demographics of the future work force

According to the U.S. Bureau of Labor Statistics (BLS), population is the single most important factor in determining the size and composition of the labor force, comprising people who are either working or looking for work. The civilian labor force is projected to increase by 17 million, or 12 percent, to 158 million over the 2000–2010 period.

The U.S. workforce will become more diverse by 2010. White, non-Hispanic persons will continue to make up a decreasing share of the labor force, falling from 73.1 percent in 2000 to 69.2 percent in 2010. However, despite relatively slow growth, white, non-Hispanics will have the largest numerical growth in the labor force between 2000 and 2010, reflecting the large size of this group. Hispanics, non-Hispanic African Americans, and Asian and other ethnic groups are projected to account for an increasing share of the labor force by 2010, growing from 10.9 percent to 13.3 percent, 11.8 percent to 12.7 percent, and 4.7 percent to 6.1 percent, respectively. By 2010, for the first time Hispanics will constitute a greater share of the labor force than will African Americans. Asians and others continue to have the fastest growth rates, but still are expected to remain the smallest of the four labor force groups.

The numbers of men and women in the labor force will grow, but the number of men will grow at a slower rate than the number of women. The male labor force is projected to grow by 9.3 percent from 2000 to 2010, compared with 15.1 percent for women. As a result, men's share of the labor force is expected to decrease from 53.4 to 52.1 percent, while women's share is expected to increase from 46.6 to 47.9 percent.

The youth labor force, aged 16 to 24, is expected to increase its share of the labor force to 16.5 percent by 2010, growing more rapidly than the overall labor force. The large group, 25 to 54 years old, who made up 71 percent of the labor force in 2000, is projected to decline to 66.6 percent of the labor force by 2010. Workers 55 and older, on the other hand, are projected to increase from 12.9 percent to 16.9 percent of the labor force between 2000 and 2010, as a result of the aging of the baby-boomer generation.

Employment in occupations requiring at least a bachelor's degree is expected to grow 21.6 percent and account for five out of the six fastest growing education or training categories. Two categories—jobs requiring an associate degree (projected to grow 32 percent over the 2000–2010 period, faster than any other category) and jobs requiring a postsecondary vocational award—together will grow 24.1 percent. The four categories of occupations requiring work-related training are projected to increase 12.4 percent, compared with 15.2 percent for all occupations combined.

4.4   Developing or expanding a training program

Identifying where employees need the most training is important to help allocate resources. One of the greatest sources of information is in the help-desk logs. These logs identify where users are having the most frequent problems as well as which users are having the most frequent problems. Another source of information about training needs is the supervisors who can monitor and observe the behavior and problems that employees have on a day-to-day basis.

For those organizations that already have an organized training effort under way, expanding efforts to more comprehensively address computer skills is relatively easy. However, those organizations that do not have a formal training program in place must recognize that developing a training program can be a very time-consuming process.

The key to success in both expanding existing programs or launching new programs is having a good training coordinator and experienced trainers.

IT training specialists plan, prepare, present, and evaluate training programs covering a variety of computer and telecommunications topics. Training specialists recommend whether specific content is best learned through classroom instruction, self-paced instruction, on-line courses, or training manuals. Annual salaries for in-house IT training staff vary by

Table 4.3 *Annual Salaries for In-House IT Training Specialist*

Experience Level	Region			
	East	Central	Mountain	Pacific
More than 8 years' experience	$51,435	$48,349	$45,777	$53,492
4 to 7 years' experience	$39,862	$37,470	$35,477	$41,457
1 to 3 years' experience	$29,832	$28,042	$26,551	$31,026

Source: Computer Economics

Table 4.4   *2002 Hourly Rates for Contract Trainers*

Experience Level	Hourly Rate
Training Specialist	$32.50
Senior Training Specialist	$45.20

Source: Computer Economics

region, as is shown in Table 4.3. Additional salary information for trainers by city can be found in Chapter 3.

Average hourly rates for contract trainers will vary by skill area and the topics for which they are training. Computer Economics surveyed a variety of training organizations to determine the hourly rate for a trainer capable of teaching basic computer skills and widely used applications such as Microsoft Office. Table 4.4 shows the hourly rate for a senior training specialist as $45.20 per hour for 2002 and a less than senior specialist at $32.50 per hour.

4.5   Sources of training

If your organization decides that hiring a training coordinator or a trainer is not costeffective, then you need to seek other sources of training. There are numerous companies that offer training for computer users as well as IT professionals. Prices vary considerably, as does the quality of instruction. It is advisable to check the references of any training company. The type of training needed also dictates some parameters for selecting a training organization.

For highly technical training for IT professionals it is advisable to utilize the best training organization available in your area or to send employees to remote training sites. For training in basic computer skills and office functions such as word processing the local community college may be your best option. Many local two-year schools offer training both in a traditional academic format as well as in condensed and accelerated formats.

Computer Economics benchmarks the costs of training by reviewing programs offered by several commercial training companies to determine costs (low and high) for several software packages and programming languages. Table 4.5 provides the level of training, number of days, and low and high costs of training for each software package.

Table 4.5   *Costs for Instructor-led Training in 2002*

Description of Training	Level	Number of days	Low ($)	High ($)
Accelerated Training for MS SQL Server 6.5	Advanced	5	1,890	2,310
Accelerated Training for MS Win NT 4.0	Advanced	5	1,890	2,310
Accelerated Training for MS Win NT 4.0	Advanced	5	1,890	2,310
Accelerated Training for MS Win NT 3.51	Advanced	5	1,890	2,310
Access 7.0 or 2000	Advanced	1	210	260
Access 7.0 or 2000	Introductory	1	210	260
Access 7.0 or 2000	Intermediate	1	210	260
Access 97 or 2000	Advanced	1	210	260
Access 97 or 2000	Introductory	1	210	260
Access 97 or 2000	Intermediate	1	210	260
Administering and Supporting MS FrontPage 97	Intermediate	2	680	830
Administering MS SMS 2.0	Intermediate	3	1,040	1,280
Administering MS Win NT 4.0	Intermediate	3	1,040	1,280
Adobe FrameMaker 5.0 or 5.5	Introductory	1	210	260
Adobe FrameMaker 5.0 or 5.5	Advanced	1	210	260
Adobe Illustrator 7.0 or 8.0	Advanced	1	210	260
Adobe Illustrator 7.0 or 8.0	Intermediate	1	210	260
Adobe Illustrator 7.0 or 8.0	Introductory	1	210	260
Adobe PageMaker 6.5	Advanced	1	210	260
Adobe PageMaker 6.5	Intermediate	1	210	260
Adobe PageMaker 6.5	Introductory	1	210	260
Adv. C Language Programming	Advanced	5	2,000	3,250
Adv. C++ Programming	Advanced	5	2,000	3,250
Adv. JAVA Programming	Advanced	5	2,000	3,250
Adv. UNIX Concepts	Introductory	5	2,000	3,250
Application Development on the World Wide Web	Advanced	5	2,000	3,250

Table 4.5   *Costs for Instructor-led Training in 2002 (continued)*

Description of Training	Level	Number of days	Low ($)	High ($)
Applying MS Internet Information Server 4.0	Advanced	1	350	430
Borland Dbase 5.0	Advanced	1	210	260
Borland Dbase 5.0	Intermediate	1	210	260
Borland Dbase 5.0	Introductory	1	210	260
C and UNIX Interface System Calls	Advanced	5	2,000	3,250
C Language Programming	Advanced	5	2,000	3,250
C++ Programming	Advanced	5	2,000	3,250
C++ Programming for Non-C Programmers	Advanced	5	2,000	3,250
COM Development Using MS Visual C++	Advanced	5	1,770	2,160
Core Technologies of MS Exchange Server 5.0	Advanced	5	1,770	2,160
Corel Paradox 8.0 or 9.0	Advanced	1	210	260
Corel Paradox 8.0 or 9.0	Intermediate	1	210	260
Corel Paradox 8.0 or 9.0	Introductory	1	210	260
Corel QuattroPro 8.0	Advanced	1	210	260
Corel QuattroPro 8.0	Intermediate	1	210	260
Corel QuattroPro 8.0	Introductory	1	210	260
Corel WordPerfect 8.0	Advanced	1	210	260
Corel WordPerfect 8.0	Intermediate	1	210	260
Corel WordPerfect 8.0	Advanced	1	210	260
Corel WordPerfect Suite 8	Introductory	1	210	260
CorelDraw 7.0 or 9.0	Advanced	1	210	260
CorelDraw 7.0 or 9.0	Intermediate	1	210	260
CorelDraw 7.0 or 9.0	Introductory	1	210	260
Creating and Configuring a Web Server Using MS Tools	Advanced	3	1,040	1,280
Database Fundamentals Using Access 2000	Intermediate	5	1,770	2,160
Deploying & Managing Microsoft Office 2000	Advanced	5	1,770	2,160

Table 4.5   *Costs for Instructor-led Training in 2002 (continued)*

Description of Training	Level	Number of days	Low ($)	High ($)
Developing Client/Server Applications for MS SQL Server	Advanced	3	1,040	1,280
Enterprise Development Using MS Visual BASIC	Advanced	5	1,770	2,160
Enterprise Development Using MS Visual C++	Advanced	5	1,770	2,160
Excel 7.0	Advanced	1	210	260
Excel 7.0 Level 1	Intermediate	1	210	260
Excel 7.0 Level 2	Introductory	1	210	260
Excel 97 or 2000	Advanced	1	210	260
Excel 97 Organizing & Charting Data	Intermediate	1	210	260
Excel 97 Worksheets	Introductory	1	210	260
Exchange 4.0 Electronic Mail for Win95	Advanced	1	210	260
Filemaker Pro 4.0 for Win95	Advanced	1	210	260
Filemaker Pro 4.0 for Win95	Intermediate	1	210	260
Filemaker Pro 4.0 for Win95	Introductory	1	210	260
Fundamentals of UNIX with Tools and Techniques	Introductory	5	1,770	2,160
HTML and CGI Programming	Advanced	3	1,800	2,300
Implementing a Database in MS SQL Server 7.0	Advanced	5	1,800	2,300
Implementing MS Internet Explorer 4.0	Advanced	2	680	830
Implementing MS Site Server 3.0	Advanced	4	1,360	1,670
Installing & Configuring Microsoft Windows 98	Advanced	3	1,040	1,280
Installing and Administering MS Win NT 5.0	Advanced	5	1,770	2,160
Installing and Configuring MS Exchange Server 5.0	Advanced	1	350	430
Installing and Configuring MS Site Server 3.0	Advanced	1	350	430
Installing and Configuring MS Win NT Server 4.0	Advanced	1	350	430
Installing and Configuring MS Win NT Workstation 4.0	Advanced	1	350	430
Installing and Configuring MS Win95	Advanced	2	680	830
Installing and Supporting MS Office 97	Advanced	2	680	830

Table 4.5   *Costs for Instructor-led Training in 2002 (continued)*

Description of Training	Level	Number of days	Low ($)	High ($)
Internetworking MS TCP/IP on MS Win NT 4.0	Advanced	5	1,770	2,160
Internetworking MS TCP/IP on MS Windows NT 3.5	Advanced	4	1,360	1,670
Lotus 1-2-3 97	Advanced	1	210	260
Lotus 1-2-3 97	Intermediate	1	210	260
Lotus 1-2-3 97	Introductory	1	210	260
Lotus Approach 8.0	Advanced	1	210	260
Lotus Approach 8.0	Intermediate	1	210	260
Lotus Approach 8.0	Introductory	1	210	260
Lotus SmartSuite 97	Advanced	1	210	260
MFC Development Using MS Visual C++	Advanced	5	1,900	2,400
MFC Development Using MS Visual C++ 5	Advanced	5	1,900	2,400
MFC Fundamentals Using MS Visual C++	Advanced	5	1,900	2,400
Microsoft Access 2000 Development	Advanced	5	1,770	2,160
Microsoft Access 2000 Programming	Advanced	5	1,770	2,160
Microsoft BackOffice Small Business Server 4.5	Advanced	1	350	430
Microsoft Windows 2000 First Look	Advanced	1	350	430
Migrating from Novell NetWare to MS Windows NT 4.0	Advanced	2	680	830
MS Exchange Server 5.5 Series	Advanced	4	1,360	1,670
MS Exchange Server Performance and Troubleshooting	Advanced	2	680	830
MS Internet Explorer 4.0	Introductory	1	210	260
MS Office 95 Document Integration	Introductory	1	210	260
MS Office 95 Transition from Win 3.1	Introductory	1	210	260
MS Office 97 Development	Advanced	5	1,770	2,160
MS Project 4.1 Level 1 Creating a Project	Introductory	1	210	260
MS Project 4.1 Level 2 Managing a Project	Introductory	1	210	260
MS SQL Server 7.0 Overview	Advanced	1	350	430

Table 4.5   *Costs for Instructor-led Training in 2002 (continued)*

Description of Training	Level	Number of days	Low ($)	High ($)
MS SQL Server 7.0 Upgrade and Migration	Advanced	3	1,040	1,280
MS SQL Server for Developers	Advanced	5	13,650	16,650
MS Visual BASIC 6 Development	Advanced	5	1,770	2,160
MS Visual BASIC 6 Fundamentals	Advanced	5	1,770	2,160
MS Visual FoxPro 5.0	Advanced	1	210	260
MS Visual FoxPro 5.0	Intermediate	1	210	260
MS Visual FoxPro 5.0	Introductory	1	210	260
MS Visual J++	Advanced	5	1,770	2,160
MS Web Essentials	Intermediate	1	350	430
MS Win Architecture for Developers	Advanced	5	1,770	2,160
MS Win NT 5.0 First Look	Intermediate	1	350	430
MS Win NT Server 4.0: Analysis and Optimization	Advanced	1	350	430
MS Win NT Server 4.0: Network Analysis and Optimization	Advanced	2	680	830
MS Windows NT Server 3.51 Expert Series	Advanced	5	1,770	2,160
Netscape Communicator for Win95	Introductory	1	210	260
Netscape Navigator for Win95	Introductory	1	210	260
Networking Microsoft Windows 98	Introductory	2	680	830
Networking MS Win95	Advanced	3	1,040	1,280
New Features of Microsoft SQL Server 6	Advanced	3	1,040	1,280
Object-Oriented Analysis and Design	Advanced	5	6,500	9,500
OO Analysis/Design/and Implementation	Advanced	5	6,500	9,500
Oracle Database Administration	Advanced	3	7,500	11,060
Oracle for Developers	Advanced	5	7,500	12,000
Oracle Perforce and Tuning	Advanced	5	7,500	12,000
Outlook 97	Advanced	1	210	260
Outlook 97	Introductory	1	210	260

Table 4.5 *Costs for Instructor-led Training in 2002 (continued)*

Description of Training	Level	Number of days	Low ($)	High ($)
Overview of Microsoft BackOffice 4.5	Advanced	1	350	430
Overview of MS Exchange Collaboration	Advanced	2	680	830
Overview of MS Exchange Server 5.5	Advanced	1	350	430
Performance Tuning & Optimization of MS SQL Server 6.5	Advanced	5	1,770	2,160
Planning and Implementing Active Directory	Advanced	3	1,040	1,280
Planning/implementing and Supporting MS SMS 2.0	Advanced	5	1,770	2,160
PowerPoint 7.0	Advanced	1	210	260
PowerPoint 7.0	Introductory	1	210	260
PowerPoint 97	Advanced	1	210	260
PowerPoint 97	Introductory	1	210	260
Programming in JavaScript	Advanced	2	2,500	4,500
Programming in MS Visual FoxPro 3.0 for MS Windows	Advanced	5	1,650	2,250
Programming in Perl	Advanced	5	13,650	16,650
Programming with MS Access for Win95	Advanced	5	1,500	2,200
Schedule+ 7.0	Introductory	1	210	260
Secure Web Access Using MS Proxy Server 2.0	Advanced	2	680	830
Securing MS Win NT Server	Advanced	2	680	830
Supporting Microsoft BackOffice Small Business Server 4.5	Advanced	1	350	430
Supporting Microsoft Proxy Server 1.0	Advanced	2	680	830
Supporting Microsoft SNA Server 3.0	Advanced	4	1,360	1,670
Supporting MS Cluster Server	Advanced	2	680	830
Supporting MS SNA Server 4.0	Advanced	5	1,600	2,200
Supporting MS Systems Management Server 1.2	Advanced	5	1,600	2,200
Supporting MS Win 98	Advanced	5	1,600	2,200
Supporting MS Win NT 4.0—Core Technologies	Advanced	5	1,600	2,200
Supporting MS Win NT 5.0	Advanced	5	1,600	2,200

Table 4.5   *Costs for Instructor-led Training in 2002 (continued)*

Description of Training	Level	Number of days	Low ($)	High ($)
Supporting MS Win NT Server 4.0—Enterprise Technologies	Advanced	5	1,600	2,200
Supporting MS Win Terminal Server 4.0 Hydra	Advanced	3	1,600	2,200
Supporting MS Win95	Advanced	5	1,600	2,200
System Administration for MS SQL Server 6.5	Advanced	5	1,770	2,160
System Administration for MS SQL Server 7.0	Advanced	5	1,770	2,160
TCP/IP Networking3	Advanced	3	2,500	4,000
The C++ Standard Template Library	Advanced	5	1,770	2,160
UNIX Shell Programming	Advanced	5	2,500	4,000
UNIX System Administration	Advanced	5	2,500	4,000
Upgrading to MS Win 98	Advanced	2	680	830
Upgrading to MS Win NT 5.0	Advanced	2	680	830
Visual BASIC 5.0 Fundamentals	Introductory	5	1,770	2,160
Visual BASIC Programming	Advanced	5	2,500	4,000
Web Page Development	Advanced	3	2,500	4,000
Web Site Development Using MS Visual InterDev	Advanced	5	1,770	2,160
Web Site Fundamentals	Introductory	5	1,770	2,160
Word 97 or 2000 for Win	Advanced	1	210	260
Word 97 or 2000 for Win	Introductory	1	210	260
Word 97 or 2000 for Win	Intermediate	1	210	260
Word for Win 7.0	Advanced	1	210	260
Word for Win 7.0	Introductory	1	210	260
Word for Win 7.0	Intermediate	1	210	260
WordPro 97	Advanced	1	210	260
WordPro 97	Intermediate	1	210	260
WordPro 97	Introductory	1	210	260

Source: Computer Economics

4.6   Selling the need for training to management

Most organizations do not spend enough money and time to properly train their employees on how to use computers. Although the benefits of improved productivity and the ability of individual employees to better contribute to their organization are compelling to IT professionals, many managers have not bought into the need for training.

In addition, adequately trained computer users are becoming more critical. The issues of computer security, the protection of information privacy, and the management of intellectual property—all of which are discussed in other chapters of this book—illustrate how the inappropriate use of a computer system can lead to high-dollar liabilities for an organization.

Thus, with improved computer skills, employees will not only be more productive, they may also avoid mistakes that could end up costing hundreds of thousands or even millions of dollars in court costs resulting from damage-seeking litigation, and in some cases fines for noncompliance with a growing myriad of laws. This may be the most compelling argument of all.

When management is confronted with litigation or fines, rest assured the argument that an inadequately trained employee made a mistake will not win the day. In fact, it is likely that investigators will examine the training levels of employees and benchmark that against other organizations. Management then faces the situation of not exercising due care in providing adequate training.

4.7   The future need for computer-trained workers

According to the U.S. Bureau of Labor Statistics (BLS), business services—including personnel supply services and computer and data processing services, among other detailed industries—will add 5.1 million jobs. The personnel supply services industry, consisting of employment agencies and temporary staffing services, is projected to be the largest source of numerical employment growth in the economy, adding 1.9 million new jobs.

However, employment in computer and data processing services—which provides prepackaged and specialized software, data and computer systems design and management, and computer-related consulting services—is projected to grow by 86 percent between 2000 and 2010, ranking as the fastest growing industry in the economy. Desktop publishers will be among the fastest growing occupations, growing 66.7 percent over the decade.

Table 4.6 *Changing Employment between 2000 and 2010*

Growth Rate	Employment is projected to
Grow much faster than average	increase 36% or more
Grow faster than average	increase 21% to 35%
Grow about as fast as average	increase 10% to 20%
Grow more slowly than average	increase 3% to 9%
Little or no change	increase 0% to 2%
Decline	decrease 1% or more

Source: Bureau of Labor Statistics

Employment in professional computer positions and the need for workers with computer skills will increase much faster than the average for all occupations through the year 2010. Rapid growth in employment can be attributed to the explosion in information technology and the fast-paced expansion of the computer and data processing services industry. Table 4.6 explains the meaning of BLS employment growth rates between 2000 and 2010.

Due to the explosive growth of electronic commerce and the ability of the Internet to create new relationships with customers, the role of computer and information systems managers will continue to evolve in the future. They will continue to become more vital to their companies and the environments in which they work. The expansion of e-commerce will spur the need for computer and information systems managers with both business savvy and technical proficiency. In order to remain competitive, firms will continue to install sophisticated computer networks and set up more complex Internet and intranet sites.

Employment in the communications sector is expected to increase by 16.9 percent, adding 277,000 jobs by 2010. Half of these new jobs—139,000—will be in the telephone communications industry; however, cable and other pay television will be the fastest growing segment of the sector over the next decade, with employment expanding by 50.6 percent. Increased demand for residential and business wireline and wireless services, cable service, and high-speed Internet connections will fuel the growth in the communications industries.

The BLS contends that employment of programmers, however, is expected to grow much slower than that of other computer specialists. With the rapid gains in technology, sophisticated computer software now has the capability to write basic code, eliminating the need for more programmers to do this routine work. The consolidation and centralization of systems and applications; developments in packaged software; advanced programming languages and tools; and the growing ability of users to design, write, and implement more of their own programs mean more of the programming functions can be transferred to other types of workers. As the level of technological innovation and sophistication increases, programmers should continue to face increasing competition from programming businesses overseas, where much routine work can be contracted out at a lower cost.

In addition, systems analysts, computers scientists, database administrators, computer support specialists, and systems administrators are projected to be among the fastest growing occupations over the 2000–2010 period. Employment is expected to increase much faster than the average for all occupations as organizations continue to adopt and integrate increasingly sophisticated technology. Job growth will continue to be driven by rapid gains in computer and data processing services, which is projected to be the fastest growing industry in the U.S. economy.

End-user organizations will also face more recruitment competition with computer service firms. Services provided by this industry include prepackaged software; customized computer programming services and applications and systems software design; data processing, preparation, and information retrieval services, including on-line databases and Internet services; integrated systems design and development and management of databases; on-site computer facilities management; rental, leasing, and repair of computers and peripheral equipment; and a variety of specialized consulting services.

Employment in computer and data processing services grew by more than 1.3 million jobs from 1990 to 2000. In 2000, there were about 2.1 million wage and salary jobs, and an additional 164,000 self-employed workers, making the industry one of the largest in the economy. Most self-employed workers are independent consultants. Since the late 1980s, employment has grown most rapidly in the computer programming services, information retrieval services, and prepackaged software segments of the industry. From 1990 to 2000, about 368,000 jobs were created in programming services, 196,000 in information retrieval services, and another 187,000 in prepackaged software. Table 4.7 shows growth in employment by education from 2000 to 2010.

While the industry has both large and small firms, the average establishment in computer and data processing services is relatively small; approxi-

Table 4.7   *Growth in Employment by Education from 2000 to 2010*

Education/Training Level	Fastest Growing Occupations	Occupations Having the Largest Category Numerical Increases in Employment
First-professional degree	Veterinarians	Lawyers
	Pharmacists	Physicians and surgeons
	Chiropractors	Pharmacists
	Optometrists	Clergy
	Lawyers	Veterinarians
Doctoral degree	Computer and information scientists, research	Postsecondary teachers
	Medical scientists	Biological scientists
	Postsecondary teachers	Computer and information scientists, research
	Biological scientists	Medical scientists
	Astronomers and physicists	Astronomers and physicists
Master's degree	Audiologists	Educational, vocational, and school counselors
	Speech-language pathologists	Physical therapists
	Mental health and substance abuse social workers	Speech-language pathologists
	Substance abuse and behavioral disorder counselors	Psychologists
	Physical therapists	Mental health and substance abuse social workers
Work experience plus bachelor's or higher degree	Public relations managers	General and operations managers
	Advertising and promotions managers	Computer and information systems managers
	Sales managers	Management analysts
	Medical and health services managers	Financial managers
		Sales managers
Bachelor's degree	Computer software engineers, applications	Computer software engineers, applications

Table 4.7   *Growth in Employment by Education from 2000 to 2010 (continued)*

Education/Training Level	Fastest Growing Occupations	Occupations Having the Largest Category Numerical Increases in Employment
	Computer software engineers, systems software	Computer software engineers, systems software
,	Network and computer systems administrators	Computer systems analysts
	Network systems and data communications analysts	Elementary schoolteachers, except special education
	Database administrators	Network and computer systems administrators
Associate degree	Computer support specialists	Registered nurses
	Medical records and health information technicians	Computer support specialists
	Physical therapist assistants	Medical records and health information technicians
	Occupational therapist assistants	Paralegals and legal assistants
	Veterinary technologists and technicians	Dental hygienists
Postsecondary vocational award	Desktop publishers	Automotive service technicians and mechanics
	Fitness trainers and aerobics instructors	Licensed practical and licensed vocational nurses
	Surgical technologists	Welders, cutters, solderers, and braziers
	Respiratory therapy technicians	Hairdressers, hairstylists, and cosmetologists
	Gaming dealers	Fitness trainers and aerobics instructors
Work experience in a related occupation	First-line supervisors/managers of correctional officers	First-line supervisors/managers of retail sales workers
	Aircraft cargo handling supervisors	First-line supervisors/managers of construction trades and extraction workers
	First-line supervisors/managers of protective service workers, except police, fire, and corrections	First-line supervisors/managers of office and administrative support workers

Table 4.7   *Growth in Employment by Education from 2000 to 2010 (continued)*

Education/Training Level	Fastest Growing Occupations	Occupations Having the Largest Category Numerical Increases in Employment
		First-line supervisors/managers of food preparation and serving workers
	Private detectives and investigators	First-line supervisors/managers of mechanics, installers, and repairers
	Transportation, storage, and distribution managers	
Long-term on-the-job training (more than 12 months)	Telecommunications line installers and repairers	Cooks, restaurant
	Actors	Police and sheriff's patrol officers
	Recreational vehicle service technicians	Electricians
	Interpreters and translators	Carpenters
Moderate-term on-the-job training (1 to 12 months)	Police and sheriff's patrol officers	Maintenance and repair workers, general
	Medical assistants	Customer service representatives
	Social and human service assistants	Truck drivers, heavy and tractor-trailer
	Dental assistants	Medical assistants
	Pharmacy technicians	Executive secretaries and administrative assistants
	Ambulance drivers and attendants, except emergency	Social and human service assistants
	Medical technicians	
Short-term on-the-job training (0 to 1 months)	Personal and home care aides	Combined food preparation and serving workers, including fast food
	Home health aides	Retail salespersons
	Physical therapist aides	Cashiers, except gaming
	Occupational therapist aides	Office clerks, general
	Veterinary assistants and laboratory animal caretakers	

mately 80 percent of establishments employ fewer than 10 workers. The majority of jobs, however, are found in establishments that employ 50 or more workers. Many small establishments in the industry are startup firms that hope to capitalize on a market niche.

Relative to the rest of the economy, there are significantly fewer workers 45 years of age and older in computer and data processing establishments; this industry's workforce remains younger than most, with large proportions of workers in the 25 to 44 age range, as shown in Table 4.8. This reflects the industry's explosive growth in employment since the early 1980s. The huge increase in employment afforded thousands of opportunities to younger workers possessing the newest technological skills.

About 6.2 percent of the workers in computer and data processing services firms work part time, compared with 15.3 percent of workers throughout all industries. For some professionals or technical specialists, evening or weekend work may be necessary to meet deadlines or solve problems. Professionals working for large establishments may have less freedom in planning their schedules than do consultants for very small firms, whose work may be more varied.

Employment of medical records and health information technicians is expected to grow much faster than the average for all occupations through 2010, due to rapid growth in the number of medical tests, treatments, and procedures, which will be increasingly scrutinized by third-party payers, regulators, courts, and consumers. Hospitals will continue to employ a large

Table 4.8   *Percent Distribution of Employment in Computer and Data Processing Services by Age Group, 2000*

Age Group	Workers in Computer and Data Processing Services	Workers in All Industries
16–19	1.4	5.4
20–24	9.3	9.9
25–34	36.9	22.6
35–44	30.0	27.1
45–54	16.0	22.0
55–64	5.7	10.0
65 and older	0.7	3.0

percentage of health information technicians, but growth will not be as fast as in other areas. Increasing demand for detailed records in offices and clinics of physicians should result in fast employment growth, especially in large group practices. Rapid growth is also expected in nursing homes and home health agencies.

Overall employment of information and records clerks is expected grow about as fast as the average for all occupations through 2010. In addition to many openings occurring as businesses and organizations expand, numerous job openings for information and records clerks will result from the need to replace experienced workers who transfer to other occupations or leave the labor force.

Principle Four: Provide Ergonomic User Environments

If you can make an employee happy by spending $800 on a comfortable office chair, what's $800?

—James R. Uffelman

5.1　The state of ergonomic activity

Even though the Republican Congress dismantled ergonomic requirements established by the Democrats when Bill Clinton was in office, ergonomics remains a critical issue. Furthermore, problems are likely to mount in the future, and within two decades the negative impact of poorly designed office furniture and information technology will result in considerable economic impact on individuals, corporations, the government, and ultimately the taxpayer.

The Occupational Safety and Health Administration (OSHA) unveiled a plan in April 2002 that is designed to dramatically reduce ergonomic injuries through a combination of industry-targeted guidelines, tough enforcement measures, workplace outreach, advanced research, and dedicated efforts to protect Hispanic and other immigrant workers.

OSHA plans to begin work on developing industry and task-specific guidelines to reduce and prevent ergonomic injuries, often called musculoskeletal disorders (MSDs), that occur in the workplace. OSHA expects to begin releasing guidelines ready for application in selected industries in late 2002.

The department's ergonomics enforcement plan will crack down on bad actors by coordinating inspections with a legal strategy designed for successful prosecution. The department will place special emphasis on industries with the sorts of serious ergonomics problems that OSHA and DOL attorneys have successfully addressed in prior 5(a)(1) or General Duty clause cases, including the Beverly Enterprises and Pepperidge Farm cases. For the first time, OSHA will have an enforcement plan designed from the start to target prosecutable ergonomic violations. Also for the first time, inspections will be coordinated with a legal strategy developed by DOL attorneys that is based on prior successful ergonomics cases and is designed to maximize successful prosecutions. Further, OSHA will have special ergonomics inspection teams that will, from the earliest stages, work closely with DOL attorneys and experts to successfully bring prosecutions under the General Duty clause.

The new ergonomics plan also calls for compliance assistance tools to help workplaces reduce and prevent ergonomic injuries. OSHA will provide specialized training and information on guidelines and the implementation of successful ergonomics programs. It will also administer targeted training grants, develop compliance assistance tools, forge partnerships, and create a recognition program to highlight successful ergonomics injury reduction efforts.

The plan also includes the announcement of a national advisory committee; part of the committee's task will be to advise OSHA on research gaps. In concert with the National Institute for Occupational Safety and Health, OSHA will stimulate and encourage needed research in this area.

The new plan was announced barely a year after Republicans and Democrats in Congress rejected the Clinton administration's rule, which was developed over a period of eight years and was broadly denounced as being excessively burdensome and complicated.

OSHA named regional coordinators for ergonomics for each of its ten regional offices to assist OSHA staff, employers, employees, and other stakeholders with ergonomic issues. (See Table 5.1.) The coordinators all have considerable experience in identifying ergonomic hazards and suggesting practical solutions for common problems that may be associated with musculoskeletal disorders. They will serve as a resource for OSHA compliance officers in conducting and documenting hazards during inspections. Regional ergonomics coordinators will also assist with and track the outreach and education efforts of OSHA compliance assistance specialists as they offer training and guidance on best practices in ergonomics and respond to specific questions from employers and employees.

The four-pronged OSHA approach to ergonomics is based on the principles outlined by the Secretary for an effective approach to ergonomics:

Table 5.1   *OSHA Regional Ergonomics Coordinator*

Region	City	Coordinator	Phone Number
Region I	Boston	Fred Malaby	(617) 565-9860
Region II	New York	Paul Cherasard	(212) 337-2378
Region III	Philadelphia	Jim Johnston	(215) 861-4900
Region IV	Atlanta	Jim Drake	(404) 562-2300
Region V	Chicago	Dana Root	(312) 353-2220
Region VI	Dallas	Susan Monroe	(214) 767-4731
Region VII	Kansas City	JoBeth Cholmondeley	(816) 426-5861
Region VIII	Denver	Terry Mitton Terry	(303) 844-1600
Region IX	San Francisco	Barbara Goto	(415) 975-4310
Region X	Seattle	Steve Gossman	(206) 553-5930

preventing injuries; using sound science in formulating a strategy; providing incentives for cooperation between OSHA and employers; maximizing flexibility and avoiding a one-size-fits all approach; creating a feasible program, especially for small businesses; and ensuring clarity, including short, simple, common-sense solutions.

The four segments of OSHA's strategy for successfully reducing injuries and illnesses from musculoskeletal disorders (MSDs) in the workplace are specified in the following subsections.

5.1.1   Guidelines

- OSHA will develop industry- or task-specific guidelines for a number of industries based on current incidence rates and available information about effective and feasible solutions. This work will take into account guidelines and best practices already developed, including OSHA's own Meatpacking Guidelines, issued in 1990.

- OSHA will encourage other industries to develop ergonomic guidelines to meet their own specific needs.

- The goal is to encourage industry to implement measures as quickly as possible to reduce work-related MSDs. OSHA expects to start releasing guidelines in selected industries by late 2002 or early 2003.

5.1.2   Enforcement

- OSHA's primary goal is the reduction of injuries and illnesses in the workplace.

- Employers must keep their workplaces free from recognized serious hazards under the OSHA Act's General Duty clause. This includes ergonomic hazards.

- OSHA will not focus its enforcement efforts on employers who have implemented effective ergonomic programs or who are making good-faith efforts to reduce ergonomic hazards.

- OSHA will conduct inspections for ergonomic hazards and issue citations under the General Duty clause and issue ergonomic hazard alert letters where appropriate. OSHA will conduct follow-up inspections or investigations within 12 months of certain employers who receive ergonomic hazard alert letters.

- OSHA has announced a National Emphasis Program in the nursing home industry to guide inspections of nursing homes and to focus significant efforts on addressing ergonomic hazards related to patient lifting.

- OSHA will conduct specialized training of appropriate staff on ergonomic hazards and abatement methods and designate ten regional ergonomic coordinators and involve them in enforcement and outreach.

- OSHA will address ergonomic hazards in its national emphasis program, notifications, and inspections of employers in the Site-Specific Targeting program, and will offer assistance to those employers in this group that have a high percentage of MSDs.

5.1.3   Outreach and assistance

- OSHA will provide assistance to businesses, particularly small businesses, and help them proactively address ergonomic issues in the workplace. OSHA will also provide advice and training on the voluntary guidelines and implementation of a successful ergonomics program.

- OSHA will target its Fiscal Year 2002 training grants to address ergonomics and other agency priorities, including support for the development of ergonomic training materials and the direct training of employers and employees to promote a better understanding of ergonomic risks and the prevention of MSDs.

- OSHA will develop a complete and comprehensive set of compliance assistance tools, including Internet-based training and information, to support understanding of guidelines and proactively defining and addressing ergonomic problems.

- OSHA will provide courses at its 12 nonprofit educational partner organizations, known as education centers, for private sector and other federal agency personnel, and will develop and utilize distance learning to make training materials available to a wider audience.

- OSHA will focus on developing new partnerships to implement and highlight the value and effectiveness of voluntary ergonomic guidelines and will use its existing partnership programs to facilitate the development of guidelines. Voluntary protection program (VPP) sites will be used to help model effective ergonomic solutions. VPP volunteers will mentor other worksites and provide training assistance.

- OSHA will also develop new recognition programs to highlight the achievements of worksites with exemplary or novel approaches to ergonomics.

- As part of the Department of Labor's cross-agency commitment to protecting immigrant workers, especially those with limited English proficiency, the new ergonomics plan includes a specialized focus to help Hispanic and other immigrant workers, many of whom work in industries with high ergonomic hazard rates.

5.1.4   Research

- While there is a large body of research available on ergonomics, there are many areas where additional research is necessary, including gaps identified by the National Academy of Science (NAS). OSHA will serve as a catalyst to encourage researchers to design studies in areas where additional information would be helpful.

- OSHA will charter an advisory committee that will be authorized to, among other things, identify gaps in research related to the application of ergonomics and ergonomic principles to the workplace. This advisory committee will report its findings to the Assistant Secretary and to the National Institute for Occupational Safety and Health (NIOSH).

- OSHA will work closely with NIOSH and through the National Occupational Research Agenda process to encourage research in needed areas.

5.2   Liability is still a threat

The threat of litigation and the filing of widespread worker's compensation claims are forcing companies to find remedies for the poor ergonomics of standardized off-the-shelf IT products. Computer Economics estimates that end-user companies will spend over $3.5 billion by 2005 on addressing IT ergonomic issues.

Many legal consultants agree that it is better to start addressing the ergonomics of IT than to sit in hope that your company will never face liability issues. We discussed the various programs that the members of our focus group have in place with our panel of legal experts. They concurred that at a minimum, companies should provide on-demand ergonomic remedy services.

The implementation of an enterprise-wide ergonomics program is not an absolute necessity, according to our consultants. They noted that the implementation of a comprehensive approach is grounded in corporate philosophies toward risk management. These philosophies can range from waiting to be sued to forecasting the potential of future litigation, and from practicing due diligence to reducing liability and court award amounts.

Regardless of the path a company selects, there will be an impact on the total cost of ownership for IT products. Additional costs will be incurred in either personnel and product expenses or in litigation expenses.

All of the members of the legal team that worked on the analysis conducted by Computer Economics discussed recent and pending settlements in tobacco-related lawsuits as an analogy. They all agreed that ergonomics could become a far bigger issue in the future because of the volume and outcome of recent tobacco cases.

The relationship is not between ergonomics and tobacco, but in the united activities of the states' attorneys general offices. The tobacco lawsuits illustrated that these organizations can have a profound impact when attacking an issue with a high degree of cooperation and unity. State attorneys general can also use such people-oriented cases to further their own political agendas.

5.3   Employee injuries in computer services

Compared with other occupational areas, IT professionals are still relatively injury free. However, there is still an incidence of work-related injuries in computer and data processing services organizations. Since the work in computer services and data processing services organizations is virtually replicated in each in-house IT organization, it is likely that the rate of injury in your organization will be similar to that shown in Table 5.2.

Table 5.2   *Cases of Nonfatal Illness Associated with Repeated Trauma (by Industry)*

		1995		2000	
Industry	SIC Code	Annual Average Employment (Thousands)	Number of Cases (Thousands)	Annual Average Employment (Thousands)	Number of Cases (Thousands)
Air transportation, scheduled	451	626.3	2.0	1,101.3	3.0
Aircraft and parts	372	449.0	6.4	463.1	6.0
Commercial banks	602	1,461.1	2.3	1,428.9	2.1
Computer and data processing services	737	1,084.0	2.7	2,148.3	2.0
Electronic components and accessories	367	581.4	4.3	681.9	3.0
Fire, marine, and casualty insurance	633	530.8	2.3	548.0	2.7
Grocery stores	541	2,983.2	5.1	3,069.2	5.4
Hospitals	806	3,742.9	6.1	3,958.2	8.2
Meat products	201	470.5	36.7	505.1	25.2
Medical instruments and supplies	384	263.8	2.7	283.7	3.0
Medical service and health insurance	632	—	—	379.3	2.9
Metal forgings and stampings	346	251.5	5.2	254.9	3.9
Miscellaneous electrical equipment & supplies	369	156.2	3.9	144.6	2.5
Miscellaneous fabricated textile products	239	221.7	2.5	214.3	3.5
Miscellaneous plastics products (n.e.c.)	308	709.5	5.9	744.9	4.7
Motor vehicles and equipment	371	967.6	49.5	1,016.5	39.3

Table 5.2   *Cases of Nonfatal Illness Associated with Repeated Trauma (by Industry) (continued)*

Industry	SIC Code	1995		2000	
		Annual Average Employment (Thousands)	Number of Cases (Thousands)	Annual Average Employment (Thousands)	Number of Cases (Thousands)
Offices and clinics of medical doctors	801	1,609.9	2.4	1,936.9	3.3
Refrigeration and service machinery	358	201.6	4.0	212.3	2.4
Ship and boat building and repairing	373	158.3	2.6	168.6	2.2
Telephone communications	481	886.6	4.6	1,155.3	3.6

Source: Bureau of Labor Statistics, U.S. Department of Labor

Note: Excludes firms with fewer than 11 employees. The n.e.c. abbreviation means that the category includes those components not elsewhere classified.

As Table 5.2 shows, in 1995 there were 2,700 cases of work-related injuries associated with repeated trauma. This dropped to 2,000 cases in 2000. In contrast, the meat products industry, for example, had 36,700 work-related injury cases associated with repeated trauma.

IT managers can expect that less than 1 percent of their workers will suffer from work-related injuries associated with repeated trauma every year. As Table 5.3 shows, this is considerably lower than many occupational areas. In the meat products occupation 7.8 percent of workers suffered from work-related injuries associated with repeated trauma.

The Bureau of Labor Statistics published rates of nonfatal work-related injuries per hundred employees for a number of industries and occupations. As Table 5.4 shows, IT managers can expect that on an annual basis there will be 3.1 cases per 100 employees per year of nonfatal occupational injuries. This rate includes all types of injuries, not just those associated with repeated trauma.

Table 5.3   *Percent of Workers with Nonfatal Illness Associated with Repeated Trauma (by Industry)*

Industry	SIC Code	1995 Percent of Workers Injured	2000 Percent of Workers Injured
Air transportation, scheduled	451	0.319%	0.272%
Aircraft and parts	372	1.425%	1.296%
Commercial banks	602	0.157%	0.147%
Computer and data processing services	737	0.249%	0.093%
Electronic components and accessories	367	0.740%	0.440%
Fire, marine, and casualty insurance	633	0.433%	0.493%
Grocery stores	541	0.171%	0.176%
Hospitals	806	0.163%	0.207%
Meat products	201	7.800%	4.989%
Medical instruments and supplies	384	1.024%	1.057%
Medical service and health insurance	632	—	—
Metal forgings and stampings	346	2.068%	1.530%
Miscellaneous electrical equipment & supplies	369	2.497%	1.729%
Miscellaneous fabricated textile products	239	1.128%	1.633%
Miscellaneous plastics products (n.e.c.)	308	0.832%	0.631%
Motor vehicles and equipment	371	5.116%	3.866%
Offices and clinics of medical doctors	801	0.149%	0.170%
Refrigeration and service machinery	358	1.984%	1.130%
Ship and boat building and repairing	373	1.642%	1.305%
Telephone communications	481	0.519%	0.312%

Source: Bureau of Labor Statistics, U.S. Department of Labor

Table 5.4   *Nonfatal Occupational Injuries in Computer and Data Processing Service*

Consequences of Cases	1995 Number of Cases (per 100 Workers)	2000 Number of Cases (per 100 Workers)
Annual average employment	1,084.0	2,148.3
Cases without days away from work	0.5	1.6
Lost workdays cases	0.2	0.9
Cases with restricted work activity	0.3	1.5
Total cases	0.8	3.1

Source: Bureau of Labor Statistics, U.S. Department of Labor

5.3.1   How ergonomics is being addressed

To determine how large corporations are dealing with this problem Computer Economics conducted a focus group of 16 companies that reported they had remedies in place. We also contacted five of our associates in the legal field and asked their opinion about potential corporate liability of IT ergonomics.

All focus group participants reported that they have had worker's compensation claims filed resulting from IT ergonomics. Each of the focus group companies has had on-demand ergonomic assistance for their employees in place for at least two years.

The on-demand approach provides employees with assistance in evaluating their needs and selecting appropriate products to ease the strain they experience when using IT equipment. The group reported a wide variety of methods for providing on-demand services. These included telephone hotlines, e-mail request systems, and walk-in showcase centers, where employees can test-drive IT products designed to provide more comfort and to help minimize IT-related worker injuries.

Four Fortune 500 companies in the focus group reported that in addition to on-demand services, they had initiated proactive evaluation programs to address ergonomics. These programs include employee training, supervisor training, videos and other learning aids in corporate libraries, awareness campaigns, bulletin boards, Web pages, and corporate-wide workstation evaluation. In all of these cases the central IT department had a role in creating or supporting the programs.

The most thorough program offered by a focus group member is a corporate-wide workstation evaluation program. This program is an interdepartmental effort with an estimated budget of $1.5 million per year. The goal of this program is to address ergonomics at every workstation in the organization. The interdepartmental team is composed of staff from the IT department, employee health and safety, training, and facilities management. To start the program the team used consultants and attended outside training courses.

In addition to the evaluation effort, the program provides in-house training for management and supervisory staff to increase awareness and understanding of ergonomic approaches and liability issues.

5.3.2   Applied ergonomics

OSHA has compiled the following pointers to help office workers address the ergonomic management of their workstations.

The desk chair

A properly designed and adjusted chair will provide appropriate support to the back, legs, buttocks, and arms. This support can reduce contact stress, overexertion, and fatigue. It will also promote proper circulation to the extremities.

Improper size, shape, or choice of materials for the seatpan and backrest may result in uneven weight distribution, contact stress, decreased circulation to the extremities, and awkward posture. The seat and backrest of the chair should support a comfortable posture that allows frequent changing of the seating position.

Chairs should be height adjustable, especially in work areas in which they are shared by a number of employees. The chair height is correct when the entire sole of the foot can rest on the floor or a footrest and the back of the knee is slightly higher than the seat of the chair. This position allows blood to circulate freely in the legs and feet.

Armrests that are too high or too low can produce awkward postures, create contact stress to the elbow, provide inadequate support, and may prevent the operator from moving close enough to the workstation. Adjustable armrests can be lowered to fit under work surfaces. This allows the user to work from a comfortable distance. The armrests should support both forearms while the employee performs tasks and should not interfere with movement.

The keyboard and mouse

The proper position of the keyboard and mouse is essential in creating a comfortable workstation. Consideration of the following factors can help prevent musculoskeletal disorders such as carpal tunnel syndrome and tendonitis.

Improper height and angle of the keyboard, mouse, or working surface can cause employees to bend their wrists or lift their arms for extended periods. The work surface may need to be raised or lowered to keep the operator's arms in a comfortable position. This can be achieved by installing an adjustable keyboard extender or tray, by providing an adjustable table or working surface, or by raising the chair and providing a footrest if needed.

Adjust the keyboard and/or chair height so the employee's elbows can hang comfortably at the side of the body, the shoulders are relaxed and the wrist is not bent up or down or to either side during keyboard use. The angle of the keyboard should also be considered when determining the preferred height. The preferred working position for most keyboard operators is with the forearms parallel to the floor and elbows at the sides; this allows the hands to move easily over the keyboard.

A keyboard or mouse that is not directly in front of or close to the body forces the employee to repeatedly reach during use. Make sure the keyboard is placed directly in front of the user. The mouse should be positioned at the operator's side with his or her arm close to the body. A straight line should be maintained between the hand and the forearm. The upper arm should not be elevated or extended while using the mouse. The employee should not have to reach to use the mouse. Consider using a mouse platform that rotates above the keyboard while maintaining about the same plane. This design allows the mouse to be used above the ten-key pad, which gives the user a better wrist angle and reduces reach.

Wrists should be extended straight, not bent up or down. A mouse pad or wrist rest can be used to help maintain straight wrists. Wrist/palm rests should not be used while keying but to rest the wrists between periods of keying.

Monitor and document placement

Monitor and document placement is important in creating a comfortable workstation. Consider the following items in order to reduce awkward head and neck postures along with fatigue and/or headaches: The monitor and document are related to the placement of the keyboard, mouse, and properly adjusted chair.

A display screen that is too high, too low, or placed to the side of the user, may, over time, cause awkward postures and increased stress on the muscles of the neck, shoulders, and upper back. Keep the monitor directly in front of the user. The topmost line of the screen should not be higher than the user's eyes. Screens that swivel horizontally and tilt or elevate vertically enable the operator to select a comfortable viewing angle. Generally, placing the monitor on top of the computer will raise it too high.

The preferred viewing distance is 18 to 24 inches. If there is not enough table depth to accommodate this distance, install a keyboard extender or tray underneath the desk. The table depth should generally be at least 30 inches from the wall to properly accommodate monitors. Pull tables and desks away from the wall and dividers to provide more space for monitors.

The screen and document holder should be close enough together that the operator can look from one to the other without excessive movement of the head, neck, or back. If writing needs to be performed, a document holder can be positioned directly beneath the monitor. This provides a sturdy writing surface and prevents frequent movement of the head, neck, or back.

5.3.3   Focus on work habits

Many problems caused by poor ergonomics are exacerbated even more by poor work habits. OSHA has also compiled pointers about modifying work habits to reduce the impact of working at computers.

Prolonged and repetitive activities are potential hazards

Computer work may appear to be easy and require little overall exertion of force. While this is true for the body in general, repetitive movements or prolonged awkward postures can lead to localized pain and injury. For example, a person using a mouse may move or activate a few small muscles and tendons of the hand hundreds or even thousands of times per hour. This can lead to localized fatigue, wear and tear, and injury in those small localized areas. Likewise, looking at the monitor for a prolonged period of time requires that the head be supported by only a few muscles of the neck and shoulder. These muscles may need to be activated for hours without significant rest, leading to fatigue and overuse. While work on the computer may appear to be a low-impact activity, the lack of motion and presence of high repetitions and awkward postures can lead to pain and serious injury if not recognized and dealt with.

A workstation at which employees can easily change their working postures is helpful. Changing the way one sits allows different muscles to provide support while others rest. Employees should also have enough workspace so they can change the hand with which they perform mouse tasks to allow the tendons and muscles of the hand to rest.

Highly repetitious jobs or jobs that require long periods of static posture may require a different strategy for break periods. Taking very short rest breaks in addition to the standard industrial break schedule (about every two hours) can provide needed rest. Some companies have found that employees experience fewer MSDs when a 15- to 30-second break is taken every 10 to 20 minutes or a five-minute break is taken every hour. During these breaks employees should be encouraged to stand, stretch, and move around a bit. This provides rest and allows the muscles enough time to recover.

Job duties should be alternated whenever possible by introducing non-computer-related tasks into the workday. This encourages body movement and the use of different muscle groups.

Inappropriate production requirements are potential hazards

Employees may work through their break periods if production standards are set too high. Without these rest periods the tissues of the body do not have time to rest and recover. Workers who consistently work through their breaks are at greater risk of musculoskeletal disorders (MSDs), accidents, and poor-quality work performance due to operating at higher muscular fatigue levels.

A competent work-time consultant can survey work and an appropriate work rate. High work rates may benefit the company in the short run by reducing the number of employees hired. However, these benefits will be lost over time as a result of higher injury rates if work standards require rates that exceed the capabilities of individuals.

Incorporate a work ramp-in period rate for new hires. Work rates set for experienced employees may be too high for those who are new to the work. It is common practice to allow a gradual ramp-up work rate for new hires that increases production over several weeks or until employees can work at the same pace as experienced workers.

Working excessive overtime is a potential hazard

Working overtime, especially when the overtime is performed as an extension of the normal workday, may overstress the body's muscles and tissues by reducing rest and recuperation times.

If overtime cannot be eliminated, reduce the overtime as much as possible to reduce the cumulative effects of stress. Limit overtime to off-days instead of tacking it onto the end of a shift. This will allow a period of recovery between shifts when muscles and other tissues can recover. This is related to adequately staffing IT operations, as discussed in Chapter 2.

Inadequate training courts disaster

Employees may not be adequately trained to recognize hazards or understand effective work practices to reduce these hazards. General ergonomics training and task-specific training at the time of new-hire orientation is recommended, and risk factors and proper work practices to minimize these hazards should be explained.

It is important for employees to understand how to report an injury and how the company prefers its employees to seek medical attention. This can expedite assistance, reduce costs, and improve lines of communication. (This is related to adequately training computer users, as discussed in Chapter 4.)

5.3.4   The office environment

Lighting that is not appropriate for computer work is a major factor in producing visual discomforts such as eyestrain, burning or itchy eyes, headaches, and blurred or double vision. Lighting should be adequate for the operator to see the text and the screen, but not so bright as to cause glare or discomfort. The following guidelines should be considered:

- Use light diffusers so that desk tasks (writing, reading papers) can be performed without direct brightness on the computer screen.

- Place rows of lights parallel to the operator's line of sight.

- Use operator-adjustable task and desk lighting.

- If diffusers or alternative lights are not available, removing the middle bulbs of 4-bulb fluorescent light fixtures can also reduce the brightness of the light.

- Use blinds or drapes on windows to eliminate bright light. Blinds should be adjusted during the day to allow light into the room, but not directly into the operator's field of view.

- Lamps should have glare shields or shades, and the line of sight from the eye to the light should be at an angle greater than 30 degrees.

- Reorient the workstation so that bright lights from open windows are not in the field of view.

- Use indirect or shielded lighting where possible and avoid intense or uneven lighting in the field of vision.

- For computer work, well-distributed diffuse light is best. The advantages of diffuse lighting are twofold: There will be fewer hot spots or glare surfaces in the visual field, and the contrasts created by the shapes of objects tend to be softer.

- Use light, matte colors and finishes on walls and ceilings in order to better reflect indirect lighting and reduce dark shadows and contrast.

- Clean the monitor frequently. A layer of dust can contribute to glare.

- To limit reflection from walls and work surfaces around the screen, these areas should be painted a medium color and have a nonreflective finish. Workstations and lighting should be arranged to avoid reflected glare on the display screen or surrounding surfaces.

5.3.5   The checklist

OSHA has also compiled a checklist, which can be helpful in making a quick assessment of various related factors. (See Table 5.5.)

Passing score

"YES" answer on all "working postures" items (A–J) and no more than two "NO" answers on remainder of checklist (1–23).

Table 5.5   *OSHA Workstation Checklist*

Working conditions: The workstation is designed or arranged for doing VDT tasks so it allows the employee's . . .	Yes	No
A. Head and neck to be about upright (not bent down/back).		
B. Head, neck, and trunk to face forward (not twisted).		
C. Trunk to be about perpendicular to floor (not leaning forward/backward).		
D. Shoulders and upper arms to be about perpendicular to floor (not stretched forward) and relaxed (not elevated).		
E. Upper arms and elbows to be close to body (not extended outward).		
F. Forearms, wrists, and hands to be straight and parallel to the floor (not pointing up/down).		
G. Wrists and hands to be straight (not bent up/down or sideways toward little finger).		

Table 5.5   *OSHA Workstation Checklist (continued)*

H. Thighs to be about parallel to floor and lower legs to be about perpendicular to the floor.

I. Feet to rest flat on the floor or to be supported by a stable footrest.

J. VDT tasks to be organized in a way that allows employee to vary VDT tasks with other work
   activities or to take microbreaks or recovery pauses while at the VDT workstation.

Seating: The chair	Yes	No
1. Backrest provides support for the employee's lower back (lumbar area).		
2. Seat width and depth accommodate a specific employee (seatpan not too big or small).		
3. Seat front does not press against the back of employee's knees and lower legs (seatpan not too long).		
4. Seat has cushioning and is rounded or has "waterfall" front (no sharp edge).		
5. Armrests support both forearms while employee performs VDT tasks and do not interfere with movement.		

Keyboard/input device: The keyboard/input device is designed or arranged for doing VDT tasks so that . . .	Yes	No
6. Keyboard/input device platform(s) is stable and large enough to hold keyboard and input device.		
7. Input device (mouse or trackball) is located right next to keyboard so it can be operated without reaching.		
8. Input device is easy to activate and shape/size fits hand of specific employee (not too big or small).		
9. Wrists and hands do not rest on sharp or hard edge.		

Monitor: The monitor is designed or arranged for VDT tasks so that . . .	Yes	No
10. Top line of screen is at or below eye level so employee is able to read it without bending head or neck down/back. (For employees with bifocals or trifocals, see next item.)		
11. Employee with bifocals or trifocals is able to read screen without bending head or neck backward.		
12. Monitor distance allows employee to read screen without leaning head, neck, or trunk forward or backward.		
13. Monitor position is directly in front of employee so employee does not have to twist head or neck.		
14. No glare (e.g., from windows or lights) is present on the screen that might cause employee to assume an awkward posture to read the screen.		

Table 5.5   *OSHA Workstation Checklist (continued)*

Work area: The monitor is designed or arranged for VDT tasks so that . . .	Yes	No
15. Thighs have clearance space between chair and VDT table/keyboard platform (thighs not trapped).		
16. Legs and feet have clearance space under VDT table so employee is able to get close enough to keyboard/input device.		

Accessories:	Yes	No
17. Document holder, if provided, is stable and large enough to hold documents that are used.		
18. Document holder, if provided, is placed at about the same height and distance as monitor screen so there is little head movement when employee looks from document to screen.		
19. Wrist rest, if provided, is padded and free of sharp and square edges.		
20. Wrist rest, if provided, allows employee to keep forearms, wrists, and hands straight and parallel to the ground when using keyboard/input device.		
21. Telephone can be used with head upright (not bent) and shoulders relaxed (not elevated) if employee does VDT tasks at the same time.		

General:	Yes	No
22. Workstation and equipment have sufficient adjustability so that the employee is able to be in a safe working posture and to make occasional changes in posture while performing VDT tasks.		
23. VDT workstation, equipment, and accessories are maintained in serviceable condition and function properly.		

Principle Five: Maintain Secure and Virus-Free Computer Systems

The Internet is giving terrorists and rogues easier access to all types of systems around the world. Information warfare may well become the preferred tool of terrorists in the future. Rogue criminal organizations that work for hire will also pursue information strategies for profit. Alarming thoughts, perhaps, but evidence is quickly stacking up in favor of the proposition, as was discovered through interviews with prosecutors, law enforcement personnel, and corporate security planners. Many expressed grave concerns about the future information warfare and computer crime activities of outlaw groups around the world.

—Michael Erbschloe

6.1   How much bad security costs

All IT managers would agree that protecting their IT resources against security breaches is a necessity, but many are not willing to commit to the continual effort required. Without adequate security, the organization is open to a variety of risks, all of which are detrimental to the bottom line.

Based on Computer Economics' projections, the likelihood that your organization will be hit with a security attack is growing. Computer crime will grow by an estimated 230 percent during 2002. Similar trends are expected with Internet fraud, which will be up over 100 percent, and viruses, which will increase by 22 percent during the same period. These statistics are even more disturbing than they first appear, because the data used as the basis for these projections are probably underreported. According to government and industry sources, only about 20 percent of computer security violations are actually reported.

The sixth annual Computer Crime and Security Survey conducted by the Computer Security Institute (CSI) with the participation of the Computer Intrusion Squad of the San Francisco office of the Federal Bureau of Investigation (FBI) provides an updated look at the impact of computer crime in the United States. Responses from 538 computer security practitioners in U.S. corporations, government agencies, financial institutions, medical institutions, and universities confirm that the threat from computer crime and other information security breaches continues unabated and that the financial toll is mounting.

Eighty-five percent of respondents (primarily large corporations and government agencies) detected computer security breaches within the past 12 months. Thirty-five percent (186 respondents) were willing and/or able to quantify their financial losses. These 186 respondents reported $377,828,700 in financial losses. (In contrast, the losses from 249 respondents in 2000 totaled only $265,589,940. The average annual total over the three years prior to 2000 was $120,240,180.)

A CIO KnowPulse Poll of 170 CIOs conducted in fall 2001 revealed that the majority (67 percent) of CIOs are not very confident or not at all confident that law enforcement will provide their companies with sufficient advance warning of a threat to computer systems. Twenty-seven percent are somewhat confident, with only 2 percent very confident, and 2 percent extremely confident. While nearly half (49 percent) of CIOs have had additional responsibility and/or accountability for security infrastructure placed on them since September 11, more than one-third (39 percent) still do not have cyber security experts on staff or contracted. Just under half (47 percent) will increase the company's budget for information security following the September 11, 2001, terrorist attacks on the United States.

As for national security, CIOs are split in their confidence level regarding the technologies, plans, and procedures currently in place to protect the nation's critical infrastructure. Following speculation that the next terrorist assault on the United States could be a cyber attack, just over half (54 percent) of CIOs are extremely, very, or somewhat confident in the ability of the United States to protect critical infrastructures. The remainder are not very confident (32 percent) or not at all confident (13 percent).

Companies in Europe are divided over the potential threat to business from viruses, hack attacks, and other forms of sabotage, according to research conducted by security specialist Evidian. In France, Benelux, Spain, and Germany, viruses are seen as the major threat, with 40 percent of companies identifying this form of attack as the most prevalent.

In the United Kingdom, deliberate sabotage by employees or ex-employees was identified as the area of greatest concern, while in Scandinavia over

50 percent cited accidental damage caused by an employee as the major concern. In Italy, financial fraud was identified as the biggest headache.

Evidian surveyed 250 companies in the finance, retail, and public sectors in the United Kingdom, France, Germany, Italy, Benelux, Scandinavia, and Spain. The company asked IT managers and directors to identify what they believed to be the main threat, which solutions were needed to deal with it, and the area of their internal systems most at risk.

The research also identified considerable differences in the areas of the business infrastructure perceived to be most at risk. In Germany and Spain, intranets were identified by the majority of respondents as being most in need of protection, whereas in France, Scandinavia, and Benelux it was Web sites. In the United Kingdom, 60 percent of companies identified corporate databases as the most vulnerable.

6.1.1   A case study: Weak security allows sales reps to defraud

As reported by the *Wall Street Journal* in mid-February 2002, WorldCom suspended three star employees and froze the commissions of at least 12 salespeople as it investigated an order-booking scandal that boosted sales commissions in three of its branch offices. Security gaps in WorldCom's accounting system apparently permitted domestic sales executives to dou-ble-book international sales deals as their own, enabling them to cash in on up to $4 million in commissions they did not earn.

Only weeks after WorldCom revealed that some of its top sales represen-tatives had manipulated its antiquated incentive compensation system to defraud the company of millions of dollars, a survey of executives was con-ducted at Synygy's spring Incentive Compensation Conference, held in Phoenix in March 2002.

In the survey, 64 percent of the respondents reported that an employee had manipulated data to affect the payout of their company's incentive plan. An additional 29 percent weren't sure whether such things had occurred. Only 10 percent were confident that their systems hadn't been exploited.

In the survey, high-tech firms in the computer, communications, and software industries were more likely to report that an employee had manip-ulated data (76 percent of respondents), and financial services companies were the most likely to assert that such things had never happened.

The smaller the company, the greater the uncertainty about what employees were doing (47 percent of the respondents from companies with revenues of less than $50 million reported that they didn't know whether an employee had manipulated data or not). The larger companies at least knew they were being cheated (68 percent of the companies with revenues greater than $1 billion).

In 1998, the National Institute of Standards and Technology (NIST) categorized and analyzed 237 computer attacks that were published on the Internet out of an estimated 400 published attacks. This sample yielded the following statistics:

- Twenty-nine percent of attacks can launch from Windows hosts; attackers do not need to understand UNIX to be dangerous anymore.

- Twenty percent of attacks are able to remotely penetrate network elements (e.g., routers, switches, hosts, printers, and firewalls).

- Three percent of the attacks enable Web sites to attack those who visited the site.

- Four percent of attacks scan the Internet for vulnerable hosts.

- Five percent of attacks are effective against routers and firewalls.

6.1.2   2001 economic impact of malicious code attacks

Viruses and other malicious code attacks are growing in number, and so is the cost incurred by companies, government organizations, and private individuals to clean up systems and get them back into working order. Incidents that have occurred following the "Love Bug" attack had less economic impact, primarily because the process of cleaning up virus damage has been highly automated since that attack.

Table 6.1   *Economic Impact of Malicious Code Attacks—Analysis by Incident*

Year	Code Name	Worldwide Economic Impact (U.S. $)	Cyber Attack Index
2001	Nimda	635 Million	0.73
2001	Code Red(s)	2.62 Billion	2.99
2001	SirCam	1.15 Billion	1.31
2000	Love Bug	8.75 Billion	10.00
1999	Melissa	1.10 Billion	1.26
1999	Explorer	1.02 Billion	1.17

The Computer Economics Cyber Attack Index, shown in Table 6.1, measures the relative economic impact of specific incidents in relationship to the "I Love You" ("Love Bug") outbreak, which occurred in 2000 and to date remains the incident with the greatest economic impact. The "Love Bug" attack has a rating of 10, and all other attacks are rated according to their relative economic impact. Table 6.2 shows the economic impact of malicious code attacks by year.

6.2   A grim future awaits us in cyber space

Dale L. Watson, Executive Assistant Director, Counter-terrorism and Counterintelligence of the FBI, testified before the Senate Select Committee on Intelligence on February 6, 2002. Watson pointed out that during the past several years the FBI had identified a wide array of cyber threats, ranging from defacement of Web sites by juveniles to sophisticated intrusions sponsored by foreign powers.

Some of these incidents pose more significant threats than others. The theft of national security information from a government agency or the interruption of electrical power to a major metropolitan area obviously would have greater consequences for national security, public safety, and the economy than the defacement of a Web site. But even the less serious categories have real consequences and, ultimately, can undermine public confidence in Web-based commerce and violate privacy or property rights. An

Table 6.2 *Economic Impact of Malicious Code Attacks—Analysis by Year*

Year	Worldwide Economic Impact (U.S. $)
2001	13.2 Billion
2000	17.1 Billion
1999	12.1 Billion
1998	6.1 Billion
1997	3.3 Billion
1996	1.8 Billion
1995	0.5 Billion

attack on a Web site that closes down an e-commerce site can have disas-
trous consequences for a Web-based business. An intrusion that results in
the theft of millions of credit-card numbers from an on-line vendor can
result in significant financial loss and, more broadly, reduce consumers'
willingness to engage in e-commerce.

Watson contends that beyond criminal threats, cyber space also faces a
variety of significant national security threats, including increasing threats
from terrorists. Terrorist groups are increasingly using new information
technology and the Internet to formulate plans, raise funds, spread propa-
ganda, and engage in secure communications. Cyber terrorism—meaning
the use of cyber tools to shut down critical national infrastructures (e.g.,
energy, transportation, or government operations) for the purpose of coerc-
ing or intimidating a government or civilian population—is clearly an
emerging threat.

On January 16, 2002, the FBI disseminated an advisory via the National
Law Enforcement Telecommunications System regarding possible attempts
by terrorists to use U.S. municipal and state Web sites to obtain information on local energy infrastructures, water reservoirs, dams, highly enriched
uranium storage sites, and nuclear and gas facilities. Although the FBI pos-
sesses no specific threat information regarding these apparent intrusions,
such activities on the part of terrorists pose serious challenges to our
national security.

In *Information Warfare: How to Survive Cyber Attacks*, the author,
Michael Erbschloe, concludes that a wide range of information warfare
strategies exist and that countries need to be prepared to defend against
them. The ten types of information warfare and their potential impact on
private companies are listed in Table 6.3. However, each of the ten categories of information warfare has a price tag, a required organizational structure, and a timeline for preparation and implementation.

Given these cost structures, the types of information warfare that will
most likely be waged against large industrial computer-dependent countries
are sustained terrorist information warfare, random terrorist information
warfare, sustained rogue information warfare, random rogue information
warfare, and amateur rogue information warfare.

To be able to finance, organize, and mount offensive ruinous information warfare and offensive containment information warfare is so expensive
that the publicly political enemies of the large industrial countries cannot
afford to use such strategies. But that does not mean that the lesser tactics
would not be extremely damaging to infrastructures and economies.

The strategies that would be most effective against smaller, somewhat computer-dependent countries are offensive ruinous information warfare and offensive containment information warfare. In the case of aggressor countries or groups, defensive responsive containment information warfare is the most likely tactic. The strategies that will be the most effective against countries that have done little in terms of developing a computer dependency are those of offensive containment information warfare.

The smaller, less-developed countries in no way can afford to mount and sustain defensive ruinous information warfare or defensive responsive containment information warfare strategies. At best, they could mount random

Table 6.3   *The Potential Impact of Information Warfare Strategies on Private Companies*

Type of Information Warfare	Potential Direct Impact on Private Companies in Full-Scale Information Wars	Potential Indirect Impact on Private Companies in Less Than Full-Scale Wars
Offensive ruinous information warfare	Destructive attacks on corporate systems by aggressors	Residual viruses or other destructive code launched during attacks or loss of communications systems
Offensive containment information warfare	Destructive attacks on corporate systems by aggressors	Residual viruses or other destructive code launched during attacks or loss of communications systems
Sustained terrorist information warfare	Repeated or sustained destructive targeted attacks on corporate systems by terrorist groups	Hits by viruses and other destructive code launched to attack general populations or loss of communications systems
Random terrorist information warfare	Random destructive targeted attacks on corporate systems by terrorist groups	Hits by viruses and other destructive code launched to attack general populations or loss of communications systems
Defensive preventive information warfare	Accidental disruption of communications during the initiation of preventive measures	Accidental disruption of communications during the initiation of preventive measures
Defensive ruinous information warfare	Destructive attacks on corporate systems by attacked countries to destroy an aggressor	Hits by viruses and other destructive code launched during defensive responses or loss of communications systems
Defensive responsive containment information warfare	Destructive attacks on corporate systems from countries attempting to contain an aggressor	Hits by viruses and other destructive code launched during defensive responses or loss of communications systems

Table 6.3   *The Potential Impact of Information Warfare Strategies on Private Companies (continued)*

Type of Information Warfare	Potential Direct Impact on Private Companies in Full-Scale Information Wars	Potential Indirect Impact on Private Companies in Less Than Full-Scale Wars
Sustained rogue information warfare	Repeated or sustained targeted attacks on corporate systems by criminal groups	Hits by viruses and other destructive code launched to attack general populations or loss of communications systems
Random rogue information warfare	Random targeted attacks on corporate systems by criminal groups	Hits by viruses and other destructive code launched to attack general populations or loss of communications systems
Amateur rogue information warfare	Random targeted attacks on corporate systems by amateur groups	Hits by viruses and other destructive code launched to attack general populations or loss of communications systems

Source: Information Warfare: How to Survive Cyber Attacks (New York: McGraw-Hill, 2001)

terrorist information warfare or random rogue information warfare strategies and most likely would depend on amateur rogue information warfare carried out by a few patriots or geographically dispersed allies.

The private sector in industrial computer-dependent countries does need to be concerned about large-scale offensive ruinous information warfare in widespread conflicts that get out of hand. However, the most likely immediate threats to corporate operations outside of organized conflicts are random terrorist information warfare, sustained rogue information warfare, random rogue information warfare, and amateur rogue information warfare.

The most vulnerable corporations are those that are heavily involved in and derive the majority of their revenues from electronic commerce, or what we so lovingly call dot-coms. It will cost corporations much more to defend themselves against these information warfare strategies than it will cost terrorist or rogues to mount such attacks.

In addition, the only organizations in the industrialized countries that can afford to effectively counter or ultimately eliminate the attackers, especially if they are outside the country of the corporation that is being attacked, are maintained and controlled by the military. Because civilian law enforcement is in a weak position to deal with information warfare attacks on private corporations, those companies without strong ties to the military will become easy targets with little recourse.

6.3   **Countering security threats**

A firm foundation is required to develop satisfactory security protection, and that foundation is an organizational security policy that covers all the necessary contingencies. Among those contingencies are procedures for installing applications, e-mail and Internet practices, IT user policies, password protection, downloading data considerations, and network monitoring. The policy must provide a plan for responding to security attacks, and that plan must be rehearsed through dry runs and other simulated methods.

The security policy must be accepted and acknowledged by each employee. This goal can be accomplished through a combination of briefings at the time of hiring; notices in the employee handbook; and frequent reminders through posters, e-mail, and Web sites.

Fighting back against security violators requires that an organizational policy be developed and implemented. The first step in any security plan is to instill an awareness of the vulnerability in all users of computer systems. Physical security is particularly important. Implementing technical security measures is wasted effort if anyone can walk into your facility or log on to your network. Equally vital is not throwing sensitive IT system data into the dumpster.

If the organization does not employ security experts, bring in an outside consultant. Be prepared to respond to the consultant's recommendations. Even using the advice of the best of consultants, however, a security breach is inevitable. Accepting this reality, be prepared with a response to a security attack. Be sure to report the attack to the appropriate law enforcement agency.

When employees leave the organization, cancel their user IDs and passwords immediately. Passwords should be randomized to avoid the possibility of having a hacker guess them. All default passwords must be changed before applications are brought on-line.

Be wary of network holes. For example, simple network management protocol (SNMP) messages should not be allowed to transit the firewall. While SNMP is handy for passing system error messages, it can reveal too much about the inner workings of the network. Prevent routers from responding to SNMP commands that originate outside the network.

Keep in mind that your system will eventually experience a security attack. Preparing ahead of time is the only way to minimize the damage that attack may cause to your IT systems and to your company's future. It is important that an overall risk assessment be performed on critical information assets. As a starting point you should answer the following questions and take steps necessary to eliminate weaknesses:

- Does your organization have a written security policy?
- Does the policy identify all individuals responsible for implementing that policy and what their duties are?
- Does the policy identify the steps to be taken if there is a security breach?
- Does the policy identify what information it is most important to protect?
- Does the policy identify enforcement procedures that identify the penalties associated with a security breach?
- Is the policy known by all individuals who have the responsibility for implementing that policy?
- Has a security plan been developed based on the security policy?
- Are only authorized individuals allowed to move and install computer equipment?
- What password rules are enforced (e.g., length, alphanumeric combinations)?
- Has your organization developed a computer security incident response capability (CSIRC)?
- Have users and system administrators received training on how to carry out their respective responsibilities when an incident occurs?
- Does your organization maintain a knowledge base of past incidents and "lessons learned" for future use?
- Does your organization have written system maintenance policies and procedures?
- Are maintenance records kept to indicate what was done, when, and by whom?
- Is sensitive and/or critical information clearly defined and labeled?
- Are employees trained on proper labeling procedures for hard copies, electronic files, e-mail attachments, diskettes, backup tapes, and disks, and so on?
- Does your organization have a policy and procedures for sanitizing and disposing of sensitive material on floppy disks, CDs, and so on?

- Is there an orientation course on good security practices for new employees?

- Is there a formal information security training program within your organization?

- Are new employees required to receive security awareness training within a specified number of days after hiring?

- Are employees required to get updated security training at regular intervals?

6.4   Reporting a computer crime

If your systems are hacked or intruded upon by an unauthorized party, you should call your local FBI office or contact the National Infrastructure Protection Center (NIPC) Watch Operations Center, 1-888-585-9078. In the event that you experience a crime against your computer systems, the FBI and the NIPC recommend that you act as follows:

- Respond quickly. Contact law enforcement. Traces are often impossible if too much time is wasted before alerting law enforcement or your own incident response team.

- If unsure of what actions to take, do not stop system processes or tamper with files. This may destroy traces of intrusion.

- Follow organizational policies and procedures. (Your organization should have a computer incident response capability and plan in place.)

- Use the telephone to communicate. (Attackers may be capable of monitoring e-mail traffic.)

- Contact the incident response team for your organization. (Quick use of technical expertise is crucial in preventing further damage and protecting potential evidence.)

- Establish points of contact with general counsel, emergency response staff, and law enforcement. (Preestablished contacts will help in a quick response effort.)

- Make copies of files an intruder may have altered or left. If you have the technical expertise to copy files, this action will assist investigators as to when and how the intrusion may have occurred.

- Identify a primary point of contact to handle potential evidence. Establish a chain of custody for evidence. (Potential hardware and software evidence that is not properly controlled may lose its value.)

- Do not contact the suspected perpetrator.

6.4.1   Information to help investigators

Compile as much information and data possible about the incident. Information that law enforcement investigators will find helpful includes:

- Date, time, and duration of incident.

- The name, title, telephone number, fax number, and e-mail of the point of contact for law enforcement as well as the name of your organization, address, city, state, zip code, and country.

- The physical locations of computer systems and/or networks that have been compromised.

- Whether the systems are managed in-house or by a contractor.

- Whether the affected systems or networks are critical to the organization's mission.

- If it is a part of the critical infrastructure, which sector was affected:
  - Banking and finance
  - Emergency services
  - Gas or oil storage and delivery
  - Government operations
  - Power
  - Transportation
  - Telecommunications
  - Water supply systems

- The nature of the problem, which could include intrusion, system impairment, denial of resources, unauthorized root access, Web site defacement, compromise of system integrity, theft, or damage.

- Whether the problem had been experienced before.

- The suspected method of intrusion or attack, which could include a virus, an exploited vulnerability, a denial of service, a distributed denial of service, a trapdoor, or a Trojan Horse.

- The suspected perpetrators and the possible motivations of the attack, which could include an insider or disgruntled employee, a former employee, or a competitor. If the suspect is an employee or former employee, you should determine and report the type of system access that the employee has or had.

- An apparent source (IP address) of the intrusion or attack if known and if there is any evidence of spoofing.

- What computer system (hardware, operating system, or applications software) was affected.

- What security infrastructure was in place, which could include an incident response team, encryption, a firewall, secure remote access or authorization tools, an intrusion detection system, security auditing tools, access control lists, or packet filtering.

- Whether the intrusion or attack resulted in a loss or compromise of sensitive, classified, or proprietary information.

- Whether the intrusion or attack resulted in damage to systems or data.

- What actions to mitigate the intrusion or attack have been taken, which could include the system being disconnected from the network, system binaries checked, backup of affected systems, or log files examined.

- What agencies have been contacted, which could include state or local police, CERT, or FedCIRC.

- When your system was last modified or updated and the name of the company or organization that did the work (address, phone number, point of contact information).

6.4.2   Information to determine damages or loss

It is also necessary to determine a dollar value of damage, business loss, and cost to restore systems to normal operating conditions. The following information is helpful in determining dollar amounts.

- In the event that repairs or recovery were performed by a contractor, you should determine the charges incurred for services.

- If in-house staff were involved in determining the extent of the damage, repairing systems or data, or restoring systems to normal operating conditions, you should determine the number of hours staff expended to accomplish these tasks and the hourly wages, benefits, and overhead associated with each employee involved in the recovery.

- If business was disrupted in some way, you should determine the number of transactions or sales that were actually disrupted and their dollar value.

- If systems were impaired to the point that actual disrupted transactions or sales cannot be determined, then you should determine the dollar value of transactions or sales that would occur on a comparable day, for the duration of the system outage.

- If systems are used to produce goods, deliver services, or manage operations, then what is the value of the loss due to that disruption. (You may have had similar experiences if operations were disrupted because of inclement weather, fires, earthquakes, or other disruptive incidents.)

- If systems were physically damaged, you need to know what you paid to acquire and install the systems.

- If systems were stolen, you need to know what you paid to acquire and install the systems and the cost of actions taken to ensure that information on the stolen systems cannot be used to access systems.

- If intellectual property or trade secrets were stolen, then you need to determine the value of that property.

- If intellectual property or trade secrets were used by a competitor or other party, then you need to determine the impact on your business.

6.4.3   Participate in InfraGard to improve cyber defense

The National Infrastructure Protection Center (NIPC), with help from representatives of private industry, the academic community, and government agencies, developed the InfraGard initiative to share information about cyber intrusions, exploited vulnerabilities, and infrastructure threats. The 56 field offices of the FBI have each established an InfraGard chapter, and more than 800 organizations across the United States are members. The National InfraGard Program provides four basic services to members:

- An alert network using encrypted e-mail.

- A secure Web site for communication about suspicious activity or intrusions.

- Local chapter activities and a help desk for questions.

- The ability of industry to provide information on intrusions to the local FBI Field Office using secure communications.

General membership in InfraGard is open to all parties interested in supporting the purposes and objectives of InfraGard. On the local level InfraGard is organized into 56 chapters, each of which is associated with a field office of the FBI. InfraGard members are responsible for promoting the protection and advancement of the critical infrastructure, cooperating with others in the interchange of knowledge and ideas, supporting the education of members and the general public, and maintaining the confidentiality of information obtained through involvement.

6.5   Steps to prevent viruses from spreading

There are several basic steps that you can take and should train employees to take also when applicable.

6.5.1   Use antivirus software and keep it up-to-date

Make sure you have antivirus software on your computer! Antivirus software is designed to protect you and your computer against known viruses so you don't have to worry. But with new viruses emerging daily, antivirus programs need regular updates, like annual flu shots, to recognize these new viruses. Be sure to update your antivirus software regularly! The more often you keep it updated—say once a week—the better. Check with the Web site of your antivirus software company to see some sample descriptions of viruses and to get regular updates for your software.

6.5.2   Don't open e-mail from unknown sources

A simple rule of thumb is that if you don't know the person who is sending you an e-mail, be very careful about opening the e-mail and any file attached to it. Should you receive a suspicious e-mail, the best thing to do is to delete the entire message, including any attachment. Even if you do know the person sending you the e-mail, you should exercise caution if the message is strange and unexpected, particularly if it contains unusual hyperlinks. Your friend may have accidentally sent you a virus. Such was the case with the "I Love You" virus that spread to millions of people in 2001. When in doubt, delete!

6.5.3   Use hard-to-guess passwords

Passwords will keep outsiders out only if they are difficult to guess! Don't share your password, and don't use the same password in more than one place. If someone should happen to guess one of your passwords, you don't want him or her to be able to use it in other places. The golden rules of passwords are: (1) A password should have a minimum of eight characters; be as meaningless as possible; and use a mix of uppercase letters, lowercase letters, and numbers (e.g., xk28LP97). (2) Change passwords regularly, at least every 90 days. (3) Do not give out your password to anyone!

6.5.4   Protect your computer from Internet intruders—use firewalls

Equip your computer with a firewall! Firewalls create a protective wall between your computer and the outside world. They come in two forms—software firewalls that run on your personal computer and hardware firewalls that protect a number of computers at the same time. They work by filtering out unauthorized or potentially dangerous types of data from the Internet while still allowing other (good) data to reach your computer. Firewalls also ensure that unauthorized persons can't gain access to your computer while you're connected to the Internet. You can find firewall hardware and software at most computer stores nationwide.

6.5.5   Don't share access to your computers with strangers

Your computer operating system may allow other computers on a network, including the Internet, to access the hard drive of your computer in order to share files. This ability to share files can be used to infect your computer with a virus or look at the files on your computer if you don't pay close attention. So, unless you really need this ability, make sure you turn off file sharing. Check your operating system and your other program help files to learn how to disable file sharing. Don't share access to your computer with strangers!

6.5.6   Disconnect from the Internet when not in use

Remember that the digital highway is a two-way thoroughfare. You send and receive information on it. Disconnecting your computer from the Internet when you're not on-line lessens the chance that someone will be able to access your computer. And if you haven't kept your antivirus software up-to-date or don't have a firewall in place, someone could infect your computer or use it to harm someone else on the Internet.

6.5.7 Back up your computer data

Experienced computer users know that there are two types of people: those who have already lost data and those who are going to experience the pain of losing data in the future. Back up small amounts of data on floppy disks and larger amounts on CDs. If you have access to a network, save copies of your data on another computer in the network. Most people make weekly backups of all their important data. And make sure you have your original software start-up disks handy and available in the event your computer system files get damaged

6.5.8 Regularly download security protection update patches

Most major software companies today have to release updates and patches to their software every so often. Sometimes bugs are discovered in a program that may allow a malicious person to attack your computer. When these bugs are discovered, the software companies or vendors create patches that they post on their Web sites. You need to be sure you download and install the patches! Check your software vendors' Web sites on a regular basis for new security patches, or use the new automated patching features that some companies offer. If you don't have the time to do the work yourself, download and install a utility program to do it for you. There are available software programs that can perform this task for you.

6.5.9 Check your security on a regular basis

When you change your clocks for daylight saving time, reevaluate your computer security. The programs and operating system on your computer have many valuable features that make your life easier but can also leave you vulnerable to hackers and viruses. You should evaluate your computer security at least twice a year—do it when you change the clocks for daylight saving! Look at the settings on applications that you have on your computer. Your browser software, for example, typically has a security setting in its preferences area. Check what settings you have and make sure you have the security level appropriate for you.

6.5.10   Make sure your employees know what to do if your computer becomes infected

It's important that everyone who uses a computer be aware of proper security practices. People should know how to update virus protection software, how to download security patches from software vendors, and how to create a proper password.

6.6   How the United States has organized for critical infrastructure protection

The U.S. General Accounting Office (GAO) has conducted an ongoing analysis of the ability of the United States to protect critical infrastructures, including computer systems. The GAO has reported to Congress that the security of these computer systems and data is essential to avoiding disruptions in critical operations and preventing data tampering, fraud, and inappropriate disclosure of sensitive information. However, federal computer systems contain weaknesses that continue to put critical operations and assets at risk. In particular, deficiencies exist in entity-wide security programs that are critical to agencies' success in ensuring that risks are understood and effective controls are implemented. GAO found weaknesses in the following six areas:

1.   Security program management

2.   Access controls

3.   Software development and change controls

4.   Segregation of duties

5.   Operating systems controls

6.   Service continuity

Weaknesses in these areas place a broad range of critical operations and assets at risk for fraud, misuse, and disruption. The GAO notes that federal agencies have tried to address these problems, and many have good remedial efforts underway. Still, these efforts will not be fully effective and lasting unless they are supported by a strong agency-wide security management framework.

The GAO contends that establishing such a management framework requires that agencies take a comprehensive approach that involves both senior agency program managers, who understand which aspects of their missions are the most critical and sensitive, and technical experts, who know the agencies' systems and can suggest appropriate technical security control techniques.

In Executive Order (EO) 13231 of October 16, 2001, Critical Infrastructure Protection in the Information Age, the president redesignated the National Security Telecommunications and Information Systems Security Committee (NSTISSC) as the Committee on National Security Systems (CNSS). The Department of Defense continues to chair the committee under the authorities established by NSD-42. As a standing committee of the President's Critical Infrastructure Protection Board, the CNSS reports fully and regularly on its activities to the board.

The EO directs the protection of information systems for critical infrastructure, including emergency preparedness communications and the physical assets that support such systems. The Secretary of Defense and the Director of Central Intelligence are responsible for developing and overseeing the implementation of government-wide policies, principles, standards, and guidelines for the security of systems with national security information.

The CNSS provides a forum for the discussion of policy issues; sets national policy; and promulgates direction, operational procedures, and guidance for the security of national security systems through the CNSS Issuance System. National security systems contain classified information or:

- Involve intelligence activities

- Involve cryptographic activities related to national security

- Involve command and control of military forces

- Involve equipment that is an integral part of a weapon or weapons systems

- Is critical to the direct fulfillment of military or intelligence missions (not including routine administrative and business applications)

The primary functions of the CNSS include but are not limited to:

- Developing and issuing national policy and standards

- Developing and issuing guidelines, instructions, advisory memoranda, technical bulletins, and incident reports

- Assessing the health of national security systems

- Approving release of INFOSEC products and information to foreign governments

- Creating and maintaining the National Issuance System

- Developing liaison and partnerships with other security organizations

The CNSS accomplishes its tasks through a combination of subcommittees, issue groups, and working groups. All of these groups, as well as the day-to-day activities of the CNSS, are supported by a secretariat. There are two main subcommittees: the Subcommittee on Information Systems Security (SISS) and the Subcommittee on Telecommunications Security (STS). These subcommittees have several working groups, which are as follows:

- Key management infrastructure

- National assessment

- Glossary

- Tempest

- CNSS information assurance

- Foreign influence on U.S. information technology

- Education, training, and awareness

- Key management infrastructure training

- Space policy

- Assurance of sensitive information

- Cryptographic modernization

6.6.1   The Subcommittee on Information Systems Security

The Subcommittee on Information Systems Security (SISS) was established under the Committee on National Security Systems (CNSS). It considers technical matters and develops operating policies, guidelines, instructions, and directives associated with information systems security. It also addresses related topics such as compromising emanations, electronic key management, and computer security aspects of telecommunications and network security. Its overall responsibilities include:

- Developing, formulating, and recommending for CNSS approval specific operating policies, objectives, and priorities affecting such matters under the cognizance of the SISS required to achieve the broad information systems security policies and objectives.

- Maintaining cognizance of the security initiatives that are undertaken with the private sector in accordance with the National Policy.

- Providing a forum for the exchange of security guidelines pertaining to information systems among all departments and agencies that participate in the CNSS process.

- Overseeing, with the STS, the development of the annual assessment on the security status of national security systems with respect to established objectives and policies.

- Developing information systems security guidance for the CNSS to provide to activities of the U.S. government.

- Interacting with other permanent or temporary subcommittees of the CNSS in order to coordinate or advise on the implementation of appropriate security protective measures.

- Providing status reports to and identify actions and topics that require the attention of the CNSS in promoting and expediting the implementation of security programs for national security telecommunications systems.

6.6.2   The Subcommittee on Telecommunications Security

The Subcommittee on Telecommunications Security (STS) is also under the Committee on National Security Systems (CNSS). The subcommittee develops operating policies, guidelines, instructions, and directives associated with telecommunications technology, security voice systems, secure record and data systems, and space and satellite telecommunications systems. The subcommittee also addresses security for weapons and strategic defense telecommunications systems, command and control telecommunications systems, compromising emanations, and electronic key management. Overall responsibilities are to:

- Develop, formulate, and recommend for CNSS approval specific operating policies, objectives, and priorities to achieve telecommunications security.

- Ensure that security initiatives are undertaken with the private sector in accordance with national policy.

- Provide a forum for the exchange of telecommunications security guidelines among all departments and agencies that participate in the CNSS process.

- Oversee, with the SISS, the development of the annual assessment on the security status of national security systems with respect to established objectives and policies.

- Develop telecommunications system security guidance for the CNSS to provide to activities of the U.S. government.

- Interact with other permanent or temporary subcommittees of the CNSS in order to coordinate or advise on the implementation of appropriate security protective measures.

- Provide status reports to and identify actions and topics that require the attention of the CNSS in promoting and expediting the implementation of security programs for national security telecommunications systems.

6.6.3   Electronic Key Management Working Group

This working group was established in 1990 to investigate the requirements of the civil community in the area of key management. In 1992, the working group wrote and the CNSS promulgated the National Policy on Electronic Keying. This policy established the national objective of virtually eliminating, by the year 2000, a dependence on paper-based nonelectronic keying methods. The working group has developed a strategy for providing training on electronic keying systems and has assisted civil agencies to budget for these programs and to complete their implementation plans. In 1997, the group expanded the scope of its responsibilities to include all matters involving key management issues, including public key infrastructure (PKI), certificate management infrastructure (CMI), and key management infrastructure (KMI). The working group was renamed the Key Management Infrastructure Working Group (KMIWG).

6.6.4   The National Assessment Working Group

This group was established to fulfill an NSD-42 requirement that stated that the CNSS will submit annually to the Executive Agent an evaluation of the security status of national security systems with respect to established objectives and priorities.

6.6.5   The Glossary Working Group

The working group was reactivated in 1994 to update the 1992 version of the glossary. NSTISSI 4009 was revised and reissued in 1997 and a new evolving document took its place. The goal of this document is to keep pace with changes in information systems security terminology through periodic reviews and, therefore, will be in a continuous state of coordination.

6.6.6   The TEMPEST Working Group

This group was formed in 1990 to streamline national-level TEMPEST activities and serve as a forum for TEMPEST matters of interest to the CNSS community in support of national TEMPEST security objectives. The TAG develops national TEMPEST policy, standards, and guidelines and oversees community TEMPEST training needs.

6.6.7   The CNSS Information Assurance Working Group

The goal of this working group is to develop a government-wide information assurance program to safeguard the national and economic security of the country. The program must achieve a balance between the strong information warfare stance of the Department of Defense (DoD) and the broader needs of the civil government and the private sector. Specific focus areas include security infrastructure, interoperability, e-mail, multiple-level security, and certification and accreditation.

6.6.8   The Foreign Influence on U.S. Information Technology Working Group

This group was formed in March 2001 to develop appropriate draft policies to address foreign ownership, operations, and influence on U.S. telecommunications and Internet providers and services. Policies address transnational implications, law enforcement, security concerns, and public safety concerns.

6.6.9   Education, Training, and Awareness Working Group

The purpose of this working group is to serve as a national-level forum for training issues of concern to the CNSS membership and to support the training of INFOSEC professionals. The group also participates in a government/private industry effort to establish training guidelines and standards and to promote sharing of information among all federal agencies. Under this group there are three specialized groups: Curriculum and Certification, KMI Training, and Tools and Standards.

6.6.10   The Key Management Infrastructure Training Committee

This group was established under the Education, Training, and Awareness Working Group (ETAWG) and the Key Management Infrastructure Working Group (KMIWG) to facilitate the development of government-wide training solutions for KMI. To ensure focus and efficiency of operation and to prevent duplication of effort, it receives direction from and reports back to both of these groups.

6.6.11   The Space Policy Working Group

The Space Policy Working Group was formed in September 1998 and is co-chaired by NSA and NASA. Its goal is to develop National Space Information Assurance (IA) Policy to ensure that IA is factored into the planning, design, launch, and operation of space systems used to collect, generate, process, sort, display, or transmit national security information.

6.6.12   The Assurance of Sensitive Information Working Group

The purpose of this working group is to provide policy and guidance to properly manage the risk in placing caveated material on the Internet while taking advantage of all the resources the Internet can provide for the community. Established in October 2000, the membership is composed of more than 19 agencies. The goals include cataloging existing terminology, engaging the CIO Council, establishing written standards and guidance, and reaching the widest possible intended audience.

6.6.13   The Cryptographic Modernization Working Group

This working group was recently established to address the high-assurance cryptographic needs of the CNSS community, an effort critical to future information technology security. The intent is to review all federal government cryptographic modernization needs so that these can be leveraged against ongoing defense department efforts.

Principle Six: Safeguard the Privacy of Information

The fantastic advances in the field of communication constitute a grave danger to the privacy of the individual.

—Earl Warren, former chief justice
of the U.S. Supreme Court

7.1 The state of privacy management

Maintaining the privacy of enterprise information is a meticulous process, one that requires coordination across all departments and functions within an organization. It is important that everyone on the privacy management team understand the basic issues and concepts of privacy management as well as enterprise policies and procedures. An understanding of the concept and the basic issues will help managers make operational decisions about privacy during the day-to-day course of events. It also enables them to more fully participate in formulating policies and procedures.

Privacy plans have been developed in 51.1 percent of the organizations that participated in the thirteenth annual "Information Systems and E-Business Spending" study conducted by Computer Economics. This is a considerable increase from 2001; when only 33.3 percent of the respondents had developed their privacy plans. Table 7.1 shows the status of privacy planning by industry sector for 2002 along with what was reported in 2001.

A big question is: Do all organizations need a privacy plan? A total of 23.4 percent of organizations have not started developing their privacy plan but need a plan as they evolve their Web site and e-commerce practices. Of the organizations in the 2002 study, 97.2 percent have Web sites, 53.2 percent have implemented at least one e-commerce application, and an additional 27.4 percent are in the process of implementing an e-commerce application.

Table 7.1   *Status of Privacy Planning 2002 Compared with 2001*

Sector	No Activity (%)	Researching (%)	Piloting ($)	Implementing (%)	In Place (%)
All sectors					
2002	23.4	10.9	3.2	11.5	51.1
2001	23.5	26.2	4.4	12.0	33.3
Banking and Finance					
2002	19.0	4.8	0.0	19.0	57.2
2001	17.5	17.5	7.9	25.0	32.1
Discrete Manufacturing					
2002	34.6	7.7	0.0	0.0	57.7
2001	24.2	17.5	9.2	18.8	30.3
Health Care					
2002	13.0	3.9	17.4	26.1	39.6
2001	11.9	34.3	0.0	17.9	35.9
Insurance					
2002	13.6	22.7	4.5	27.3	31.9
2001	12.2	33.1	0.0	8.9	45.8
Process Manufacturing					
2002	32.1	14.3	3.6	10.7	39.3
2001	46.4	10.8	3.5	0.0	39.3
Professional Services					
2002	24.1	10.3	3.4	13.8	48.4
2001	31.0	26.2	7.1	11.9	23.8
Retail Distribution					
2002	33.3	12.5	4.2	8.3	41.7
2001	28.6	22.5	3.2	7.5	38.2
State and Local Government					
2002	8.7	21.9	0.0	4.3	65.1
2001	11.1	45.8	0.0	16.7	26.4

Table 7.1   *Status of Privacy Planning 2002 Compared with 2001 (continued)*

Sector	No Activity (%)	Researching (%)	Piloting ($)	Implementing (%)	In Place (%)
Trade Services					
2002	23.6	5.9	0.0	17.6	52.9
2001	26.9	29.3	7.3	12.1	24.4
Transportation					
2002	38.5	0.0	0.0	0.0	61.5
2001	46.6	13.3	0.0	9.0	31.1
Utilities					
2002	13.0	8.0	5.3	10.5	63.2
2001	5.3	42.1	10.5	5.3	36.8
Wholesale Distribution					
2002	27.3	18.2	0.0	0.0	54.5
2001	23.1	24.4	4.5	14.4	33.6

Source: Computer Economics

This means that there are a considerable number of organizations in the study that have Web sites but do not have privacy plans. In addition, there are more organizations that will be engaging in e-commerce than have privacy plans. Although there may be organizations that do not have a great need for a privacy plan, certainly those involved in e-commerce and have a Web site do need a privacy plan.

7.2   Privacy is a concern with consumers

There have been numerous studies on consumer perspectives on privacy. Regardless of when the studies were conducted or the type of organization that conducted the research, all findings point toward consumers being concerned about privacy.

In a study conducted by AT&T Labs entitled "Beyond Concern: Understanding Net Users' Attitudes about Online Privacy" only 13 percent of respondents reported they were "not very" or "not at all" concerned about on-line privacy. Forty-eight percent said they would be more likely to provide more information to Web sites if there was a law that prevented the site from using the information for any purpose other than processing the request; 28 percent said they would be more likely to provide it if the site had a privacy policy; and 58 percent said they would be more likely to provide it if the site had both a privacy policy and a seal of approval from a well-known organization such as the Better Business Bureau or the AAA. These data were derived from the analysis of 381 questionnaires completed between November 6 and November 13, 1998, by American Internet users. The sample was drawn from the *Family PC* magazine/Digital Research, Inc.

A survey of those who seek medical and health information on-line reveals that 81 percent would like to have the right to sue a medical company that gave away or sold information in violation of its privacy promises. The study was conducted by the Pew Internet & American Life Project from a survey of 521 Internet users who have obtained health information on-line during fall 2000. Of those who seek health and medical information on-line, 60 percent say they don't want to have their health records posted on-line because they worry about other people seeing their health records. In another survey of 1,101 Internet users during August 2000, Pew found that 86 percent of health site users are concerned that a Web site might sell or give away information about their activity at health sites.

In a spring 2002 study conducted by Star Systems, 35 percent of consumers said they are more concerned about their financial privacy than they were one year before. The other 65 percent, however, report either the same level (59 percent) or a lower level (6 percent) of concern. The survey also showed that when consumers are unfamiliar with their financial institutions' privacy policies, they are more likely to be concerned about their financial privacy. Interestingly, respondents to the Star survey believe the privacy of their financial information varies with the type of electronic payment method they use. They rated credit-card transactions the least private and PIN-secured ATM/debit-card transactions the most private. They said signature-authorized ATM/debit-card transactions fall between the other two categories.

Further, despite two federal laws enacted in the 1970s to limit government access to financial information, survey respondents view the government as one of the main recipients of such information. Asked which entities can access information collected electronically at the time of purchase, government agencies (76 percent) ranked ahead of the store where the purchase was made (73 percent), marketing companies (65 percent), and the company that makes the product that was purchased (48 percent). Only the financial institution that issued the card (85 percent) and the companies involved with processing the electronic transaction (80 percent) were perceived to have greater access than government agencies.

7.3   **Getting a grip on privacy issues**

Unfortunately, the definition of privacy is not straightforward. There are cultural, societal, political, legal, and national viewpoints as to what privacy is and what constitutes a violation of privacy. Thus, it is important to establish an operational definition of privacy in an enterprise. A strong definition of privacy will help prevent inadequate interpretations of policies and procedures as well as poor decisions regarding the privacy of information when there is a lack of specific procedures covering specific incidents or information elements.

At the most basic level, the privacy of information is tied to ownership of information. Ownership of information is clear in many cases. If an enterprise, for example, creates information about its products, business strategies, or operations, that information is the property of the enterprise. Managers in the enterprise then get to determine who has the right to know that information and when and where it can be disseminated.

Disseminating the information, however, is not the same as giving away ownership and the rights that are inherent in that ownership. This is where the definition of privacy becomes more complicated. It is common practice for an organization to provide another organization with proprietary information in order to facilitate a business relationship. During this process the two organizations establish a basis for the exchange of information and expectations, as well as requirements as to how that information can be used are agreed on.

When organizations exchange information to help facilitate business processes, the importance of privacy has been fairly well established and has become customary. An organization wants its information kept confidential to prevent damage that may occur if the information was obtained by competitors or other parties that could use that information to negatively impact the competitive position or the well-being of the company providing the information. The provider of the information has a public image to protect, and the misuse of confidential information could result in bad publicity. In the case of publicly held companies, improper dissemination of proprietary information could negatively impact stock value.

Individuals who provide information to businesses or government organizations can also be negatively affected by the misuse of information.

Such misuse may impact their job, career choices, and lifetime earnings. An individual who is gay or lesbian may choose to keep this information private in order to avoid dealing with potential social or financial negative consequences. People who are making investment decisions, considering changing jobs, or planning to get divorced may suffer damages from the release of information related to their lives or their plans.

Because there is a lack of universal definitions as to what constitutes the ownership of information and the privacy of information, the privacy contract is essential to establish an agreement between the information provider and the information recipient as to the use of the information exchanged. The example of a business-to-business exchange of information to facilitate business processes is done under specific conditions with agreed-on procedures and rights to use the information. Similarly, the exchange of information between a consumer and a business needs to be governed by a contract that establishes rights and expectations.

When information is exchanged, there must a contract between the parties who are giving and receiving information as to the scope of use of that information. It is neither reasonable nor prudent to expect both parties to share a common view of the rights to use the information. Where there are local or national laws governing the use of information, the contract should, of course, be in compliance with such laws. Where there is a lack of specific laws, the exchange of information should be governed by a contract that binds them and that both parties can understand.

The concept of the privacy contract is exemplified in the privacy statement on a Web site. To be in compliance with the safe harbor principles of the European Union, an organization must inform individuals as to why information about them is collected. The privacy statement must also indicate how to contact the organization with inquiries or complaints as well as state the types of third parties to which the information will be disclosed. This notice must be provided to individuals in clear language at the point when individuals are first asked to provide personal information or as soon thereafter as is practicable. In all circumstances the organization must inform individuals before it uses information for any purpose other than that for which it was originally collected or before it discloses information to a third party.

The social nature of privacy and rising concerns among citizen groups and governments will likely keep privacy issues at the forefront of social concerns. This will be fueled in part by a desire to deal with many of the issues that have emerged because of the Internet. State attorneys general, the

U.S. Justice Department, the Federal Trade Commission, and the Securities and Exchange Commission are expected to step up their efforts to enforce existing laws in Internet communications and business as well as eventually push for additional laws and regulations.

The U.S. Congress, state legislatures, and governments in countries around the world are also expected to become more aggressive in the regulation of the Internet, and those privacy issues will be a subpart of those efforts. Internet regulation will not be easy for governments to cope with, and therefore many false starts, high levels of rhetoric, and the pursuit of test cases to show regulatory prowess or to reinforce the popularity of political entities or candidates can be anticipated.

7.4   Is your organization at risk?

One of an organization's greatest points of vulnerability internally is lack of knowledge about what types of data it has and how they are being used. Those companies without a privacy plan in place are the most vulnerable. Although companies with a track record in collecting and using a wide variety of data may be better versed in privacy issues, they may still not understand what is happening with the data that may create privacy problems.

One of the key steps in developing a privacy plan is to conduct a privacy vulnerability audit. A privacy vulnerability audit is a complex and meticulous process. It involves all departments in an enterprise and requires an examination of how data and information are protected, how they are used inside the enterprise, and how they are shared with its business partners. The privacy vulnerability audit is an important step in determining how to develop a privacy plan, as well as the type and scope of privacy-related policies and procedures that need to be established to avoid privacy problems.

In the management of privacy there are two types of threats within an organization. First is deliberate misuse or theft of information. This can range from incidents whereby employees deliberately remove proprietary information—including trade secrets, customer lists, or financial data—and provide that information to unauthorized parties. The second type of internal threat stems from ignorance or carelessness as to how proprietary data and information are used. This can result in information being unnecessarily compromised, putting an organization at risk or having a negative impact on its ability to function or compete. In addition, improper disclosure can result in civil litigation by the parties who believe their privacy rights have been violated.

A lesser threat has to do with how professionals interact with each other at conferences, workshops, or scientific or engineering meetings and now even over the Internet in communities and chat rooms. Professionals like to network, share ideas, and learn from each other. They like to help each other solve problems and accomplish research or advance their professions in some way. This, of course, may be good for society as a whole or for the professionals involved in the networking activity, but it may not be the best thing for an organization. It is essential that the privacy plan define appropriate behavior in these circumstances.

There are certainly privacy threats from outside an organization. Competitors, market researchers, and even social action groups can benefit from obtaining another organization's proprietary information. In many cases such groups will work with people inside the organization and plot to steal trade secrets or customer lists. In other cases researchers will use extreme means to find out about operations or business plans. Although much of this type of activity is deemed legitimate and is a customary business practice in many countries, it is still possible to experience a negative impact if the wrong type of information is revealed to individuals outside the organization.

Even the most innocent-looking research effort can be detrimental to an organization. There are numerous survey organizations, for example, that send questionnaires to purchasing or information technology departments or conduct telephone surveys about issues or buying plans.

The necessity for good data security is absolute and is a fiduciary responsibility of corporate management. However, even though data security and privacy have a relationship, it is important to remember that the concept and practice of data security are generally geared toward restricting access to data. Restricting access to data does not automatically assure that privacy is not being abused or violated. If organizational policies and practices regarding the use or sale of sensitive information are not appropriate for a specific environment, privacy problems will still surface even though there is a secure information and technology infrastructure.

In theory, law enforcement agencies in most major countries will get involved when unauthorized parties access information systems or misappropriate trade secrets. It is important to note that most law enforcement agencies are rather under-equipped to deal with cyber crimes. Thus, the reality of getting help from law enforcement agencies is far different from the theory. Law-enforcement officials may write a report and may be of help when physical property is stolen, but organizations should be wary of counting on them to be of much assistance when the theft of information or the intentional violation of the privacy of information is involved.

Organizations need to check their policies to make sure; however, it is doubtful that their insurance policies can or will cover the potential extent of damage that major privacy violations could produce. Unless an organization has demonstrated due care in protecting its data and information and has clear policies for the management of privacy in place, its insurance company representative may just laugh and tell stories back at the office about how dumb the organization was to think that it had coverage. It is important to conduct an insurance audit to determine whether there is coverage as well as the extent of any possible coverage. This includes a legal review of the policies as well as conferences with the insurance companies.

Privacy laws also differ considerably from country to country. It is important to note that if an organization is doing business in multiple countries, its privacy plan must address requirements to comply with the privacy laws of all of the countries in which it conducts business or has operations. The management team in each country, or those managers in the corporate headquarters responsible for business operations in each country, need to address specific requirements. In addition, an organization's privacy plan, policies, and procedures must address varying privacy requirements by country. Further, If a company plans on expanding its operations or sales efforts into new countries, it should evaluate privacy requirements and modify its privacy policies and procedures before it expands into a new country.

Every company needs an enterprise-wide privacy plan from which to formulate policies and procedures and should produce that plan in written form so department managers and individuals responsible for managing information or data can refer to the document for guidance when making decisions. It is also recommended that organizations have a standing privacy task force or committee that systematically reviews the plan and updates it as new business efforts are launched or new technology is implemented.

It is also critical that managers inform their clients, customers, and business partners about the company privacy policies and procedures to ensure that they understand their position and how seriously they take properly managing privacy. The process of building an enterprise-wide privacy management program is broken down into four major phases. Phase one is organizing and research; phase two is actually conducting the privacy needs audit; phase three is developing policies and plans; and the final phase is implementing those policies and plans.

Organizations with Web sites are generally more vulnerable, depending on how the organization uses its Web site. If it does not post sensitive material or collect, compile, or process customer data on its Web server, it is not more vulnerable for having a Web site. If the Web site is used to collect, compile, or process customer data, then the company has an added point of vulnerability. The increased vulnerability in this situation arises from the potential of a hacker breaking into the Web site and stealing data such as names, addresses, account information, or credit-card numbers. In addition, if the Web site is integrated with back-end applications or connected to other systems in the enterprise, there is a greater possibility that hackers and information thieves can access more sensitive information that otherwise would be kept private. Therefore, organizations with Web sites should pay special attention to these types of vulnerabilities when conducting a privacy audit and developing privacy plans.

Organizations with customer/client data are more at risk. The reason for this is that customer/client data are not only confidential, they are the type of information that thieves and hackers seek out. This is especially true when financial records or credit-card numbers are at risk. There is also the burden of added social pressure because of the sensitive nature of information that is considered personal. Pressure to protect personal data will increase over the next several years as privacy legislation is passed in countries around the world. This means that organizations that collect or use personal data about customers or business partners will need to take extraordinary steps to ensure privacy and, of course, to avoid potentially costly litigation or embarrassing public relations incidents.

7.5   How privacy laws are evolving

As the concern for privacy increases, governments around the world are working on legislation or have formed cross-border task forces to deal with privacy issues. We expect that the outcome of international privacy efforts will take several years to unfold and even longer to be implemented on a global basis. We also expect that national laws regarding privacy will continue to evolve around the world.

Historically, the Organization for Economic Cooperation and Development (OECD) has been the leading international organization addressing privacy issues, especially issues related to cross-border flow of data and the development of national laws governing privacy. We have traced the origins of OECD privacy-related activities back to 1960.

The European Union's (EU) privacy legislation, called the Directive on Data Protection, became effective on October 25, 1998. It and many national laws have been formulated following the guidelines developed over the years by the OECD. The directive requires that transfers of personal data take place only to non-EU countries that provide acceptable levels of privacy protection. This resulted in a long series of negotiations between the United States and the EU and the development of safe-harbor standards. As it now stands, compliance with safe-harbor requirements are voluntary, and organizations may qualify for safe harbor in different ways. Organizations that do decide to voluntarily adhere to safe-harbor principles can obtain and retain the benefits of the safe harbor and publicly declare that they have done so. The principles of safe harbor are as follows:

- An organization must inform individuals as to why information about them is collected, how to contact the organization with inquiries or complaints, what types of third parties the information will be disclosed to, and the options and means the organization provides individuals to limit its use and disclosure of information. Notice must be provided to individuals in clear language at the point at which individuals are first asked to provide personal information or as soon thereafter as is practicable. In all circumstances the organization must inform individuals before it uses information for any purpose other than that for which it was originally collected or before it discloses information to a third party.

- An organization must provide individuals with an opportunity to choose (opt out) whether and how personal information that they provide is used or disclosed to third parties if such use is not compatible with the original purpose for which the information was collected. Individuals must be provided with clear, readily available, and affordable mechanisms to exercise this option. When information is sensitive, such as medical and health information, racial or ethnic origin, political opinions, religious or philosophical beliefs, trade union membership, or information concerning the sex life of the individual, the individual must be given the opportunity to specifically affirm (opt in) that the information can be used.

- An organization is allowed to disclose personal information to third parties in manners that are consistent with the original principles of notice and choice. When an organization is passing on information that an individual has approved the use of, it must first determine that the receiving party subscribes to the safe-harbor principles. As an alternative to meeting general safe-harbor requirements, the receiving party must enter into a written agreement with the organization providing the information assuring, that the receiver will provide at least the same level of privacy protection as is required by relevant safe-harbor principles.

- Organizations that create, maintain, use, or disseminate personal information must take reasonable measures to ensure that it is reliable for the intended use. In addition, organizations must take reasonable precautions to protect their information from loss, misuse, unauthorized access, disclosure, alteration, and destruction.

- An organization may process personal information only for the purposes for which the information was originally collected. In doing so, an organization is responsible for ensuring that data are accurate, complete, and current.

- Individuals who provide information must have reasonable access to personal information about them that an organization holds and be able to correct or amend that information where it is inaccurate.

In addition to the steps that an organization must take internally, countries and states face the need for providing privacy protection mechanisms to assure compliance with the safe-harbor principles. There must also be recourse for individuals affected by noncompliance with the principles, and there must be consequences for an organization that violates safe-harbor principles. Such mechanisms must include readily available and affordable independent recourse for an individual's complaints and a method by which disputes can be investigated and resolved, as well as damages awarded where the applicable law or private sector initiatives so provide. There must also be procedures to verify that the assertions businesses make about their privacy practices are true and that privacy practices have been implemented as they were stated at the time the information was originally collected. Sanctions against organizations that violate the principles must be rigorous enough to ensure compliance.

7.6   Potential privacy problems in different sectors

In June 2001 Computer Economics released the results of a study of potential privacy problems in different industry sectors. Banking and finance organizations were determined to be the most susceptible to privacy management problems. The transportation, wholesale, and retail industries also rank high on the privacy problem susceptibility index compiled by Computer Economics.

The index is based on several factors, including the speed at which these sectors are moving into electronic commerce and Web-based customer service activities and the level of privacy planning and protection that has been put into place by organizations within the sectors. The sectors that are the

Table 7.2   *Privacy Problem Susceptibility Index*

Relative Vulnerability	Sector
100	Banking and Finance
97	Transportation
85	Wholesale
83	Retail
76	Discrete Manufacturing
71	Professional Services
66	Trade Services
66	Utilities
64	Process Manufacturing
61	State and Local Government
59	Health Care
51	Insurance
46	Federal Government

Source: Computer Economics

most vulnerable to privacy management problems along with their relative vulnerability, are shown in Table 7.2.

The global nature of the Internet and e-commerce is fueling the debate over the protection of privacy. As a result, privacy is a growing political, social, and business issue, and government policy makers and regulators around the world are focusing considerable attention on privacy issues. This makes privacy protection a management issue that cannot be ignored. It is important to focus on the business costs and benefits associated with risks in order to determine the best privacy management approach for a given organization. The risk analysis process involves the following three considerations:

- Assessing the range of risks associated with privacy management practices in your organization

- Selecting a risk level that best fits the business style of your organization

- Developing a course of action for privacy management that is appropriate for business goals

7.7   Establishing a privacy task force

An important first step in any organization is to establish a privacy task force or committee composed of representatives from all departments in the enterprise. The privacy task force can determine whether a full-time staff person will be required to oversee the implementation of the privacy plan. Although it is becoming rather in vogue to appoint a privacy director or czar, such a position may not be required in all organizations. The process of developing a privacy management plan is explained in depth in *Net Privacy: A Guide to Developing & Implementing an Ironclad ebusiness Privacy Plan,* coauthored by Michael Erbschloe and John Vacca.

The amount of time it takes to develop a privacy plan will obviously vary depending on the nature of an organization as well as on the type of data and information that need to be protected. Generally speaking, the first draft of a good privacy plan with appropriate input from all departments should take from three to six months to develop. Once developed, it will take three to six months to implement a privacy plan. Note, however, that managing privacy is a continuing effort, and after the plan is implemented outcomes must be measured and policies and procedures must be updated as business and legislative condition change. In other words, the work on privacy management is an ongoing process and should not be considered finished once the privacy plan is implemented.

There are several technologies that can help protect privacy but none that will ensure that privacy efforts are being managed effectively. Technologies are useful in protecting data processing and storage facilities as well as data transmitted over networks and the Internet. It is self-deceptive to think that technology is all that is needed to protect privacy. Technology helps, but privacy protection is a human effort that requires coordinated effort across all departments in the enterprise.

Net Privacy: A Guide to Developing & Implementing an Ironclad ebusiness Privacy Plan states that the privacy task force should be guided by the principles established for managing risks during the risk-assessment process. The privacy task force will require several months to compile the information needed to determine what data and information must be protected and to formulate policies and procedures to ensure that privacy is maintained. The process of building an enterprise-wide privacy management program is broken down into four principal phases, which are as follows:

- Organizing and research

- Conducting a privacy needs audit

- Developing policies and plans

- Implementing the plan

In phase one, the organizing and research phase, a privacy task force leader is appointed and the privacy task force is put into place. Departments identify and staff their departmental-level privacy teams, and the skill base of the task force and department teams is assessed. Training to round out the skills of the staff working on the privacy plan is conducted, and outside help, if necessary, is identified and selected. A schedule for the work of the task force is developed, and an internal awareness campaign should be launched.

In phase two, the privacy needs audit phase, an organization must begin to understand the many types of data and information it collects and uses. Identifying data, determining where or who they come from, establishing how and where these date are used, and if and where they are disseminated are accomplished during the privacy needs audit. In addition, the audit process identifies laws, government regulations, and internal requirements that could possibly govern the collection, use, and dissemination of the data.

In the third phase of privacy planning, enterprise privacy statements, policies, and procedures are developed and written. Actual implementation of the plan is accomplished in phase four.

7.8   Making the case for privacy management

Privacy has become a hot button of the information age. Politicians are debating new laws. Countries and economic blocs are taking positions on privacy management and are attempting to leverage privacy issues for political and economic gain. Advocacy groups are taking extreme positions and lobbying to influence how privacy is regulated. This mix of emotion, politics, and economics, has resulted in more chaos than order. Organizations that collect and maintain information about their customers, clients, or markets are caught in the middle of this chaos.

It seems that with new laws, the growth of the global Internet, and consumer opinions regarding privacy protection there is little to argue about when an organization starts facing privacy management issues. But the reality of it is that many organizations flounder when it comes to developing a solid privacy plan and, once the plan is developed, face an even more difficult time getting necessary procedures implemented.

When laws are clear and an organization operates in an environment such as health care or banking where there are well-formulated laws regarding privacy protection, there is little room left for debate. When no clear legal mandate is present, however, it is important to develop an understanding as to why privacy management is important to an organization and its overall business environment. But what may be even more important is to determine how an organization can achieve a return on investment for developing and implementing privacy protection policies and procedures. This can be done in part by assessing the public relations and marketing value of privacy protection and how a reputation for ethical privacy management can be used as a tool in developing and maintaining a positive public image of an organization.

Principle Seven: Ethically Manage Intellectual Property

Just as man can't exist without his body, so no rights can exist without the right to translate one's rights into reality, to think, to work and keep the results, which means: the right of property.

—Ayn Rand

8.1 The breadth of intellectual property management problems

The challenge that businesses face in managing intellectual property has greatly increased during the past decade. Some companies have been caught deliberately violating copyright laws. There have been many cases in which management was unaware that laws were being broken. Cases of carelessness or independent acts by employees can put an organization in jeopardy.

The Software and Information Industry Association (SIIA) and KPMG LLP released a report in November 2001 entitled "Doesn't Everybody Do It? Internet Piracy Attitudes and Behaviors." The survey, conducted to examine the acquisition and use of software and digital content via the Internet, found that nearly 30 percent of business people could be classified as pirating through a variety of electronic methods.

Of the 1,004 business people surveyed, more than half of the business users surveyed said they were unaware of corporate policies governing intellectual property that may be in place. According to the study, 54 percent of business users indicated they do not know whether it is permissible to redistribute information from on-line sites they subscribe to, while 23 percent said they believe it is permitted.

According to the study, most users of Internet content and software products said they were unaware of the proper legal use of such products, yet roughly seven out of ten (69.5 percent) reported they have used the Internet to acquire software and 22 percent subscribe to business information services.

While individuals may consciously and illegally download software, 12 percent of those surveyed claim that no one gets hurt when software is shared. Their behaviors tend to moderate with respect to redistribution of software. Fewer than 10 percent of consumers and 16 percent of business users admit to redistribution, more closely aligning with their expressed beliefs.

Redistribution of subscription business content is much more frequent. Nearly half of those who access unauthorized subscription services report having redistributed content at least once, but only 7 percent report redistributing content more than once a week.

In addition, 21 percent of business users indicated that they have downloaded digital content from information services to which their employer does not have a paid subscription. Fully one-third said they receive content once a week and one-sixth at least once a day. Forty-six percent of the content is received from business colleagues.

Other findings from the survey include the following:

- Eighty-one percent state that they would not violate copyright laws.

- Forty-eight percent agree that everyone who uses the Internet violates copyright laws at some point.

- Forty-one percent say that there should be stricter regulations to protect copyright laws at some point.

- Thirty-eight percent say that all information on the Internet should be free.

- Sixty-one percent claimed that they would never share software downloaded from the Internet without appropriate licensing.

- Sixty-seven percent say that any newsworthy article in print or published on the Internet should be fully accessible without a fee attached.

The Internet poses a serious threat to the economic viability of digital industries as well as to all creators of intellectual property. According to the Business Software Alliance (BSA) there are three factors that define the emerging threat:

- The Internet has become a staple in many offices and homes. The result is a vast, borderless, sleepless marketplace for goods, including pirated software. One need only contrast the number of people who can crowd around a card table where pirated software is being sold with the number who can simultaneously access an auction site listing or a pirate Web site to appreciate the exponential increase in the scope of the problem.

- Ease of access to the Internet has increased dramatically alongside advances in technology. Many of the barriers to entry that once existed, including cost, technical limitations, and the need for computer sophistication, have been lowered or removed. Where navigation of the Internet once required knowledge of UNIX or DOS commands, the World Wide Web has delivered point-and-click maneuverability. Where it once took abundant time and patience to download pirated software programs, high-speed Internet connections and advances in compression technology make some of the largest files available in a matter of minutes. Now, even the most novice of users can find his or her way to pirated software.

- At present, Internet piracy offers a lower risk of detection than many other forms of unauthorized distribution. Software can be downloaded off the Internet in the privacy of one's home or office. The pirated program can be transferred from host computer to PC untouched by human hands and out of the view of third parties. The very nature of the Internet—unrestricted, self-regulated, and largely anonymous—requires that users exercise self-restraint and voluntarily comply with the law.

8.2   The world of software piracy

Results of the fifth annual benchmark survey on global software piracy illustrate the serious impact of copyright infringement to the software industry. Piracy losses exceeded $12 billion worldwide in 1999 and topped $59 billion during the past five years. The survey, conducted by an independent research firm, was commissioned by the Software & Information Industry Association (SIIA) and the Business Software Alliance.

In a broader analysis, Computer Economics projects that by 2005 there will be over $55 billion in annual revenue losses due to software piracy. The Asia Pacific region will account for the largest dollar amount in software piracy. Table 8.1 shows projections for annual losses due to software piracy by country. The types of software in the analysis include off-the-shelf,

Table 8.1   *Software Piracy Losses (U.S. $)*

Country	2001 ($)	2003 ($)	2005 ($)
Algeria	326,700	715,413	1,939,933
Angola	571,725	1,231,175	3,294,225
Benin	263,175	565,675	1,427,498
Botswana	245,025	525,745	1,354,293
Burkina Faso	178,475	382,663	988,268
Cameroon	326,700	700,772	1,573,908
Egypt	14,913,250	32,609,500	69,947,378
Ethiopia	285,863	612,260	1,354,293
Gabon	89,843	192,995	486,813
Ghana	530,888	1,147,988	2,470,669
Ivory Coast	245,025	525,745	1,134,678
Kenya	1,143,450	2,445,713	5,318,343
Madagascar	122,513	266,200	622,243
Mauritius	163,350	352,715	756,574
Morocco	1,470,150	3,194,400	6,851,988
Mozambique	392,040	865,150	1,855,747
Namibia	228,690	499,125	1,079,774
Nigeria	130,075	282,838	721,069
Senegal	261,360	565,675	1,213,373
South Africa	121,060,500	166,458,188	201,496,763
Swaziland	148,225	319,440	695,448
Tanzania	285,863	612,260	1,314,030
Tunisia	367,538	798,600	1,712,997
Uganda	204,188	465,850	999,248
Zambia	229,900	499,125	1,079,774
Zimbabwe	1,143,450	2,129,600	3,865,224

Table 8.1   *Software Piracy Losses (U.S. $) (continued)*

Country	2001 ($)	2003 ($)	2005 ($)
Other Africa	1,102,613	2,495,625	13,542,925
Total Africa	$146,430,570	$221,460,432	$329,097,470
Australia	340,131,000	401,130,125	482,054,925
Bangladesh	612,563	915,063	1,354,293
China	3,432,000,000	12,340,584,795	30,933,166,472
Hong Kong	283,140,000	342,599,400	415,072,350
India	136,397,250	397,303,500	917,771,085
Indonesia	20,418,750	30,346,800	45,064,998
Japan	1,165,725,000	1,731,101,625	2,194,153,500
Malaysia	118,428,750	143,082,500	172,763,800
New Zealand	42,259,250	51,133,693	59,662,075
Philippines	61,256,250	90,973,850	135,429,250
Singapore	68,198,625	82,520,336	95,166,500
South Korea	825,000,000	998,250,000	1,156,946,154
Sri Lanka	1,347,638	2,894,925	5,490,375
Taiwan	384,780,000	507,909,600	614,189,950
Thailand	43,287,750	73,870,500	158,854,850
Vietnam	3,575,000	16,259,375	89,010,625
Total Asia Pacific	$6,926,557,825	$17,210,876,087	$37,476,151,201
Austria	43,696,125	64,886,250	75,858,681
Belgium	80,613,225	113,001,900	146,263,590
Czech Republic	36,753,750	54,571,000	72,472,950
Denmark	93,018,750	109,807,500	150,985,313
Estonia	692,725	1,031,525	1,683,715

Table 8.1   *Software Piracy Losses (U.S. $) (continued)*

Country	2001 ($)	2003 ($)	2005 ($)
Finland	104,665,000	121,786,500	144,945,900
France	257,276,250	316,278,875	362,547,763
Germany	750,750,000	1,073,572,500	1,535,208,675
Great Britain	559,473,750	828,547,500	1,061,472,500
Greece	22,052,250	32,742,600	46,119,150
Hungary	36,753,750	54,571,000	72,472,950
Ireland	38,795,625	57,565,750	85,485,139
Italy	322,616,250	479,160,000	711,552,600
The Netherlands	124,781,250	156,392,500	281,839,250
Norway	60,031,125	89,177,000	132,427,845
Poland	141,297,750	209,632,500	311,304,263
Portugal	19,193,625	28,516,675	42,347,262
Russia	515,625,000	713,900,000	981,612,500
Slovakia	28,957,500	42,955,000	63,788,175
Spain	162,593,750	223,608,000	289,159,750
Sweden	217,421,875	262,872,500	303,800,750
Switzerland	61,407,500	83,187,500	95,166,500
Turkey	124,962,750	185,674,500	275,726,633
Other Europe	93,926,250	139,755,000	207,536,175
Total Europe	$3,897,355,825	$5,443,194,075	$7,451,778,027
Israel	53,088,750	78,836,794	116,761,975
Jordan	1,510,988	2,246,063	5,014,543
Kuwait	3,484,800	4,591,950	6,061,374
Lebanon	6,534,000	8,624,880	11,383,378
Oman	1,837,688	2,728,550	4,051,897
Qatar	1,410,750	2,117,500	3,527,150

Table 8.1   *Software Piracy Losses (U.S. $) (continued)*

Country	2001 ($)	2003 ($)	2005 ($)
Saudi Arabia	4,002,075	5,946,243	9,333,638
United Arab Emirates	7,623,000	10,062,360	13,286,708
Yemen	266,200	395,973	1,024,870
Total Middle East	$79,758,250	$115,550,311	$170,445,531
Canada	664,365,625	915,062,500	1,258,210,938
Caribbean	3,705,625	7,154,125	25,621,750
Mexico	300,836,250	645,535,000	1,384,672,575
United States	3,542,000,000	4,337,043,333	5,618,794,317
Total North America	$4,510,907,500	$5,904,794,958	$8,287,299,579
Argentina	38,877,300	57,898,500	92,970,350
Bolivia	1,781,725	3,041,335	7,100,885
Brazil	380,428,125	642,812,500	1,095,995,313
Chile	43,621,875	65,037,500	87,346,875
Colombia	21,484,375	29,493,750	40,553,906
Costa Rica	4,522,375	5,719,973	8,089,153
Ecuador	1,763,438	2,624,188	5,823,125
Paraguay	895,125	1,542,750	3,893,175
Peru	12,713,250	16,089,975	22,959,750
Uruguay	3,118,500	4,628,250	6,887,925
Venezuela	10,580,625	15,726,975	24,956,250
Total South America	$519,786,713	$844,615,695	$1,396,576,706
Total Worldwide	$16,080,796,683	$29,740,491,558	$55,111,348,514

Source: Computer Economics

shrink-wrapped business software; custom software; games; operating systems; utilities; communications software; and industrial process software.

8.2.1 The response to piracy

The Business Software Alliance's global Internet piracy plan consists of several components, three of which fall under the heading of enforcement.

- The BSA has established high-volume notice and takedown programs in North America and Europe and is working to bring Latin America and Asia up to speed.

- The BSA is seeking to promote criminal prosecution of Internet pirates through a range of activities, including ensuring coverage under the law; providing training; and developing, referring, and supporting criminal cases.

- The BSA is seeking to bring high-profile, high-impact civil litigation.

The BSA's notice and takedown programs are designed to enable high-volume removal of infringing content by enlisting the cooperation of Internet service providers (ISPs), auction sites, and other Internet intermediaries. Generally, BSA investigators process leads from outside sources and proactively search the Internet to identify member company products being offered for unauthorized download or sale. In the majority of cases, the BSA seeks to terminate the infringing activity by calling upon the relevant ISP(s) to remove the offending content or take other appropriate action.

During 2000, the BSA's notice and takedown programs in North America and Europe generated thousands of notices directed at infringing activity. Notices were sent to Internet auction sites, Web sites (including so-called Warez sites), file transfer protocol (FTP) sites, Internet relay chat (IRC) channels, Gnutella, Hotline and other P2P services, redirect services, mail-order sites, and news groups. In the great majority of these cases, the notice resulted in a takedown of the offending content.

Internet auction sites provide an electronic forum to sell and bid upon virtually any consumer product or collectible imaginable. But they are also a popular venue for software pirates to move their illicit wares. The apparent legitimacy and growing popularity of Internet auction sites among cost-conscious consumers afford software pirates a unique opportunity to reach a large pool of software users, many of whom would not knowingly purchase illegal software. These pirates sometimes defraud bidders by claiming that the illegal software is an authorized backup copy or a genuine product obtained at a discount through wholesale channels, inventory liquidations, or bankruptcy sales. Test purchases confirm that these claims are almost universally false. To help stem these sales and raise awareness among consumers, the BSA has targeted auction site listings for notice and takedown and pirate vendors for civil litigation and criminal prosecution.

Operation Buccaneer

In January 2002 the first criminal cases resulting from Operation Buccaneer were brought against two Los Angeles men for criminal copyright infringement and their involvement in an Internet piracy or Warez group known as DrinkOrDie.

According to plea agreements with the defendants, the two men, Kartadinata and Nguyen, were both members of DrinkOrDie. Kartadinata operated an electronic mail server for the group, and Nguyen managed several of the file servers that contained thousands of pirated software titles, including Windows operating systems and various utility programs. The file servers also contained video games and DVD movies, which were often made available to group members prior to commercial release at movie theaters. According to information that had appeared on the DrinkOrDie Web site, the group said it acquired, hacked, and distributed various software products, including Windows 95, weeks before the commercial release of the products.

DrinkOrDie was the Warez group targeted in Operation Buccaneer, in which 58 search warrants were simultaneously executed on December 11, 2001, in the United States, Australia, Finland, England, and Norway. The searches led to the seizure of more than 100 computers linked to the distribution of pirated copyrighted material on the Internet.

The plea agreements with Kartadinata and Nguyen also reflect how Warez group members operated. It had strategically situated members, often information technology specialists who worked with corporate or university computer systems, who would locate Warez computers within the corporate or university infrastructure. Warez computers, which could contain thousands of pirated software and movie titles, were hidden within the computer systems of businesses such as Bank of America and prominent universities such as MIT and UCLA. The Warez computers were located in these places so the Warez operators could take advantage of the enormous communications bandwidth available at these institutions without having to incur the tremendous costs associated with the high-speed service.

DVD pirates

On January 11, 2002, the U.S. Attorney for the Eastern District of New York and the New York Office of the U.S. Secret Service indicted Abdullah Qaza and Khalid Ghnaim for copyright and trademark infringement in connection with the large-scale manufacture and distribution of counterfeit compact discs (CDs) and digital video discs (DVDs).

From March through December 2001, the defendants operated a distribution center out of a storefront on Myrtle Avenue in Brooklyn, New York. The operation, which law enforcement officials estimate distributed thousands of counterfeit newly released CDs and DVDs weekly, was a principal source of supply for a network of outdoor flea market vendors in the metropolitan area.

On December 13, 2001, agents of the U.S. Secret Service executed search warrants at the factory and a nearby storage facility where the defendants warehoused the counterfeit goods, effectively shutting down their enterprise. Law enforcement's mid-December operation resulted in the largest seizure of counterfeit DVDs in U.S. history, consisting of more than 30,000 counterfeit movies and an equal number of counterfeit musical recordings with a total retail value of approximately $1 million. In addition to mass-producing a wide variety of popular musical recordings from rock to rap, including popular recording artists such as Santana, Jennifer Lopez, and R. Kelly, the defendants distributed movies that were either newly released or soon to be released on DVD, including the *Godfather* trilogy, *Cats and Dogs*, and *The Grinch*.

Operation White Horse

In November 2001, Operation White Horse, an 18-month undercover investigation conducted by the U.S. Customs Service in Los Angeles, resulted in three arrests and the all-time record seizure of $100 million worth of counterfeit computer software. Customs special agents from the Los Angeles Offices of Investigations and Internal Affairs targeted suspects involved in smuggling merchandise, including pirated computer software and counterfeit cigarettes, into the United States.

During the course of the investigation, suspects Tony Lu, 47, of Hacienda Heights, California, and Vincent Koo, 44, of Monterrey Park, California, were alleged to have repeatedly bribed a man whom they believed to be a corrupt U.S. Customs special agent. The agent, however, actually was working in an undercover capacity in furtherance of an international smuggling and bribery investigation. A total of $57,500 was paid in bribes to facilitate the suspects' smuggling venture.

On November 6, 2001, U.S. Customs agents served three arrest warrants and executed two search warrants in conjunction with Operation White Horse. Tony Lu, Vince Koo, and Wilson Liu, 39, of Pasadena, California, were arrested on federal complaints charging them with bribery of a public official, smuggling merchandise into the United States, entry of goods by means of false statements, and conspiracy to commit an offense against the United States.

Seized in connection with these arrests were one 40-foot shipping container of counterfeit computer software along with packaging material valued in excess of $100 million and two 40-foot shipping containers of counterfeit Marlboro cigarettes totaling 85,000 cartons (17 million cigarettes).

The first search warrant, served on November 6, 2001, was executed at Yojin International, El Monte, California, the business premises of Tony Lu. The second search warrant, also served on November 6, 2001, was executed at Storage USA in La Puente, California. Customs agents seized from this previously identified storage unit over 47,000 copies of counterfeit Microsoft and Symantec software and 21 cartons of counterfeit end-user license agreements, manuals, bar codes, adhesive labels, and registration cards.

A long list of cases

The U.S. government has been busy during the past several years, increasing its efforts to counter piracy. Statistics on case activity are shown in Table 8.2. The primary U.S. laws that govern copyrights are as follows:

- Title 18, United States Code (USC), § 2318—Trafficking in Counterfeit Labels for Phonographic Records and Copies of Motion Pictures or Other Audiovisual Works

- Title 18, USC, § 2319—Criminal Infringement of a Copyright

- Title 18, USC, § 2319A—Unauthorized Fixation of and Trafficking in Sound Recordings and Music Videos of Live Musical Performances

- Title 18, USC, § 2320—Trafficking in Counterfeit Goods or Services

Samples of the many cases that have been prosecuted under the intellectual property statutes, such as 18 USC, §§ 2318, 2319, and 2320 include:

- Two Brooklyn, New York, men indicted in connection with largest seizure of counterfeit DVDs in U.S. history (January 11, 2002)

- Liberty, Mississippi, woman convicted of distributing copyrighted videotapes through her video rental business (November 21, 2001)

Table 8.2   *Nationwide Enforcement of Title 18 USC, §§ 2318, 2319, 219A, and 2320*

	FY 98	FY 99	FY 00
Referrals and Cases			
Number of Investigative Matters Received by U.S. Attorneys:	192	204	197
Number of Defendants:	298	333	314
Number of Cases Filed:	97	108	106
Number of Defendants:	132	161	162
Number of Cases Resolved/Terminated:	84	92	79
Number of Defendants:	128	141	99
Disposition of Defendants in Concluded Cases			
Number of Defendants Who Pled Guilty:	104	105	71
Number of Defendants Who Were Tried and Found Guilty:	8	2	5
Number of Defendants against Whom Charges Were Dismissed:	28	26	19
Number of Defendants Acquitted:	0	3	1
Other Disposition:	6	5	3
Prison Sentencing for Convicted Defendants (number represents defendants)			
No Imprisonment:	74	73	51
1–12 Months:	27	21	10
13–24 Months:	6	10	9
25–36 Months:	3	2	6
37–60 Months:	1	1	0
61+ Months:	0	0	0
Statistics on Matters/Cases Originating with the U.S. Customs Service			
Number of Investigative Matters Referred by U.S. Customs Service:	64	71	64
Number of Defendants:	104	121	101
Number of Customs Matters Pending Resolution:	75	71	77
Number of Defendants:	114	113	120
Number of Customs Matters Terminated:	33	36	23

Table 8.2   *Nationwide Enforcement of Title 18 USC, §§ 2318, 2319, 219A, and 2320 (continued)*

	FY 98	FY 99	FY 00
Number of Defendants:	61	57	40
Number of Cases Originating with U.S. Customs Service:	42	39	31
Number of Defendants:	63	64	49
Number of Customs Cases Pending Resolution:	61	60	70
Number of Defendants:	98	86	113
Number of Customs Cases Resolved/Terminated:	37	35	29
Number of Defendants:	58	66	3

Source: FBI

- Millersburg, Ohio, man pleads guilty to selling and distributing illegal satellite TV cards (October 1, 2001)

- West Valley, Utah, man sentenced to ten months in federal prison for trafficking in counterfeit video tapes (July 17, 2001)

- San Gabriel Valley, California, woman arrested for trafficking in counterfeit Microsoft computer programs (June 15, 2001)

- Former Eugene, Oregon, resident sentenced to prison for criminal copyright infringement (April 16, 2001)

- Leonid and Michael Kislyansky sentenced in Cleveland, Ohio, in organized crime software piracy case (April 3, 2001)

- Aberdeen, Washington, woman arrested on criminal copyright infringement charges for selling unauthorized copies of Sony games and movies over the Internet (March 23, 2001)

- Operators of www.fakegifts.com Web site plead guilty in South Carolina to selling counterfeit luxury goods over the Internet (March 7, 2001)

- Two indicted and arrested in South Carolina for trafficking in counterfeit luxury goods over www.fakegifts.com Web site (January 29, 2001)

- Former police lieutenant sentenced for distributing and selling satellite TV interception devices (February 23, 2001)

- Nine indicted in Chicago, Illinios, in $1 million "fastlane" software piracy conspiracy (February 16, 2001)

- Man sentenced in Michigan for offering software programs for free downloading on "Hacker Hurricane" Web site (January 30, 2001)

- Temple Hills, Maryland, man sentenced for conspiracy to distribute 23,892 bootleg video cassettes and 58,975 compact discs (January 29, 2001)

- Man pleads guilty to Internet piracy of *Star Wars* film (December, 15, 2000)

- New York Electronic Crimes Task Force arrests two individuals on charges of trafficking in counterfeit computer chips and software (June 22, 2000)

- Two Californians arrested by FBI for counterfeiting high-security computer chips used in arcade video games (June 2, 2000)

- Texas woman charged with running ring that trafficked in counterfeit software (May 23, 2000)

- Three-year investigation reveals black-market dealings in counterfeit sports and celebrity memorabilia (April 12, 2000)

8.3   Controlling digital copyrights

The Digital Millennium Copyright Act provides some new approaches to protect copyrighted material on the Internet. In particular, for sites that employ products or services to prevent unauthorized access to copyrighted works (such as video, audio, text files, or computer software) or that use a digital rights management system to identify and control access to copyrighted works, these laws allow for lawsuits (and in some cases the filing of criminal charges) against those who are violating these sections.

Section 1201 prohibits circumventing—or making, selling, or trafficking a device that circumvents—security measures designed to prevent the unauthorized access to copyrighted works. This law was used successfully by several movie studios in their suit against Web site operators who posted or provided links to DeCSS, a program that unlocks the copy protection on DVDs containing movies. In that case, the judge concluded that the DVD copy control device qualified as a security measure designed to limit access, that DeCSS circumvented that security measure, and that the Web site operators were trafficking it. The court ordered the Web site operators to cease making DeCSS available.

Filing suit under Section 1201 was a good idea because it was easier to identify those who were trafficking DeCSS than to locate and sue the thousands of individuals who were using DeCSS to copy DVDs. Furthermore, it was probably easier to prove a violation of Section 1201 than to prove copyright infringement due to the inherent complexity of infringement litigation.

Section 1202 prohibits providing false copyright management information or altering or destroying such information with the intent to induce, facilitate, or conceal copyright infringement. Copyright management information includes the title of the work, the name of the author, and the terms and conditions for use of the work, which are usually part of a digital rights management system. In one case, a photographer filed suit against a visual search engine using this law. The visual search engine displayed miniature copies of images and provided URLs based on search terms entered by a user. The photographer claimed that the miniature copies of his pictures did not contain the licensing information he added to each image. Although the court found that the search engine altered or removed the copyright management information in violation of Section 1202, the court concluded that this was a fair use of the copyrighted works.

Any person injured by a violation of Section 1201 or Section 1202 may file a suit in federal court for an injunction preventing ongoing or future violations as well as monetary damages. In some cases, a person can also file criminal charges against someone who is violating either section willfully and in order to profit commercially or personally. Penalties include fines of up to $1 million or ten years in prison.

8.4 Getting a grip on intellectual property management

Preventing workplace piracy requires adhering to a process that makes everyone in the company understand the issue of piracy, put procedures in place to ensure that only legal software is purchased and used, and get rid of any illegal software at once. The BSA provides a four-step process to achieve that goal, which is summarized in the following text. A more complete explanation, along with other information and material, is available in the BSA's *Software Management Guide*.

8.4.1 Step one

Develop a clear statement of policy for your company. It should express the company's goals to prohibit piracy and spell out how employees acquire legal software.

An effective software purchase procedure involves centralized purchasing (no expense account purchases permitted); software purchases only with written approval; only purchases that are on the company's list of supported software; purchases only from reputable, authorized resellers or direct from the manufacturer; and only purchases that include original user material such as documentation and license agreements.

Include your policy in the packet of information given to new employees, distribute it to all current employees, and post it on company bulletin boards and on company computer networks. Require every employee to acknowledge the policy and the consequences of violating it. In turn, employers must take steps to educate employees on what constitutes illegal use of software.

8.4.2   Step two

Take inventory of your software assets. You must know what software, both legal and illegal, is installed on all the computers in your organization, including copies of programs from work installed by employees on their home computers. An accurate inventory not only can identify potential illegal software but can help your organization determine whether it is using the most up-to-date versions of programs, or if there are outdated or unused programs that can be deleted to save disk space. The inventory can also identify gaps in training or the presence of employees who lack a vital piece of software.

There are several tools, including some on the BSA Web site, available to help you complete the inventory. No matter what tools you use, make sure to collect the following information for each copy of software installed on each computer: product name, version number, and serial number. Also take inventory of all material related to the software, from the original media to manuals, licenses, invoices, and receipts. Make sure to carefully store the documentation, original copies of your software, and other material in a secure place in case of problems.

8.4.3   Step three

Use the inventory to compare the software that's installed on your company's computers to what's allowed under the terms of your licenses. Simply having an original CD or floppy disk for the software doesn't necessarily mean you have authorized copies; only the original license gives you the right to use the software and spells out the terms.

Delete any illegal software you identify from your computers. This is an ideal time to remind employees about the company's software policy and the dangers associated with illegal software.

You can now match the legitimate copies of software with the needs of your company. You can make informed decisions about which software you legally have that you want to keep, upgrade, or discard. Copies can be moved from computers on which they are not needed to computers on which they are. Copies can be upgraded, if necessary, so that everyone is using the version of the program that's most appropriate for your company. And you can purchase only the new, legitimate software you need to keep your company running.

Based on the inventory, upgrades, new purchases, and input from employees, you can now create a formal list of the software that your company will allow its employees to use. It should include program names, serial numbers, version numbers, number of copies or users permitted by the license, the computers on which the copies are installed, and plans to add, upgrade, or discard the software in future.

8.4.4 Step four

Good software management is a continual process. You need to monitor adherence, guard against the introduction of illegal software, keep your list of supported software up-to-date, and plan ahead for the next three years. It makes sense to have someone within your company placed in charge of the process, in order to centralize the job. Where possible, employ the many site license programs that are available from publishers. Licensing fosters strategic, long-term planning of software expenditures.

Periodically, it's a good idea to perform spot checks on individual computers to make sure illegal software has not been inadvertently or deliberately installed. It also makes sense to conduct your inventory every year, as you might for other valuable assets, to account for everything. You should also pay special attention when employees leave the company to make sure the software they worked with remains with your company and that they do not take or keep copies.

8.5 Coping with intellectual property management

Successfully addressing problems such as intellectual property management, privacy, and security requires an aware and educated workforce. One of the key steps in bringing these issues under control in your organization is training employees on what they should do and should not do. As pointed out in Chapter 4, adequately trained employees are not only more productive, they are also less likely to take actions that may legally and economically jeopardize your organization.

Controlling digital properties in an organization can also have considerable economic benefits. In the case of software management, many organizations are not using all of the licenses they pay for and do not have as many active users of applications for which they pay per-user fees. An assessment and inventory of licensees and users can lead to considerable reduction in software costs.

Principle Eight: Utilize Energy-Efficient Technology

You know that there can be a shortage of electricity when you live in California during the rolling blackouts. Suddenly and without warning your computer, phone, and lights go out. Getting stuck in the elevator when you need to use the restroom is the worst part.

—Tonya Heartfield

9.1 What energy efficiency can mean in savings

An organization can save from $7 to $52 per year on utility bills for every energy-efficient computer or peripheral in use. This can amount to thousands of dollars in savings over a short period of time. Enabling monitor power management could save your organization approximately 200,000 kwh per year for every 1,000 monitors. This amounts to $20,000 per year saved at 10 cents/kwh, which is enough energy to power 230 households for one month.

Actual savings will depend on regional differences in electricity cost and variance in energy efficiency levels. If average savings per year per piece of equipment installed are $12 and an organization had 2,500 units installed, annual savings in electricity costs would be $30,000, five-year savings would be $150,000, and ten-year savings would be $300,000. Table 9.1 shows annual and accumulated savings when annual savings per unit are $12.

If average savings per year per piece of equipment installed are $25 and an organization had 5,000 units installed, annual savings in electricity costs would be $125,000, five-year savings would be $625,000, and ten-year savings would be $1,250,000. Table 9.2 shows annual and accumulated savings when annual savings per unit are $25.

Table 9.1 *Potential Savings from Using Energy-Efficient Units (Low Electricity Costs)*

Number of Units Installed	Annual Savings per Unit	Savings per Year	Savings in 5 Years	Savings in 10 Years
25	$12	$300	$1,500	$3,000
100	$12	$1,200	$6,000	$12,000
250	$12	$3,000	$15,000	$30,000
500	$12	$6,000	$30,000	$60,000
1,000	$12	$12,000	$60,000	$120,000
2,500	$12	$30,000	$150,000	$300,000
5,000	$12	$60,000	$300,000	$600,000
10,000	$12	$120,000	$600,000	$1,200,000
20,000	$12	$240,000	$1,200,000	$2,400,000
30,000	$12	$360,000	$1,800,000	$3,600,000

Table 9.2 *Potential Savings from Using Energy-Efficient Units (Medium Electricity Costs)*

Number of Units Installed	Annual Savings per Unit	Savings per Year	Savings in 5 Years	Savings in 10 Years
25	$25	$625	$3,125	$6,250
100	$25	$2,500	$12,500	$25,000
250	$25	$6,250	$31,250	$62,500
500	$25	$12,500	$62,500	$125,000
1,000	$25	$25,000	$125,000	$250,000
2,500	$25	$62,500	$312,500	$625,000
5,000	$25	$125,000	$625,000	$1,250,000
10,000	$25	$250,000	$1,250,000	$2,500,000
20,000	$25	$500,000	$2,500,000	$5,000,000
30,000	$25	$750,000	$3,750,000	$7,500,000

Table 9.3   *Potential Savings from Using Energy-Efficient Units (High Electricity Costs)*

Number of Units Installed	Annual Savings per Unit	Savings per Year	Savings in 5 Years	Savings in 10 Years
25	$40	$1,000	$5,000	$10,000
100	$40	$4,000	$20,000	$40,000
250	$40	$10,000	$50,000	$100,000
500	$40	$20,000	$100,000	$200,000
1,000	$40	$40,000	$200,000	$400,000
2,500	$40	$100,000	$500,000	$1,000,000
5,000	$40	$200,000	$1,000,000	$2,000,000
10,000	$40	$400,000	$2,000,000	$4,000,000
20,000	$40	$800,000	$4,000,000	$8,000,000
30,000	$40	$1,200,000	$6,000,000	$12,000,000

If average savings per year per piece of equipment installed are $40 and an organization had 30,000 units installed, annual savings in electricity costs would be $1,200,000, five-year savings would be $6 million, and ten-year savings would be $12 million. Table 9.3 shows annual and accumulated savings when annual savings per unit are $40.

9.2   The ENERGY STAR program

ENERGY STAR was introduced by the U.S. Environmental Protection Agency (EPA) in 1992 as a voluntary labeling program designed to identify and promote energy-efficient products, in order to reduce carbon dioxide emissions. EPA partnered with the U.S. Department of Energy in 1996 to promote the ENERGY STAR label, with each agency taking responsibility for particular product categories. ENERGY STAR has expanded to cover new homes, most of the buildings sector, residential heating and cooling equipment, major appliances, office equipment, lighting, and consumer electronics. The ENERGY STAR program is also becoming a worldwide phenomenon, with many industrial nations adopting similar approaches to energy savings.

If all consumers, businesses, and organizations in the United States made their product choices and building improvement decisions with ENERGY STAR in mind over the next decade, the national annual energy bill would be reduced by about $200 billion. With that would come a sizable contribution to reducing air pollution and protecting the global climate.

ENERGY STAR–labeled computers automatically power down to 15 watts or less when not in use and may actually last longer than conventional products because they spend a large portion of time in a low-power sleep mode. ENERGY STAR–labeled computers also generate less heat than conventional models. Upgrading your existing equipment to ENERGY STAR can lead to reduced cooling costs.

ENERGY STAR partners agree to qualify products as they are intended to be used by the end user, particularly products intended to be connected to a network. ENERGY STAR partners agree that all products marketed, advertised, or sold as network capable must meet the ENERGY STAR specifications (spelled out in section 9.2.1) when configured as network ready. If the product is shipped with the capability to be on a network, it shall have the ability to enter a sleep mode while on the network. If the product has the capability to be on a network, it shall retain in sleep mode its ability to respond to wake events directed or targeted to the product while on a network. ENERGY STAR partners also agree to qualify products according to the following specifications.

9.2.1   ENERGY STAR definitions

Printer: Imaging equipment, manufactured as a standard model, that serves as a hard copy output device and is capable of receiving information from single-user or networked computers. In addition, the unit must be capable of being powered from a wall outlet. This definition is intended to cover products that are advertised and sold as printers, including printers that can be upgraded to a multifunctional device.

Fax machine: Imaging equipment, manufactured as a standard model, that serves as a hard copy output device whose primary function is sending and receiving information. Plain paper fax machines include ink jet/bubble jet, laser/LED, and thermal transfer systems. The unit must be capable of being powered from a wall outlet. This definition is intended to cover products that are advertised and sold as fax machines.

Combination printer/fax machine: Imaging equipment manufactured as a standard model that serves as both a fully functional printer and fax machine and is intended to cover products that are marketed and sold as a combination printer/fax device.

Mailing machine: Imaging equipment that serves to print postage onto mail pieces. The unit must be capable of being powered from a wall outlet. This definition is intended to cover products that are advertised and sold as mailing machines.

Standard model: The term used to describe a product and its bundled features as marketed and sold by the Partner and as manufactured for its intended use.

Print speed: Pages per minute (ppm) measures the printing speed of a model. Print speed corresponds to the product's print speed as advertised by Partner. For line printers (e.g., dot matrix/impact printers), print speed is based on the method established in ISO 10561.

For wide-format printers designed to handle primarily A2 or 17" × 22" paper or larger, the print speed is specified in terms of monochrome text output at the default resolution. The print speed measured as A2- or A0-sized prints per minute shall be converted into A4-sized print speeds as follows:

- One A2 print per minute is equivalent to four A4 prints per minute.

- One A0 print per minute is equivalent to 16 A4 prints per minute.

- For mailing machines, pages per minute (ppm) are considered equivalent to mail pieces per minute (mppm).

Sleep mode: The condition that exists when the product is not producing hard copy output or receiving hard copy input and is consuming less power than when in a standby mode. In the transition from sleep mode to active mode, there may be some delay in the production of hard copy output; however, there shall be no delay in the acceptance of information from a network or other input sources. The product enters this mode within a specified time period after the last hard copy output was produced.

Wake event: A wake event is defined as a user, programmed, or external event or stimulus that causes the unit to transition from its standby or sleep mode to its active ode of operation.

9.2.2   The ENERGY STAR performance requirements

Table 9.4 shows the default time to sleep mode and the watts consumed by the type of product while in sleep mode. In many cases the sleep mode consumption rate can be less than 5 percent of the active mode power consumption rate.

Table 9.4   *ENERGY STAR Performance Requirements*

Product Type/Performance	Sleep Mode (Watts)	Default Time to Sleep Mode
Standard Size Printers and Printer/Fax Combinations		
0 < ppm ≤ 10	≤ 10	≤ 5 minutes
10 < ppm ≤ 20	≤ 20	≤ 15 minutes
20 < ppm ≤ 30	≤ 30	≤ 30 minutes
30 < ppm ≤ 44	≤ 40	≤ 60 minutes
44 < ppm	≤ 75	≤ 60 minutes
Impact Printers (A3 paper)	≤ 30	≤ 30 minutes
Large/Wide-Format Printers (A2 or 17" × 22" or larger paper)		
0 < ppm ≤ 10	≤ 35	≤ 30 minutes
10 < ppm ≤ 40	≤ 65	≤ 30 minutes
40 < ppm	≤ 100	≤ 90 minutes
Color Printers (A3, A4, or 8.5" × 11" paper)		
0 < ppm ≤ 10	≤ 35	≤ 30 minutes
10 < ppm ≤ 20	≤ 45	≤ 60 minutes
20 < ppm	≤ 70	≤ 60 minutes
Standalone Fax Machine (A4 or 8.5" × 11" paper)		
0 < ppm ≤ 10	≤ 10	≤ 5 minutes
10 < ppm	≤ 15	≤ 5 minutes
Mailing Machines		
0 < mppm ≤ 50	≤ 10	≤ 20 minutes
50 < mppm ≤ 100	≤ 30	≤ 30 minutes
100 < mppm ≤ 150	≤ 50	≤ 40 minutes
150 < mppm	≤ 85	≤ 60 minutes

Source: U.S. Environmental Protection Agency

9.2.3 ENERGY STAR program requirements for telephony

The ENERGY STAR program is also addressing energy efficiency of telephony products. All telephony products shipped from the factory or factories after January 1, 2002, and through December 31, 2003, must meet Tier 1 requirements in order to bear the ENERGY STAR label. All products shipped on or after January 1, 2004, must meet Tier 2 requirements in order to bear the ENERGY STAR label. Telephony products are defined as follows:

- Cordless telephone: A commercially available electronic product with a base station and a handset, whose purpose is to convert sound into electrical impulses for transmission. Most of these devices require a wall pack for power, are plugged into an AC power outlet for 24 hours a day, and do not have a power switch to turn them off. To qualify, the base station of the cordless phone or its power supply must be designed to plug into a wall outlet, and there must not be a physical connection between the portable handset and the phone jack.

- Answering machine: A commercially available electronic product— also known as a telephone answering device (TAD)—whose purpose is to provide analog or digital storage of outgoing and incoming telephone messages by connecting to the telephone line between the phone and the phone jack. Most of these devices require a wall pack for power and are plugged into an AC power outlet for 24 hours a day. To qualify, the answering machine or its power supply must be designed to plug into a wall outlet.

- Combination cordless telephone/answering machine: A commercially available electronic product in which the cordless telephone and answering machine are combined into a single unit and which meets all of the following criteria: the answering machine is included in the base station of the cordless telephone, it is not possible to measure the power requirements of the two components separately without removal of the telephone casing, and the unit is connected to the wall outlet through a single power cable. Most of these devices require a wall pack for power, are plugged into an AC power outlet for 24 hours a day, and do not have a power switch to turn them off. To qualify, the combination unit or its power supply must be designed to plug into a wall outlet.

- Spread spectrum technology (SST): There are two types of spread spectrum technology—direct sequence (e.g., digital spread spectrum or DSS) and frequency hoppers. Both types are available in some digital telephony products to provide enhanced transmission range, extendible portable numbers, and additional security. With this technology, the power requirement is typically greater than traditional analog models because the handsets and bases are always communicating with one another.

- Multihandset model: This cordless phone system requires only one base and phone jack and, as the name implies, can support multiple cordless handsets. Each handset added to the system comes with a battery and a charging base. Due to limited available data during the writing of this specification, multihandset cordless telephones and combination units are not currently eligible for the ENERGY STAR label but may be added in a future specification revision.

- Cellular telephone: A cellular telephone uses radio waves to connect to the cellular telephone carrier. Cellular telephones are not eligible to carry the ENERGY STAR label under this specification, since they are not considered cordless telephones.

- Corded telephone: Corded telephones provide the same services as cordless telephones except that there is a physical connection between the handset and the jack, which limits the user's mobility while using the telephone. Corded telephones may or may not require a wall pack for power. Corded telephones and combination units are not covered

Table 9.5 *Energy-efficiency Criteria for ENERGY STAR–Qualified Telephony*

Product Category	Tier 1 1/1/2002 to 12/31/2003 Standby Mode	Tier 2 1/1/2004 and after Standby Mode
Answering Machine, Cordless Telephone	≤ 3.3 watts	≤ 1.0 watt
Answering Machine with SST, Cordless Telephone with SST	≤ 3.6 watts	≤ 1.5 watts
Combination Cordless Telephone/Answering Machine	≤ 4.0 watts	≤ 1.0 watt
Combination Cordless Telephone/Answering Machine with SST	≤ 5.1 watts	≤ 2.0 watts

Source: U.S. Environmental Protection Agency

by this cordless telephone specification and may not qualify as ENERGY STAR.

- Wall pack: A power supply commonly shipped with consumer electronic products that plugs into an AC power outlet on the wall.

During the standby mode, telephony products are connected to a power source and are inactive and may consume energy to operate circuitry and to charge rechargeable batteries. While in the active mode, telephony products are connected to a power source and can be transmitting telephone conversation, playing/recording a message, and/or supplying current to a low battery to charge it. The power requirement in this mode is typically greater than the power requirement in standby mode. Table 9.5 shows the power requirements for telephony products in the standby mode.

9.3   Moving toward energy-efficient technology

Establishing a policy to purchase energy-efficient technology is an easy process in any organization. Larger organizations may choose to develop an approved product list or simply require that all information technology purchased have an ENERGY STAR label. Purchasing agents can be required to implement the policy or justify why energy-efficient technology was not available for a specific purpose.

It is also important to evaluate information technology that is already installed to determine whether replacement with energy-efficient units is warranted. In some cases energy cost savings can help to justify replacement of older equipment, because many older computers and peripherals were not manufactured in compliance with ENERGY STAR requirements. Fortunately, the process of upgrading systems to year 2000 (Y2K)–capable systems helped to eliminate many older systems. However, there are still many systems installed that are not designed to go into sleep mode or do not have more modern and efficient power units.

There are some basic indicators that should be considered when evaluating older equipment. One of the best indicators is the age of the equipment. If the equipment was manufactured or installed before 1995, it is very likely that it is not ENERGY STAR compliant. If the manufacturer has introduced three new replacement models for a piece of equipment, it is likely that the newer equipment will be more energy efficient than the model installed. Note that this guideline may not apply to personal computers because they have such a short product cycle.

However, minicomputers and communications equipment are typically kept in service for longer periods of time than personal computers. As a rule, an organization will replace personal computers every two to four years. On the other hand, minicomputers and communications equipment can stay in place for eight to ten years and sometimes longer. Even if this equipment is not designed to enter a sleep mode, newer models generally consume a considerably smaller amount of electricity. This is because newer circuit boards and power supplies are more energy efficient.

Many organizations do not aggressively pursue comprehensive information-technology portfolio management programs because of staffing and time requirements. This often results in large numbers of systems being installed at multiple locations that are not energy efficient and can also be redundant, oversized, or no longer needed to support computing needs. Thus, rooting out older systems can result in great energy savings as well as reduce staffing, software, equipment maintenance, and overhead costs.

When pursing an energy-efficiency program, it is also advisable to look at other items that may be installed in a facility, including refrigerators, freezers, clothes washers. clothes dryers, dishwashers, ovens and ranges, heating and cooling systems, and water heaters.

9.4   Help from the EPA

The EPA has several programs to quickly and easily enable power management organization-wide. The EPA offers free software tools and services. The EPA ENERGY STAR program Web page is located at http://yosemite1.epa.gov/estar/consumers.nsf/content/computers.htm.

The EZ Save network-based software tool for large organizations with a mixture of operating systems that want to start a comprehensive monitor power management program is ideal for large government organizations with voluntary computer policies. EZ Save is a centrally administered software tool distributed by the EPA. It acts as follows:

- Polls monitors on a network to determine each monitor's power management settings

- Generates reports on the result of the polling

- Sets appropriate power management settings on monitors on the network

- Sets appropriate screen saver settings on monitors on the network so that users retain screen saver images

■ Requires no special processes on the network, no special hardware, and no client installations

■ Uses the existing power management functionality in Windows (95/98/ME/2000/XP)

To access EZ Save use this URL: http://www.energystar.gov/powermanagement/download.asp?orgtype=large.

Windows 2000/XP Enablement is for large organizations that desire a relatively homogeneous power management practice. EPA can provide technical support to assist your IT department in enabling power management through Windows 2000 and XP.

To access Windows 2000/XP Enablement, use this URL: http://www.energystar.gov/powermanagement/ windows2k.asp?orgtype=large.

The EPA also tracks the computers and peripherals that qualify for the ENERGY STAR program. Table 9.6 shows a selected list of popular computers that are ENERGY STAR compliant, organized by manufacturer and model number. The list also includes the chip installed in the computer along with the sleep mode watts consumption.

Table 9.6   *Popular Computers that Are ENERGY STAR Compliant*

Brand	Model	Chip	Sleep Mode (Watts)
Apple	iBook (M7701)	Power PC G3	4
Apple	iBook (M8597)	Power PC G3	5
Apple	iBook (M8599)	Power PC G3	5
Apple	iBook M8597	Power PC G3	5
Apple	iBook M8598	Power PC G3	5
Apple	iBook M8599	Power PC G3	5
Apple	iMac (M7677) Flat Panel	Power PC G4	7
Apple	iMac (M8492-Graphite, M8596-Snow)	Power PC G3	35
Apple	iMac (M8534-Indigo)	Power PC G3	35
Apple	iMac (M8535) Flat Panel	Power PC G4	7
Apple	iMac (M8672) Flat Panel	Power PC G4	7
Apple	PowerBook G4 M8591	Power PC G4	5

Table 9.6 *Popular Computers that Are ENERGY STAR Compliant (continued)*

Brand	Model	Chip	Sleep Mode (Watts)
Apple	PowerBook G4 M8592	Power PC G4	5
Apple	PowerBook G4 M8622	Power PC G4	6
Apple	PowerBook G4 M8623	Power PC G4	6
Apple	PowerMac G4	Power PC G4	10
Apple	PowerMac G4 (M7681)	Power PC G4	15
Apple	PowerMac G4 (M8359)	Power PC G4	10
Apple	PowerMac G4 (M8359)	Power PC G4	10
Apple	PowerMac G4 (M8359) w/15" Studio Display (M7928)	Power PC G4	15
Apple	PowerMac G4 (M8359) w/17" Studio Display (M7649)	Power PC G4	15
Apple	PowerMac G4 (M8360)	Power PC G4	10
Apple	PowerMac G4 (M8360) w/15" Studio Display (M7928)	Power PC G4	15
Apple	PowerMac G4 (M8360) w/17" Studio Display (M7649)	Power PC G4	15
Apple	PowerMac G4 (M8360) w/22" Studio Display (M8058)	Power PC G4	16
Apple	PowerMac G4 (M8361)	Dual Power PC G4	10
Apple	PowerMac G4 (M8361) w/15" Studio Display (M7928)	Dual Power PC G4	15
Apple	PowerMac G4 (M8361) w/17" Studio Display (M7649)	Dual Power PC G4	15
Apple	PowerMac G4 (M8361) w/22" Studio Display (M8058)	Dual Power PC G4	16
Apple	PowerMac G4 (M8666)	Power PC G4	10
Apple	PowerMac G4 (M8666) w/15" Studio Display (M7928)	Power PC G4	11
Apple	PowerMac G4 (M8666) w/17" Studio Display (M7649)	Power PC G4	11
Apple	PowerMac G4 (M8666) w/22" Studio Display (M8058)	Power PC G4	13
Apple	PowerMac G4 (M8666) w/23" Studio Display (M8537)	Power PC G4	13
Apple	PowerMac G4 (M8667)	Dual Power PC G4	10
Apple	PowerMac G4 (M8667) w/15" Studio Display (M7928)	Dual Power PC G4	11
Apple	PowerMac G4 (M8667) w/17" Studio Display (M7649)	Dual Power PC G4	11
Apple	PowerMac G4 (M8667) w/22" Studio Display (M8058)	Dual Power PC G4	13

Table 9.6   *Popular Computers that Are ENERGY STAR Compliant (continued)*

Brand	Model	Chip	Sleep Mode (Watts)
Apple	PowerMac G4 (M8667) w/23" Studio Display (M8537)	Power PC G4	13
Apple	PowerMac G4 (M8705) w/23" Studio Display (M8537)	Power PC G4	13
Apple	PowerMacG4 (M7681) w/15" StudioDisplay(M7681/M7928)	Power PC G4	18
Apple	PowerMacG4 (M7681) w/17" StudioDisplay(M7681/M7770)	Power PC G4	22
Apple	PowerMacG4 (M7681) w/22" StudioDisplay(M7681/M8058)	Power PC G4	18
Apple	PowerMacG4 (M8666) w/22" StudioDisplay(M8058) & VGA	Power PC G4	13
Apple	PowerMacG4 (M8667) w/22" StudioDisplay(M8058) & VGA	Dual Power PC G4	13
Apple	PowerMacG4 (M8705) w/22" StudioDisplay(M8058) & VGA	Power PC G4	13
Apple	PowerMacG4(M8360)w/17" CRTStudioDisplay(M7770)	Power PC G4	18
Apple	PowerMacG4(M8361)w/17" CRTStudioDisplay(M7770)	Power PC G4	18
Compaq	Armada 1100	486	18
Compaq	Armada 1500	P55	9
Compaq	Armada 1500C	Intel Celeron	0.13
Compaq	Armada 1500c	Intel Celeron	0.13
Compaq	Armada 1500c	Intel Celeron	0.13
Compaq	Armada 1700	Intel Pentium II	9
Compaq	Armada 1750	Intel Pentium II	0.39
Compaq	Armada 1750	Intel Pentium II	0.39
Compaq	Armada 1750	Intel Pentium II	0.39
Compaq	Armada 3500	Intel Pentium II	0.15
Compaq	Armada 3500	Intel Pentium II	0.15
Compaq	Armada 4100	P54	14
Compaq	Armada 4200	P55	14
Compaq	Armada 6500	Intel Pentium II	12.1
Compaq	Armada 7300	P55	9
Compaq	Armada 7400	Intel Pentium II	18

Table 9.6   *Popular Computers that Are ENERGY STAR Compliant (continued)*

Brand	Model	Chip	Sleep Mode (Watts)
Compaq	Armada 7700	P55	15
Compaq	Armada 7800	Intel Pentium II	19
Compaq	Armada SB	P55	9
Compaq	CM0104	Intel Celeron	20
Compaq	CM0104	Intel Celeron	15.4
Compaq	CM0104	Intel Celeron	15.4
Compaq	Contura Aero	486	8
Compaq	Deskpro 1000	Intel Pentium	27.6
Compaq	Deskpro EN	Intel Pentium II	24.7
Compaq	Deskpro EN	Intel Celeron	27.2
Compaq	Deskpro EN C	Intel Celeron	2.3
Compaq	Deskpro EN C	Intel Celeron	2.4
Compaq	Deskpro EN C	Intel Pentium III	2.5
Compaq	Deskpro EN C	Intel Pentium III	2.3
Compaq	Deskpro EN C	Intel Pentium III	2.6
Compaq	Deskpro EN C	Intel Pentium III	2.2
Compaq	Deskpro EN C	Intel Pentium III	2.3
Compaq	Deskpro EN L	Intel Celeron	2.6
Compaq	Deskpro EN L	Intel Pentium III	2.7
Compaq	Deskpro EN L	Intel Pentium III	2.4
Compaq	Deskpro EN L	Intel Celeron	2.5
Compaq	Deskpro EN L	Intel Pentium III	2.5
Compaq	Deskpro EN L	Intel Pentium III	2.4
Compaq	Deskpro EN L	Intel Pentium III	2.3
Compaq	Deskpro EN S	Intel Celeron	2.7
Compaq	Deskpro EN S	Intel Celeron	2.6

Table 9.6   *Popular Computers that Are ENERGY STAR Compliant (continued)*

Brand	Model	Chip	Sleep Mode (Watts)
Compaq	Deskpro EN S	Intel Pentium III	2.6
Compaq	Deskpro EN S	Intel Pentium III	2.3
Compaq	Deskpro EN S	Intel Pentium III	2.7
Compaq	Deskpro EN S	Intel Pentium III	2.4
Compaq	Deskpro EN S	Intel Pentium III	2.5
Compaq	Deskpro EP	Intel Pentium II	23.8
Compaq	Deskpro EP	Intel Celeron	26.7
Compaq	Deskpro EP, SB	Intel Pentium II	25.2
Compaq	LTE 5000	P54	12
Compaq	LTE Elite	486	8
Compaq	Presario 1000	P54	8
Compaq	Presario 1200	Cyrix GXm	5
Compaq	Presario 1230	AMD K6	8
Compaq	Presario 1250	Intel Pentium II	8
Compaq	Presario 1600	Intel Pentium II	5
Compaq	Presario 1710 SB	P55	7
Compaq	Presario 2240	AMD K6	24.6
Compaq	Presario 2254	AMD K6	24.6
Compaq	Presario 2255	AMD K6	24.6
Compaq	Presario 2256	AMD K6	24.6
Compaq	Presario 2510	AMD K6	24.6
Compaq	Presario 4540	AMD K6	20.3
Compaq	Presario 4550	AMD K6	20.3
Compaq	Presario 4640	Intel Pentium II	21.9
Compaq	Presario 4660	Intel Pentium II	21.9
Compaq	Presario 4860	Intel Pentium II	20.8

Table 9.6   *Popular Computers that Are ENERGY STAR Compliant (continued)*

Brand	Model	Chip	Sleep Mode (Watts)
Compaq	Presario 4880	Intel Pentium II	20.8
Compaq	Presario 5015	Intel Celeron	22.4
Compaq	Presario 5020	Intel Celeron	22.54
Compaq	Presario 5030	Intel Pentium II	21.9
Compaq	Presario 5032	Intel Pentium II	21.9
Compaq	Presario 5035	Intel Pentium II	21.9
Compaq	Presario 5140	Intel Pentium II	21.9
Compaq	Presario 5610	Intel Pentium II	20.8
Compaq	Presario 5612	Intel Pentium II	20.8
Compaq	Presario 5630	Intel Pentium II	20.8
Compaq	Presario 5635	Intel Pentium II	20.8
Compaq	Presario 705US	AMD Athlon	7
Compaq	Prosigna 142	Intel Pentium II	0.39
Compaq	Prosignia 144	Intel Pentium II	0.39
Compaq	Prosignia 162	Intel Pentium II	0.39
Compaq	T1000	Cyrix GXm	13.6
Compaq	T1010	Cyrix	10
Compaq	T1500	Cyrix GXm	13.3
Compaq	T1510	Cyrix	10
Compaq	T20	GX1	9
Compaq	T30	GX1	10
Dell	Dimension 4300	Intel Pentium IV	1.51
Dell	Dimension 8200	Intel Pentium IV	1.76
Dell	GX150	Intel Pentium III	3.7
Dell	OptiPlex GX240	Intel Pentium IV	1.8
Dell	OptiPlex GX400	Intel Pentium IV	5.23

Table 9.6   *Popular Computers that Are ENERGY STAR Compliant (continued)*

Brand	Model	Chip	Sleep Mode (Watts)
Dell	OptiPlex GX50	Intel Celeron	2.04
Dell	Precision Workstation 220	Intel Pentium III	33.3
Dell	Precision Workstation 330	Intel Pentium IV	4.46
Dell	Precision Workstation 340	Intel Pentium IV	2.74
Dell	Precision Workstation 530	Intel	5.46
Gateway	200	Intel Pentium III	1.53
Gateway	450	Intel Pentium IV	2.42
Gateway	600	Intel Pentium IV	2.02
Gateway	Astro or AN1.1	Intel Celeron	22.5
Gateway	E-1200	Intel Celeron	21
Gateway	E-1600	Intel Pentium	3
Gateway	E-3200	Intel Pentium II	26
Gateway	E-3600	Intel Pentium IV	3.2
Gateway	E-4600	P54	3.8
Gateway	E-4650	Intel Pentium IV	4.1
Gateway	Gateway	Cyrix	2.5
Gateway	Gateway 300 Series	Intel Celeron	3.3
Gateway	Gateway 500 Series	Intel Pentium IV	4.2
Gateway	Gateway 700 Series	Intel Pentium IV	4.1
Gateway	Gateway Profile	AMD K6	6
Gateway	LC2	Intel Celeron	2.5
Gateway	Profile 2	Intel Celeron	24
Gateway	Solo 1450	Intel Pentium III	2.22
Gateway	Solo 3450	Intel	1.6
HP	2000/HEZ8383	Intel Celeron	22.5
HP	5000	Intel Pentium	1

Table 9.6   *Popular Computers that Are ENERGY STAR Compliant (continued)*

Brand	Model	Chip	Sleep Mode (Watts)
HP	5010	486	25.8
HP	5500	Intel Pentium	1
HP	600CT	486	0.1
HP	7050	Intel Pentium	29.7
HP	7350P	Intel Pentium	28
HP	7360	Intel Pentium	27
HP	800	Intel Pentium	0.1
HP	Brio BA 410	Intel Pentium III	3
HP	e-pc 40	Intel Celeron	7
HP	e-pc 42	Intel Pentium IV	9
HP	epc c10/s10	Intel Pentium III	3.8
HP	E-PC C10/S10	Intel Pentium III	3.8
HP	HP GT220	Cyrix	10
HP	Kayak XM 600	Intel Pentium III	5
HP	OmniBook 2000	Intel Pentium	0.1
HP	Omnibook 2100	Intel	0.3
HP	OmniBook 3000	Intel	0.5
HP	Omnibook 3100	Intel	0.3
HP	Omnibook 4100	Intel Pentium II	0.3
HP	OmniBook 5700	Intel	0.1
HP	Omnibook 7100	Intel Pentium II	1
HP	OmniBook 800 MMX	Intel	0.1
HP	OmniBook 900	Intel	1
HP	Vectra VL 400	Intel Pentium III	4.8
HP	Vectra VL 410	Intel Pentium III	4
HP	Vectra VL 420	Intel Pentium IV	3.2

Table 9.6 *Popular Computers that Are ENERGY STAR Compliant (continued)*

Brand	Model	Chip	Sleep Mode (Watts)
HP	Vectra VL 800	Intel Pentium IV	5
HP	Vectra VL 400	Intel Pentium III	4.8
HP	Vectra VL 800	Intel Pentium IV	5
HP	XE310	Intel Pentium III	5
HP	XE320	Intel Pentium IV	4
IBM	2178-80A		24.5
IBM	2178-820		29.6
IBM	2178-830		29.6
IBM	2178-830		29.6
IBM	2178-840		29.6
IBM	2179-700	Intel Celeron	24
IBM	2179-750	Intel Pentium III	24
IBM	2198-954		19.4
IBM	2198-962		29.2
IBM	2198-964		29.2
IBM	4840-521	AMD K6	19.9
IBM	4840-541	AMD K6	19.9
IBM	4840-561	AMD K6-2	19.9
IBM	6283-22x	AMD K6	25.4
IBM	6577	Intel Pentium	25
IBM	6584-41X		27.1
IBM	6584-42X		25.5
IBM	6584-44X		26.1
IBM	6584-45X		26.1
IBM	6584-47X		25.5
IBM	6584-52X		25.7

Table 9.6   *Popular Computers that Are ENERGY STAR Compliant (continued)*

Brand	Model	Chip	Sleep Mode (Watts)
IBM	6584-53X		25.7
IBM	6584-62X		27.6
IBM	6587	Intel Pentium	25
IBM	6594-42X	Intel Pentium III	28.1
IBM	6643	Intel Pentium III	2.9
IBM	6643-11U	Intel Celeron	24
IBM	6643-12U	Intel Celeron	24
IBM	6643-13U	Intel Pentium III	24
IBM	6643-14U	Intel Pentium III	24
IBM	A20-6269-E2U (-C1U, -C2U, -D1U, -D2U, -E1U)	Intel Celeron	26
IBM	A20-6269-N2U (M1U, -M2U, -N1U)	Intel Pentium III	26
IBM	Aptiva 2134-XXX, 2176-XXX	Intel Pentium	3
IBM	Aptiva 2137-XXX	AMD K6	29
IBM	Aptiva 2139-XXX	Intel Pentium II	22
IBM	Aptiva 2153-XXX	AMD K6	21
IBM	Aptiva 2156-XXX	Power PC	27
IBM	Aptiva 2158-XXX	AMD K6	22
IBM	Aptiva 2159-XXX	Intel	3
IBM	Aptiva 2161-XXX	Intel	3
IBM	Aptiva 2162-XXX	Intel	3
IBM	Aptiva 2163-XXX	Intel Pentium II	23
IBM	Aptiva 2164-XXX	Intel Pentium III	20
IBM	Aptiva 2165	AMD K6	22
IBM	Aptiva 2168 Series	Intel Pentium	30
IBM	Aptiva 2171-XXX	Intel Pentium III	19.5
IBM	Aptiva 2172-XXX	Intel Pentium III	19.5

Table 9.6   *Popular Computers that Are ENERGY STAR Compliant (continued)*

Brand	Model	Chip	Sleep Mode (Watts)
IBM	Aptiva 2174-XXX	AMD	29.4
IBM	Aptiva 2178-850		20
IBM	Aptiva 2178-85C, -85W, -85V		21.8
IBM	Aptiva 2178-860		20.4
IBM	Aptiva 2178-89A		21.8
IBM	Aptiva 2178-98U/F		21.5
IBM	Aptiva 2178-99U/F		21.8
IBM	Aptiva 2187-XXX	AMD K6	22.6
IBM	Aptiva 2190-28J	AMD K6-2	23
IBM	Aptiva 2194-3XX	Intel Celeron	4.5
IBM	Aptiva 2198-973		19
IBM	Aptiva 2198-974		21.3
IBM	Aptiva L31/L3F	Intel	27.7
IBM	Aptiva L51	Intel Pentium II	28.7
IBM	Aptiva L5H	Intel Pentium II	28.7
IBM	Aptiva L61	Intel Pentium II	28.7
IBM	CF-17TR42AAMADS	Intel Celeron	5.5
IBM	IBM Thinkpad	Intel Pentium	6
IBM	IBM Thinkpad 310/310D	P54	6
IBM	NetVista 2251, -EAx, EBx, ECx, GAx, GBx, GCx, TAx	Intel Pentium III	2.8
IBM	NetVista 2271, -EAx,EBx,ECx,GAx,GBx,GCx,TAx,TBx	Intel Pentium III	2.7
IBM	NetVista 6058, -RAx, RBx, TAx, TBx	Intel Pentium III	2.9
IBM	NetVista 6059-NAx, NBx, PCx, PDx	Intel Pentium III	3
IBM	NetVista 6568,GAx,GBx,LAx,LBx,NAx,NBx,PAx,PBx,RAx	Intel Pentium III	3
IBM	NetVista 6569,PAx,PBx,RAx,RBx,TAx,TBx	Intel Pentium III	3
IBM	NetVista 6578	Intel Pentium III	2.9

Table 9.6   *Popular Computers that Are ENERGY STAR Compliant (continued)*

Brand	Model	Chip	Sleep Mode (Watts)
IBM	NetVista 6578-GAx, GBx, LCx, LDx, NAx, NBx	Intel Pentium III	3
IBM	NetVista 6578-L1U	Intel Pentium III	3
IBM	NetVista 6578-LAX, LBx	Intel Pentium III	3
IBM	NetVista 6578-N1U	Intel Pentium III	3
IBM	NetVista 6578-NCx, NDx	Intel Pentium III	3
IBM	NetVista 6578-P1U	Intel Pentium III	3
IBM	NetVista 6578-PAx, PBx	Intel Pentium III	3
IBM	NetVista 6578-RAx, RBx	Intel Pentium III	3
IBM	NetVista 6579	Intel Pentium III	2.9
IBM	NetVista 6579-GAx, GBx	Intel Pentium III	3
IBM	Netvista 6579-L1U	Intel Pentium III	3
IBM	NetVista 6579-LAx, LBx	Intel Pentium III	3
IBM	NetVista 6579-LDx, LEx	Intel Pentium III	3
IBM	NetVista 6579-N1U	Intel Pentium III	3
IBM	NetVista 6579-NAx, NBx	Intel Pentium III	3
IBM	NetVista 6579-NCx, NDx	Intel Pentium III	3
IBM	NetVista 6579-P1U	Intel Pentium III	3
IBM	NetVista 6579-PAx, PBx	Intel Pentium III	3
IBM	NetVista 6579-PCx, PDx	Intel Pentium III	3
IBM	NetVista 6648	Intel Pentium III	3
IBM	NetVista 6649	Intel Pentium III	3
IBM	NetVista 6830, -CAx,CBx,EAx,EBx,GAx,GBx,TAx,TBx	Intel Pentium III	2.6
IBM	NetVista 6831m -EAx,EBx,GAx,GBx,E2U,G2U	Intel Pentium III	2.6
IBM	NetVista 6837, -D1x, -E1x, -F1x	Intel Pentium III	3.1
IBM	NetVista 6840,-CAx,EAx,GAx,TAx,C1U,E1U,G1U,P2U,R2U	Intel Pentium III	2.7
IBM	NetVista 6841-EAx,GAx,TAx,E1U,G1U	Intel Pentium III	2.8

Table 9.6   *Popular Computers that Are ENERGY STAR Compliant (continued)*

Brand	Model	Chip	Sleep Mode (Watts)
IBM	NetVista 6847-D1x, -E1x, -F1x	Intel Pentium III	3.3
IBM	NetVista A20i,2255-xxx	AMD	3
IBM	NetVista A20i,2275-xxx	AMD	2.8
IBM	NetVista A21,6339-16U,24U,26U,41U,56U,57U,64U	Intel Celeron	3.5
IBM	NetVista A21,6339-B5U,B8U	Intel Celeron	3.5
IBM	NetVista A21,6341-20U,27U,41U,58U,64U,B7U	Intel Celeron	3.5
IBM	NetVista A21,6342-25U,46U,54U,62U,B3U	Intel Celeron	3.5
IBM	NetVista A22p 2292,13x,21x,33x	Intel Pentium IV	3
IBM	NetVista A22p 6343,31x	Intel Pentium IV	3
IBM	NetVista A22p 6343,91x,12-14x,93x,21x,95x,25x,97x	Intel Pentium IV	3
IBM	NetVista A22p 6349,91x,11x,92x,16x,17x,18x,71x,72x	Intel Pentium IV	3
IBM	NetVista A22p 6349,93x,21x,22x,23x,24x,94x,73x,74x	Intel Pentium IV	3
IBM	NetVista A22p 6349,95x,31x,32x,33x,34x,96x,75x,76x	Intel Pentium IV	3
IBM	NetVista A22p 6350,31x,33x	Intel Pentium IV	3
IBM	NetVista A22p 6350,91x,11x,13x,93x,95x,21x,96x,23x	Intel Pentium IV	3
IBM	NetVista A22p 6823,11x,12x,13x,14x,15x,16x,17x	Intel Pentium IV	3
IBM	NetVista A22p 6823,18x,19x	Intel Pentium IV	3
IBM	NetVista A22p 6823,21x,23x,28x,2Ex,2Ax,2Bx	Intel Pentium IV	3
IBM	NetVista A22p 6823,22x,24x,25x,27x,29x,2Cx,2Dx,2Fx	Intel Pentium IV	3
IBM	NetVista A22p 6823,31x,32x,33x,34x,35x,36x,37x,38x	Intel Pentium IV	3
IBM	NetVista A22p 6823,91x,92x,93x,94x	Intel Pentium IV	3
IBM	NetVista A22p 6825,21x,71x	Intel Pentium IV	3
IBM	NetVista A22p, 2259-C1A,C1C,C1M,C1V	Intel Pentium IV	3.7
IBM	NetVista A22p, 2259-E8C,E8M,E8V,E6A	Intel Pentium IV	3.7
IBM	NetVista A22p, 6049-Cxx	Intel Pentium IV	3.7
IBM	NetVista A22p, 6049-E3x,E4x	Intel Pentium IV	3.7

Table 9.6   *Popular Computers that Are ENERGY STAR Compliant (continued)*

Brand	Model	Chip	Sleep Mode (Watts)
IBM	NetVista A22p, 6049-G3C,G3D,G3M,G3V	Intel Pentium IV	3.7
IBM	NetVista A30p, 6824-41x,42x,43x,44x	Intel Pentium IV	3.8
IBM	NetVista M41 6790,11x,14-16x,21-23x,2A-Cx,31-33x	Intel Pentium IV	3
IBM	NetVista M41 6792,11x,16x,17x,18x,35x,36x,37x	Intel Pentium IV	3
IBM	NetVista M41 6792,1Ax,1Bx,71x,72x	Intel Pentium IV	3
IBM	NetVista M41 6792,21x,22x,23x,26x,27x,29x,2Ax,24x	Intel Pentium IV	3
IBM	NetVista M41 6792,31x,32x,3Ax,3Bx,3Cx,33x,34x,38x	Intel Pentium IV	3
IBM	NetVista M41 6793,11x,21x,22x,31x	Intel Pentium IV	3
IBM	NetVista M41 6794,11x,14-15x,21-25x,31-33x,71-72x	Intel Pentium IV	3
IBM	NetVista M41 6795, 31X	Intel Pentium IV	3
IBM	NetVista TBx, TCx, TDx, TEx	Intel Pentium III	2.8
IBM	NetVista TCx, P2U, R2U	Intel Pentium III	2.6
IBM	NetVista X41, 2283-5xx, 6xx	Intel Pentium IV	8
IBM	NetVista X41, 2283-5xx, 6xx	Intel Pentium IV	8
IBM	NetVista X41, 6274, 1xx, 2xx, 1Tx	Intel Pentium IV	8
IBM	Network Station 100 (ACT) 8361	Power PC	8
IBM	Network Station 1000, 8362-A22	Power PC	24
IBM	Network Station 1000, 8362-A23	Power PC	24
IBM	Network Station 1000/8362-A52		24
IBM	Network Station 1000/8362-A53		24
IBM	Network Station 200 (ACT) 8361	Power PC	8
IBM	Network Station 8361-341	Power PC	8
IBM	Network Station 8363-EXX	Cyrix GXm	11.7
IBM	Network Station 8363-TXX	Cyrix GXm	11.7
IBM	Network Station 8364-EXX	Intel Pentium II w/ MMX	18.5

Table 9.6   *Popular Computers that Are ENERGY STAR Compliant (continued)*

Brand	Model	Chip	Sleep Mode (Watts)
IBM	Network Station 8364-S20	Intel Pentium II w/ MMX	18.5
IBM	Network Station 8364-S21	Intel Pentium II w/ MMX	19.5
IBM	Network Station 8364-TXX	Intel Pentium II w/ MMX	18.5
IBM	PC 100 6260-XXX	Intel Pentium	18
IBM	PC 300 6576-XXX	Intel Pentium	28
IBM	PC 300 6586-XXX	Intel Pentium	28
IBM	PC 300 GL 6263-66x, 6Ax		29.54
IBM	PC 300 GL 6263-74x, 7Ax		29.9
IBM	PC 300 GL 6267-15X	Intel Celeron	24.4
IBM	PC 300 GL 6267-21X	Intel Celeron	24.4
IBM	PC 300 GL 6267-22X	Intel Celeron	24.4
IBM	PC 300 GL 6268-16x, 43x	Intel Celeron	22
IBM	PC 300 GL 6268-44x	Intel Celeron	22
IBM	PC 300 GL 6268-70x	Intel Celeron	23.8
IBM	PC 300 GL 6268-72x	Intel Celeron	23.8
IBM	PC 300 GL 6272/ -76x, -88x	P55	25
IBM	PC 300 GL 6272/ -77x	P55	25
IBM	PC 300 GL 6272/ -89x, -90x	P55	25
IBM	PC 300 GL 6272/ -91x	P55	29
IBM	PC 300 GL 6274-M4x	Intel Pentium II	29.9
IBM	PC 300 GL 6275-34x, -35x	Intel Pentium II	29.54
IBM	PC 300 GL 6275-36x	Intel Pentium II	29.54
IBM	PC 300 GL 6275-44x, -45x, -47x	Intel Pentium II w/ MMX	29.54
IBM	PC 300 GL 6275-46x	Intel Pentium II	29.54

Table 9.6   *Popular Computers that Are ENERGY STAR Compliant (continued)*

Brand	Model	Chip	Sleep Mode (Watts)
IBM	PC 300 GL 6275-54x, -55x	Intel Pentium II	29.54
IBM	PC 300 GL 6275-56x	Intel Pentium II	29.54
IBM	PC 300 GL 6275-64x, -65x	Intel Pentium II	29.54
IBM	PC 300 GL 6275-66x	Intel Pentium II	29.9
IBM	PC 300 GL 6275-73x	Intel Pentium II	29.9
IBM	PC 300 GL 6275-81x	Intel Pentium III	26.6
IBM	PC 300 GL 6275-83x	Intel Pentium III	26.6
IBM	PC 300 GL 6275-94x, -95x	Intel Pentium III	27.4
IBM	PC 300 GL 6275-B4x, -B6x	Intel Pentium II	29.9
IBM	PC 300 GL 6275-B7x	Intel Pentium II	29.9
IBM	PC 300 GL 6275-B8x, -B9x, -B3x, -B5x	Intel Pentium II	29.9
IBM	PC 300 GL 6275-M1x, -M2x, M5x	Intel Pentium II	29.9
IBM	PC 300 GL 6275-M3x	Intel Pentium II	29.9
IBM	PC 300 GL 6275-R1x	Intel Celeron	26.1
IBM	PC 300 GL 6275-R2x, -R6x	Intel Celeron	26.8
IBM	PC 300 GL 6275-R3x, -R4x	Intel Celeron	26.1
IBM	PC 300 GL 6277-24X, -27X	Intel Celeron	24.4
IBM	PC 300 GL 6277-34X, -35X	Intel Celeron	25.1
IBM	PC 300 GL 6277-4Dx, -4Fx	Intel Celeron	22.3
IBM	PC 300 GL 6277-53X, -55X	Intel Pentium II	24.4
IBM	PC 300 GL 6277-5Dx, -5Ex, -5Fx	Intel Celeron	21.6
IBM	PC 300 GL 6277-70X, -71X	Intel Pentium II w/ MMX	24.4
IBM	PC 300 GL 6277-72x	Intel Pentium II	25.2
IBM	PC 300 GL 6277-73X	Intel Pentium II	24
IBM	PC 300 GL 6277-7Dx	Intel Pentium III	25
IBM	PC 300 GL 6277-7Ex, -7Lx	Intel Pentium III	25

Table 9.6   *Popular Computers that Are ENERGY STAR Compliant (continued)*

Brand	Model	Chip	Sleep Mode (Watts)
IBM	PC 300 GL 6277-7Kx	Intel Pentium III	25
IBM	PC 300 GL 6277-87X, -89X	Intel Pentium II	24.4
IBM	PC 300 GL 6277-88X	Intel Pentium II	24.4
IBM	PC 300 GL 6277-8Kx, 8Jx	Intel Pentium III	25
IBM	PC 300 GL 6277-94x	Intel Pentium III	25.5
IBM	PC 300 GL 6277-98x	Intel Pentium III	26
IBM	PC 300 GL 6277-9Jx	Intel Pentium III	25
IBM	PC 300 GL 6277-9Kx	Intel Pentium III	25
IBM	PC 300 GL 6277-HX	Intel Pentium III	25
IBM	PC 300 GL 6278-73x, 74x	Intel Celeron	23.8
IBM	PC 300 GL 6278-S1x, S8x	Intel Celeron	22
IBM	PC 300 GL 6278-S2x, S3x	Intel Celeron	22
IBM	PC 300 GL 6278-S4x	Intel Celeron	23.9
IBM	PC 300 GL 6278-S5x	Intel Celeron	22
IBM	PC 300 GL 6278-S6x	Intel Celeron	22
IBM	PC 300 GL 6278-S9x	Intel Celeron	22
IBM	PC 300 GL 6278-SAx	Intel Celeron	22
IBM	PC 300 GL 6278-SBx	Intel Celeron	22
IBM	PC 300 GL 6278-SCx	Intel Celeron	24.2
IBM	PC 300 GL 6278-SDx, SGx, SHx, SIx	Intel Celeron	23.9
IBM	PC 300 GL 6278-SEx	Intel Celeron	23
IBM	PC 300 GL 6278-SFx, SJx	Intel Celeron	23.8
IBM	PC 300 GL 6282/ -78x	P55	25
IBM	PC 300 GL 6282/ -80x	P55	25
IBM	PC 300 GL 6282/ -81x, -82x, -84x	P55	25
IBM	PC 300 GL 6282/ -85x, 86x, 87x	P55	28

Table 9.6   *Popular Computers that Are ENERGY STAR Compliant (continued)*

Brand	Model	Chip	Sleep Mode (Watts)
IBM	PC 300 GL 6282/-79x, 83x	P55	25
IBM	PC 300 GL 6285-34x, -35x	Intel Pentium II	29.575
IBM	PC 300 GL 6285-44x, -45x	Intel Pentium II	29.575
IBM	PC 300 GL 6285-54x, -55x	Intel Pentium II	29.575
IBM	PC 300 GL 6285-56x	Intel Pentium II	29.575
IBM	PC 300 GL 6285-64x, -65x	Intel Pentium II	29.575
IBM	PC 300 GL 6285-66x	Intel Pentium II	29.575
IBM	PC 300 GL 6285-F2x		27.4
IBM	PC 300 GL 6287 -22X, -25X, -28X	Intel Celeron	24.4
IBM	PC 300 GL 6287-15X/-17X/-26X	Intel Celeron	24.4
IBM	PC 300 GL 6287-21X	Intel Celeron	24.4
IBM	PC 300 GL 6287-29X	Intel Celeron	24.4
IBM	PC 300 GL 6287-31X, 32XGM	Intel Celeron	24.5
IBM	PC 300 GL 6287-33X, -35x	Intel Celeron	25.1
IBM	PC 300 GL 6287-41X, -50X	Intel Pentium	24.4
IBM	PC 300 GL 6287-4Bx, -4Cx, -4Dx	Intel Celeron	22.3
IBM	PC 300 GL 6287-4Ex	Intel Celeron	22.3
IBM	PC 300 GL 6287-54X	Intel Pentium II	24.4
IBM	PC 300 GL 6287-5Bx, -5Cx	Intel Celeron	21.6
IBM	PC 300 GL 6287-61X	Intel Pentium II	24.4
IBM	PC 300 GL 6287-62x	Intel Pentium II	24.4
IBM	PC 300 GL 6287-69X	Intel Pentium II	24.4
IBM	PC 300 GL 6287-7Bx, 7Cx	Intel Pentium III	24.4
IBM	PC 300 GL 6287-7Fx, 7Gx	Intel Pentium III	24.4
IBM	PC 300 GL 6287-85X, -86X	Intel Pentium II	24.4
IBM	PC 300 GL 6287-8Fx	Intel Pentium III	24.4

Table 9.6   *Popular Computers that Are ENERGY STAR Compliant (continued)*

Brand	Model	Chip	Sleep Mode (Watts)
IBM	PC 300 GL 6287-9Fx, 9Gx	Intel Pentium III	23.2
IBM	PC 300 GL 6287-E5x	Intel Celeron	22.3
IBM	PC 300 GL 6288-10x	Intel Celeron	22
IBM	PC 300 GL 6288-11x	Intel Celeron	22
IBM	PC 300 GL 6288-15x, 16x	Intel Celeron	22
IBM	PC 300 GL 6288-17x	Intel Celeron	22
IBM	PC 300 GL 6288-1C, 1F	Intel Celeron	23.8
IBM	PC 300 GL 6288-1D, 1E	Intel Celeron	23.8
IBM	PC 300 GL 6288-1G	Intel Celeron	23.8
IBM	PC 300 GL 6288-1Hx	Intel Celeron	23
IBM	PC 300 GL 6288-30x, 31x	Intel Celeron	22
IBM	PC 300 GL 6288-35x, 36x, 41x	Intel Celeron	22
IBM	PC 300 GL 6288-37x, 42x	Intel Celeron	22
IBM	PC 300 GL 6288-39x, 40x	Intel Celeron	22
IBM	PC 300 GL 6288-44x, 45x	Intel Celeron	22
IBM	PC 300 GL 6288-46x, 47x	Intel Celeron	22
IBM	PC 300 GL 6288-48x	Intel Celeron	22
IBM	PC 300 GL 6288-49x	Intel Celeron	22
IBM	PC 300 GL 6288-50x	Intel Celeron	22
IBM	PC 300 GL 6288-51x, 53x	Intel Celeron	22
IBM	PC 300 GL 6288-70x	Intel Celeron	23
IBM	PC 300 GL 6288-71x, 72x	Intel Celeron	23.8
IBM	PC 300 GL 6288-76x, 77x, 79x	Intel Celeron	23.8
IBM	PC 300 GL 6288-78x, 7Ax	Intel Celeron	23.8
IBM	PC 300 GL 6288-7Bx, 7Cx	Intel Celeron	23
IBM	PC 300 GL 6338-36x, 41x	Intel Celeron	22

Table 9.6   *Popular Computers that Are ENERGY STAR Compliant (continued)*

Brand	Model	Chip	Sleep Mode (Watts)
IBM	PC 300 GL 6338-46x, 47x	Intel Celeron	22
IBM	PC 300 GL 6338-51x, 53x	Intel Celeron	22
IBM	PC 300 GL 6338-73x, 7C	Intel Celeron	23.8
IBM	PC 300 GL 6338-74x, 7B	Intel Celeron	23.8
IBM	PC 300 GL 6561-11x	Intel Pentium II	28
IBM	PC 300 GL 6561-13x	Intel Pentium II	28
IBM	PC 300 GL 6561-15x, -16x, -19x	Intel Pentium II	28
IBM	PC 300 GL 6561-28x	Intel Pentium II	26
IBM	PC 300 GL 6561-32x	Intel Pentium II	28
IBM	PC 300 GL 6561-34x, 35x	Intel Pentium II	28
IBM	PC 300 GL 6561-42x, -45x, -46x	Intel Pentium II	26
IBM	PC 300 GL 6561-53x, -54x	Intel Pentium II	26
IBM	PC 300 GL 6561-55x, 56x	Intel Pentium II	26
IBM	PC 300 GL 6563-22x	Intel Pentium III	29
IBM	PC 300 GL 6563-23x	Intel Pentium III	29
IBM	PC 300 GL 6563-24x	Intel Pentium III	29
IBM	PC 300 GL 6563-25x	Intel Pentium III	29
IBM	PC 300 GL 6563-26x	Intel Pentium III	29
IBM	PC 300 GL 6563-27x	Intel Pentium III	29
IBM	PC 300 GL 6563-42x	Intel Pentium III	29
IBM	PC 300 GL 6563-43x	Intel Pentium III	29
IBM	PC 300 GL 6563-44x	Intel Pentium III	29
IBM	PC 300 GL 6563-45x	Intel Pentium III	29
IBM	PC 300 GL 6563-64x	Intel Pentium III	29.3
IBM	PC 300 GL 6563-65x	Intel Pentium III	29.3
IBM	PC 300 GL 6563-71x	Intel Pentium III	29.3

Table 9.6   *Popular Computers that Are ENERGY STAR Compliant (continued)*

Brand	Model	Chip	Sleep Mode (Watts)
IBM	PC 300 GL 6563-88x	Intel Pentium III	28.4
IBM	PC 300 GL 6563-9Ax, 9Bx, 9Cx	Intel Pentium III	27.6
IBM	PC 300 GL 6563-9Dx	Intel Pentium III	29.1
IBM	PC 300 GL 6563-A3x	Intel Pentium III	28
IBM	PC 300 GL 6563-A5x	Intel Pentium III	21.3
IBM	PC 300 GL 6563-B1x	Intel Pentium III	24.1
IBM	PC 300 GL 6564-C1x	Intel Pentium III	18
IBM	PC 300 GL 6564-P6x	Intel Pentium III	22.3
IBM	PC 300 GL 6564-R1x, R2x, R4x	Intel Pentium III	29.2
IBM	PC 300 GL 6564-S3x	Intel Pentium III	29
IBM	PC 300 GL 6564-S4x	Intel Pentium III	29
IBM	PC 300 GL 6564-S6x	Intel Pentium III	29
IBM	PC 300 GL 6564-S7x	Intel Pentium III	29
IBM	PC 300 GL 6564-S8x	Intel Pentium III	29
IBM	PC 300 GL 6564-SFx	Intel Pentium III	29
IBM	PC 300 GL 6564-SYx	Intel Pentium III	22
IBM	PC 300 GL 6574-23x	Intel Pentium III	29
IBM	PC 300 GL 6574-28x	Intel Pentium III	29
IBM	PC 300 GL 6574-45x	Intel Pentium III	29
IBM	PC 300 GL 6574-47x	Intel Pentium III	29
IBM	PC 300 GL 6574-A3x	Intel Pentium III	25.7
IBM	PC 300 GL 6574-B1x	Intel Pentium III	26.2
IBM	PC 300 GL 6591-13x	Intel Pentium II	28
IBM	PC 300 GL 6591-15x, -16x	Intel Pentium II	28
IBM	PC 300 GL 6591-34x, -35x	Intel Pentium II	28
IBM	PC 300 GL 6591-54x	Intel Pentium II	27

Table 9.6   *Popular Computers that Are ENERGY STAR Compliant (continued)*

Brand	Model	Chip	Sleep Mode (Watts)
IBM	PC 300 GL 6591-76x	Intel Pentium II	25
IBM	PC 300 GL, 6265-12S, -12P	Intel Celeron	27.5
IBM	PC 300 GL, 6275-12x, -13x	Intel Celeron	27.5
IBM	PC 300 GL, 6275-16x	Intel Celeron	27.5
IBM	PC 300 GL, 6275-17V	Intel Celeron	27.5
IBM	PC 300 GL, 6275-18V	Intel Pentium II	28.7
IBM	PC 300 GL, 6275-22x, -23x	Intel Celeron	27.5
IBM	PC 300 GL, 6275-24x	Intel Celeron	27.5
IBM	PC 300 GL, 6275-25x	Intel Celeron	27.5
IBM	PC 300 GL, 6275-26x, -29x	Intel Celeron	27.5
IBM	PC 300 GL, 6275-27x	Intel Celeron	27.5
IBM	PC 300 GL, 6275-37x	Intel Pentium II	29.9
IBM	PC 300 GL, 6275-57x, -58x	Intel Pentium II	29.9
IBM	PC 300 GL, 6275-59x	Intel Pentium II	29.9
IBM	PC 300 GL, 6275-67x	Intel Pentium II	29.9
IBM	PC 300 GL, 6275-68x	Intel Pentium II	29.9
IBM	PC 300 GL, 6275-69x	Intel Pentium II	29.9
IBM	PC 300 GL, 6275-73x, -74x	Intel Pentium II	29.9
IBM	PC 300 GL, 6275-750	Intel Pentium II	29.9
IBM	PC 300 GL, 6275-G3x	Intel Celeron	27.5
IBM	PC 300 GL, 6275-G4x	Intel Celeron	27.5
IBM	PC 300 GL, 6275-G5x, F1x	Intel Celeron	27.5
IBM	PC 300 GL, 6275-H1x	Intel Celeron	27.5
IBM	PC 300 GL, 6275-H2x	Intel Celeron	27.5
IBM	PC 300 GL, 6275-H3x	Intel Celeron	27.5
IBM	PC 300 GL, 6285-13x	Intel Celeron	28.7

Table 9.6   *Popular Computers that Are ENERGY STAR Compliant (continued)*

Brand	Model	Chip	Sleep Mode (Watts)
IBM	PC 300 GL, 6285-14x	Intel Celeron	28.7
IBM	PC 300 GL, 6285-57x	Intel Pentium II	29.9
IBM	PC 300 GL, 6285-67x	Intel Pentium II	29.9
IBM	PC 300 GL, 6285-73x, -74x	Intel Pentium II	27.3
IBM	PC 300 GL, 6285-75x	Intel Pentium II	27.3
IBM	PC 300 GL, 6285-G1x, G2x	Intel Celeron	27.4
IBM	PC 300 PL	Intel Pentium III	20.8
IBM	PC 300 PL	Intel Pentium III	19.2
IBM	PC 300 PL, 6862-110	Intel Pentium II	29.54
IBM	PC 300 PL 6562	Intel	28.4
IBM	PC 300 PL 6562/10x, 34x, 46x	Intel Pentium II w/ MMX	28.5
IBM	PC 300 PL 6562/20x, 32x, 36x, 38x	Intel Pentium II w/ MMX	28.5
IBM	PC 300 PL 6562/50x, 52x	Intel Pentium II w/ MMX	28.5
IBM	PC 300 PL 6563-47U	Intel Pentium III	20.4
IBM	PC 300 PL 6563-62x	Intel Pentium III	18.2
IBM	PC 300 PL 6563-63x	Intel Pentium III	26
IBM	PC 300 PL 6563-66X	Intel Pentium III	17.9
IBM	PC 300 PL 6563-67X	Intel Pentium III	25.8
IBM	PC 300 PL 6563-68x	Intel Pentium III	19
IBM	PC 300 PL 6563-69x	Intel Pentium III	26
IBM	PC 300 PL 6563-82x	Intel Pentium III	19.2
IBM	PC 300 PL 6563-83x	Intel Pentium III	28.4
IBM	PC 300 PL 6563-84x	Intel Pentium III	18.8
IBM	PC 300 PL 6563-85x	Intel Pentium III	26.7

Table 9.6   *Popular Computers that Are ENERGY STAR Compliant (continued)*

Brand	Model	Chip	Sleep Mode (Watts)
IBM	PC 300 PL 6563-86x	Intel Pentium III	17.9
IBM	PC 300 PL 6563-87x	Intel Pentium III	25.8
IBM	PC 300 PL 6563-91x	Intel Pentium III	26.7
IBM	PC 300 PL 6563-92x	Intel Pentium III	18.8
IBM	PC 300 PL 6563-93x	Intel Pentium III	28.4
IBM	PC 300 PL 6563-94x	Intel Pentium III	19.2
IBM	PC 300 PL 6563-A1X	Intel Pentium III	19.9
IBM	PC 300 PL 6563-A2x	Intel Pentium III	29.3
IBM	PC 300 PL 6564-91x	Intel Pentium III	28.4
IBM	PC 300 PL 6564-SCx	Intel Pentium III	26.6
IBM	PC 300 PL 6564-SLx	Intel Pentium III	26.6
IBM	PC 300 PL 6564-SPx	Intel Pentium III	20.1
IBM	PC 300 PL 6564-SQx	Intel Pentium III	29.4
IBM	PC 300 PL 6564-SRx	Intel Pentium III	29.2
IBM	PC 300 PL 6565-41x	Intel Pentium III	29.8
IBM	PC 300 PL 6565-42x	Intel Pentium III	29.8
IBM	PC 300 PL 6565-43x	Intel Pentium III	29.8
IBM	PC 300 PL 6565-44x	Intel Pentium III	29.8
IBM	PC 300 PL 6565-61x	Intel Pentium III	29.8
IBM	PC 300 PL 6565-62x	Intel Pentium III	29.8
IBM	PC 300 PL 6565-63x	Intel Pentium III	29.8
IBM	PC 300 PL 6565-64x	Intel Pentium III	29.8
IBM	PC 300 PL 6565-66x	Intel Pentium III	28.1
IBM	PC 300 PL 6565-82X	Intel Pentium III	20.8
IBM	PC 300 PL 6565-83x	Intel Pentium III	28.1
IBM	PC 300 PL 6565-84x	Intel Pentium III	20.8

Table 9.6   *Popular Computers that Are ENERGY STAR Compliant (continued)*

Brand	Model	Chip	Sleep Mode (Watts)
IBM	PC 300 PL 6565-85x	Intel Pentium III	28.1
IBM	PC 300 PL 6565-86xd	Intel Pentium III	20.9
IBM	PC 300 PL 6565-92x	Intel Pentium III	20.5
IBM	PC 300 PL 6565-93x	Intel Pentium III	29.2
IBM	PC 300 PL 6565-96x	Intel Pentium III	20.9
IBM	PC 300 PL 6565-9Cx, 89C, 88x	Intel Pentium III	17.7
IBM	PC 300 PL 6565-E1X	Intel Pentium III	20.9
IBM	PC 300 PL 6565-F1x	Intel Pentium III	21.4
IBM	PC 300 PL 6574-61x	Intel Pentium III	26
IBM	PC 300 PL 6574-62x	Intel Pentium III	19
IBM	PC 300 PL 6574-82x	Intel Pentium III	19.2
IBM	PC 300 PL 6574-83X	Intel Pentium III	28.4
IBM	PC 300 PL 6574-A1x	Intel Pentium III	19.9
IBM	PC 300 PL 6574-A2X	Intel Pentium III	29.3
IBM	PC 300 PL 6584-82x	Intel Pentium III	26.5
IBM	PC 300 PL 6584-84x	Intel Pentium III	24.4
IBM	PC 300 PL 6584-85x	Intel Pentium III	29.7
IBM	PC 300 PL 6584-88x	Intel Pentium III	23.8
IBM	PC 300 PL 6584-89x	Intel Pentium III	28.4
IBM	PC 300 PL 6584-92x	Intel Pentium III	23.8
IBM	PC 300 PL 6584-93x	Intel Pentium III	28.6
IBM	PC 300 PL 6584-94x	Intel Pentium III	26.7
IBM	PC 300 PL 6584-98x	Intel Pentium III	24.5
IBM	PC 300 PL 6584-99x	Intel Pentium III	29.9
IBM	PC 300 PL 6584-A1x	Intel Pentium III	26.6
IBM	PC 300 PL 6584-A4x	Intel Pentium III	28.7

Table 9.6   *Popular Computers that Are ENERGY STAR Compliant (continued)*

Brand	Model	Chip	Sleep Mode (Watts)
IBM	PC 300 PL 6584-A5x	Intel Pentium III	25.3
IBM	PC 300 PL 6592	Intel	28.4
IBM	PC 300 PL 6592/12x,16x	Intel Pentium II w/ MMX	28.5
IBM	PC 300 PL 6594-E1j	Intel Pentium III	25.1
IBM	PC 300 PL 6862, W1x, W2x	Intel Pentium III	29.4
IBM	PC 300 PL 6862, W3x, W4x	Intel Pentium III	29.5
IBM	PC 300 PL 6862, W7x, W8x	Intel Pentium III	29.9
IBM	PC 300 PL 6862-140	Intel Pentium II	29.54
IBM	PC 300 PL 6862-230	Intel Pentium II	29.54
IBM	PC 300 PL 6862-27x, -34x, -C5x, -C6x, C7x	Power PC	29.9
IBM	PC 300 PL 6862-41x	Intel Pentium II	29.9
IBM	PC 300 PL 6862-5CJ, -5DJ	Intel Pentium III	28.5
IBM	PC 300 PL 6862-5JJ, -5KJ, -5LJ	Intel Celeron	26.9
IBM	PC 300 PL 6862-F30	Intel Pentium II	29.9
IBM	PC 300 PL 6862-N1x, -N0x, V1x	Intel Pentium III	28.8
IBM	PC 300 PL 6862-N2x, -V2x	Intel Pentium III	28.5
IBM	PC 300 PL 6862-N3x, -N7x	Intel Pentium III	28.8
IBM	PC 300 PL 6862-N4x, -V6x	Intel Pentium III	28.5
IBM	PC 300 PL 6862-N7x	AMD	29
IBM	PC 300 PL 6862-NOx	Intel Pentium III	29
IBM	PC 300 PL 6862-S1x, -S2x, -S3x	Intel Pentium III	29
IBM	PC 300 PL 6862-S9x, -S4x, -S5x, -C8J, -C9J	Intel Pentium III	29
IBM	PC 300 PL 686-V4x, -V5x	Intel Pentium III	29.1
IBM	PC 300 PL 6872-34x	Intel Pentium II	29.54
IBM	PC 300 PL 6872-52x	Intel Pentium II	29.54
IBM	PC 300 PL 6892-120	Intel Pentium II	29.575

Table 9.6   *Popular Computers that Are ENERGY STAR Compliant (continued)*

Brand	Model	Chip	Sleep Mode (Watts)
IBM	PC 300 PL 6892-140	Intel Pentium II	29.575
IBM	PC 300 PL 6892-160 GM	Intel Pentium II	29.575
IBM	PC 300 PL 6892-200	Intel Pentium II	29.575
IBM	PC 300 PL 6892-C8J, -C9J	Intel Pentium III	29
IBM	PC 300 PL 6892-N1x	Intel Pentium III	29.3
IBM	PC 300 PL 6892-N2x	Intel Pentium III	28.5
IBM	PC 300 PL 6892-N3x, -N4x	Intel Pentium III	28.5
IBM	PC 300 PL 6892-S1x, -S2x	Intel Pentium III	28.8
IBM	PC 300 PL F2x	Intel Pentium III	29.9
IBM	PC 300 PL, 6565-G1x	Intel Pentium III	22.4
IBM	PC 300 PL, 6862 - 240 GM	Intel Pentium II	29.54
IBM	PC 300 PL, 6862 - 250	Intel Pentium II	29.54
IBM	PC 300 PL, 6862-120, -130	Intel Pentium II	29.54
IBM	PC 300 PL, 6862-180GM, -200GM	Intel Pentium II	29.54
IBM	PC 300 PL, 6862-220, -260	Intel Pentium II	29.54
IBM	PC 300 PL, 6862-270	Intel Pentium II	29.54
IBM	PC 300 PL, 6862-29x	Intel Pentium II	28.7
IBM	PC 300 PL, 6862-30x	Intel Pentium II	29.9
IBM	PC 300 PL, 6862-31x	Intel Pentium II	29.9
IBM	PC 300 PL, 6862-32x	Intel Pentium II	29.9
IBM	PC 300 PL, 6862-34x	Intel Pentium II	29.9
IBM	PC 300 PL, 6862-35x	Intel Pentium II	29.9
IBM	PC 300 PL, 6862-41x	Intel Pentium II	29.9
IBM	PC 300 PL, 6862-43x	Intel Pentium II	29.9
IBM	PC 300 PL, 6862-44J, -45J	Intel Pentium II	29.9
IBM	PC 300 PL, 6862-52X	Intel Pentium II	29.9

Table 9.6   *Popular Computers that Are ENERGY STAR Compliant (continued)*

Brand	Model	Chip	Sleep Mode (Watts)
IBM	PC 300 PL, 6862-B1J, -B3J, -B4J	Intel Celeron	27.5
IBM	PC 300 PL, 6862-B2J, -B5J, -B6J	Intel Celeron	27.5
IBM	PC 300 PL, 6862-B7J	Intel Pentium II	29.9
IBM	PC 300 PL, 6892-37x	Intel Pentium II	27.3
IBM	PC 300 PL, 6892-45x, -47x	Intel Pentium II	27.3
IBM	PC 300 PL, 6892-47J, -48J	Intel Pentium II	27.3
IBM	PC 300 PL, 6892-5AJ, -5BJ	Intel Pentium II	27.3
IBM	PC 300 PL, 6892-B8J	Intel Pentium II	27.3
IBM	PC 365 15x	Intel Pentium Pro	26
IBM	PC 300 6344-60U	Intel Pentium III	4.5
IBM	PC 300 6344-XOU	Intel Celeron	4.5
IBM	PC 300 6345-7OU	Intel Pentium III	4.5
IBM	PC 300 6345-XOU	Intel Celeron	4.5
IBM	RISC System	Power PC	5
IBM	ThinkPad 130 1171-33x	Intel Celeron	18
IBM	ThinkPad 130 1171-37x	Intel Celeron	18
IBM	ThinkPad 235/2607-10J	Intel	3.5
IBM	ThinkPad 235/2607-20J	Intel Pentium II w/ MMX	3.5
IBM	ThinkPad 240 2609-3xx	Intel Celeron	6
IBM	ThinkPad 240, 2609	Intel Celeron	6
IBM	ThinkPad 240X, 2609, 2612	Intel Celeron	6
IBM	ThinkPad 240Z	Intel Pentium III	1.5
IBM	ThinkPad 240Z 2609-XXX	Intel Pentium III	1.5
IBM	ThinkPad 365X, 365XD	Intel Pentium	6
IBM	ThinkPad 380, 380D, 385, 385D	Intel Pentium	6
IBM	ThinkPad 380E/ED	Intel	6

Table 9.6   *Popular Computers that Are ENERGY STAR Compliant (continued)*

Brand	Model	Chip	Sleep Mode (Watts)
IBM	ThinkPad 380X	Intel Pentium II w/ MMX	6
IBM	ThinkPad 380XD 2635-9Ax	Intel Pentium II w/ MMX	6
IBM	ThinkPad 380XD 2635-Aax	Intel Pentium II w/ MMX	6
IBM	ThinkPad 380XD 2635-Eax	Intel Pentium II	6
IBM	ThinkPad 380XD 2635-Fax	Intel Pentium II	6
IBM	ThinkPad 380Z 2635-HGx	Intel Pentium II	6
IBM	ThinkPad 380Z 2635-JGx	Intel Pentium II	6
IBM	ThinkPad 385E/ED	Intel	6
IBM	ThinkPad 385XD	Intel Pentium II w/ MMX	6
IBM	ThinkPad 390, 2626-20x	Intel Pentium II w/ MMX	6
IBM	ThinkPad 390, 2626-50x	Intel Pentium II	6
IBM	ThinkPad 390, 2626-5Ax	Intel Pentium II	6
IBM	ThinkPad 390, 2626-70x	Intel Pentium II	6
IBM	ThinkPad 390E 2624-E0x	Intel Pentium II	6
IBM	ThinkPad 390E 2624-Enx	Intel Pentium II	6
IBM	ThinkPad 390E 2626-90x	Intel Celeron	6
IBM	ThinkPad 390E 2626-B0x	Intel Celeron	6
IBM	ThinkPad 390E 2626-C0x	Intel Pentium II	6
IBM	ThinkPad 390E 2626-D0x	Intel Pentium II	6
IBM	ThinkPad 390E 2626-E0x	Intel Pentium II	6
IBM	ThinkPad 390E 2626-Enx	Intel Pentium II	6
IBM	ThinkPad 390X 2626/2624-H0x	Intel Pentium II	16
IBM	ThinkPad 390X 2626/2624-HNx	Intel Pentium II	16

Table 9.6 *Popular Computers that Are ENERGY STAR Compliant (continued)*

Brand	Model	Chip	Sleep Mode (Watts)
IBM	ThinkPad 390X 2626-F0x	Intel Celeron	16
IBM	ThinkPad 390X 2626-G0x	Intel Celeron	16
IBM	ThinkPad 390X 2626-J0x	Intel Pentium II	16
IBM	ThinkPad 390X 2626-JNx	Intel Pentium II	16
IBM	ThinkPad 390X 2626-L0x	Intel Pentium III	19
IBM	ThinkPad 390X 2626-LNx	Intel Pentium III	19
IBM	ThinkPad 390X 2626-M0x	Intel Pentium III	19
IBM	ThinkPad 390X 2626-MNx	Intel Pentium III	19
IBM	ThinkPad 390X 2626-N0x	Intel Celeron	19
IBM	ThinkPad 390X 2626-NNx	Intel Celeron	19
IBM	ThinkPad 390X 2626-P0x	Intel Celeron	19
IBM	ThinkPad 390X 2626-PNx	Intel Celeron	19
IBM	ThinkPad 560	Intel Pentium	8.9
IBM	ThinkPad 570 2643-3Ax, -3Bx	Intel Pentium II	6
IBM	ThinkPad 570 2644-Aax	Intel Celeron	6
IBM	ThinkPad 570, 2644-1Ax/Bx/1Cx	Intel Pentium II	6
IBM	ThinkPad 570, 2644-2Ax	Intel Pentium II	6
IBM	ThinkPad 570, 2644-3Ax/3Bx	Intel Pentium II	6
IBM	ThinkPad 600, Model 21	Intel Pentium II	6
IBM	ThinkPad 600, Model 31	Intel	6
IBM	ThinkPad 600, Model 35	Intel Pentium II	6
IBM	ThinkPad 600, Model 41	Intel	6
IBM	ThinkPad 600, Model 45	Intel Pentium II	6
IBM	ThinkPad 600, Model 51	Intel Pentium II	6
IBM	ThinkPad 600E Model-3A	Intel Pentium II	6
IBM	ThinkPad 600E Model-4A, -8A	Intel Pentium II	6

→

Table 9.6 *Popular Computers that Are ENERGY STAR Compliant (continued)*

Brand	Model	Chip	Sleep Mode (Watts)
IBM	ThinkPad 600E Model-4Bx/8Bx	Intel Pentium II	6
IBM	ThinkPad 600E Model-5A	Intel Pentium II	0
IBM	ThinkPad 600E Model-5A (A)	Intel Pentium II	6
IBM	ThinkPad 600E Model-5Bx	Intel Pentium II	6
IBM	ThinkPad 600X Model-3Ex/7Ex	Intel Pentium III	6
IBM	ThinkPad 600X Model-4Ex/8Ex	Intel Pentium III	6
IBM	ThinkPad 600X Model-5Ex/9Ex	Intel Pentium III	6
IBM	ThinkPad 760 XD	Intel Pentium	6
IBM	ThinkPad 760 XL	Intel Pentium	6
IBM	ThinkPad 760C/CD	Intel Pentium	6
IBM	ThinkPad 760E/ED	Intel Pentium	6
IBM	ThinkPad 760ED	Intel Pentium	6
IBM	ThinkPad 760EL	Intel Pentium	6
IBM	ThinkPad 760EL/ELD	Intel Pentium	6
IBM	ThinkPad 760L/LD	Intel Pentium	6
IBM	ThinkPad 765D	Intel	6
IBM	ThinkPad 765L	Intel	6
IBM	ThinkPad 770 9548-3xU	Intel Pentium	14
IBM	ThinkPad 770 9548-40U	Intel Pentium	14
IBM	ThinkPad 770 9549-1AU	Intel Pentium	14
IBM	ThinkPad 770 E 9548-6xU	Intel Pentium II	14
IBM	ThinkPad 770 ED 9549-5AU	Intel Pentium II	14
IBM	ThinkPad 770X 9549-71U/-72U/-73U	Intel Pentium II	13
IBM	ThinkPad 770X 9549-7AU/-7BU	Intel Pentium II	13
IBM	ThinkPad 770Z 9549-81U, -82U, -83U	Intel Pentium II	6
IBM	ThinkPad 770Z 9549-8AU, -8BU	Intel Pentium II	13

Table 9.6   *Popular Computers that Are ENERGY STAR Compliant (continued)*

Brand	Model	Chip	Sleep Mode (Watts)
IBM	ThinkPad A20m 2628-1Ax/1Cx/1Ux/1Vx/1Zx	Intel Celeron	1
IBM	ThinkPad A20m 2628-3Ax/3Cx/3Ux/3Vx/3Zx	Intel Celeron	1
IBM	ThinkPad A20m 2628-3xx	Intel Celeron	10
IBM	ThinkPad A20m 2628-4Ax/4Cx/4Ux/4Vx/4Zx/3JC/3KC	Intel Pentium III	1
IBM	ThinkPad A20m, 2628-1xx	Intel Celeron	9
IBM	ThinkPad A20m, 2628-2xx	Intel Pentium III	9
IBM	ThinkPad A20m, 2628-4xx, 2633-4xx	Intel Pentium III	10
IBM	ThinkPad A20p 2629-6Ax/6Cx/6Ux/6Vx/6Zx	Intel Pentium III	1.5
IBM	ThinkPad A20p, 2629-6xx	Intel Pentium III	11
IBM	ThinkPad A21e 2628-CXX	Intel Celeron	5
IBM	ThinkPad A21e 2628-JXX	Intel Celeron	5
IBM	ThinkPad A21e, 2629-Jxx, lxx	Intel Celeron	5
IBM	ThinkPad A21e,2655-2xx,7xx	Intel Celeron	9
IBM	ThinkPad A21e,2655-3xx,8xx	Intel Celeron	9
IBM	ThinkPad A21e,2655-4xx, 9xx	Intel Celeron	9
IBM	ThinkPad A21m, 2628/2633-Gxx	Intel Pentium III	11
IBM	ThinkPad A21m, 2628-Exx/Dxx	Intel Pentium III	11
IBM	ThinkPad A21m, 2628-Fxx	Intel Pentium III	11
IBM	ThinkPad A21p, 2629-Hxx	Intel Pentium III	11
IBM	ThinkPad A22e, 2655-2xx, 3xx, 7xx, 8xx	Intel Celeron	9
IBM	ThinkPad A22e, 2655-4xx, 5xx, 9xx, Axx	Intel Pentium III	12
IBM	ThinkPad A22e, 2655-6xx, Bxx	Intel Pentium III	12
IBM	ThinkPad A22e, 2664-7xx	Intel Celeron	9
IBM	ThinkPad A22m,2628-Pxx	Intel Pentium III	12
IBM	ThinkPad A22m,2628-Qxx	Intel Pentium III	12
IBM	ThinkPad A22m,2628-Rxx	Intel Pentium III	12

Table 9.6   *Popular Computers that Are ENERGY STAR Compliant (continued)*

Brand	Model	Chip	Sleep Mode (Watts)
IBM	ThinkPad A22m,2628-Sxx	Intel Pentium III	12
IBM	ThinkPad A22m,2628-Txx	Intel Pentium III	12
IBM	ThinkPad A22m,2628-Vxx	Intel Pentium III	12
IBM	ThinkPad A22m,2628-Wxx	Intel Pentium III	12
IBM	ThinkPad A22p,2629-Uxx	Intel Pentium III	12
IBM	ThinkPad A30, 2652-1xx/2xx	Intel Pentium III	12
IBM	ThinkPad A30, 2652-33x/34x/3Bx	Intel Pentium III	11
IBM	ThinkPad A30, 2652-35x/36x/3Cx	Intel Pentium III	11
IBM	ThinkPad A30, 2652-43x/44x/4Bx	Intel Pentium III	11
IBM	ThinkPad A30, 2652-45x/46x/4Cx	Intel Pentium III	11
IBM	ThinkPad A30p, 2653-63x/64x	Intel Pentium III	12
IBM	ThinkPad A30p, 2653-65x/66x	Intel Pentium III	12
IBM	ThinkPad A31,2652/2653/2654-Axx	Intel Pentium IV	12
IBM	ThinkPad A31,2652/2653/2654-Cxx	Intel Pentium IV	12
IBM	ThinkPad A31,2652/2653/2654-Dxx	Intel Pentium IV	12
IBM	ThinkPad A31p,2652/2653/2654-Hxx	Intel Pentium IV	12
IBM	ThinkPad i Series 1200 1161-11x	Intel Celeron	16
IBM	ThinkPad i Series 1200 1161-21x	Intel Celeron	17
IBM	ThinkPad i Series 1200 1161-23x	Intel Celeron	17
IBM	ThinkPad i Series 1200 1161-25x	Intel Celeron	18
IBM	ThinkPad i Series 1200 1161-26x	Intel Celeron	18
IBM	ThinkPad i Series 1200 1161-41x	Intel Celeron	16
IBM	ThinkPad i Series 1200 1161-43x	Intel Celeron	10
IBM	ThinkPad i Series 1200 1161-51x, -71x	Intel Celeron	16
IBM	ThinkPad i Series 1200 1161-61x	Intel Pentium III	16
IBM	ThinkPad i Series 1200, 1161-12x	Intel Celeron	18

Table 9.6   *Popular Computers that Are ENERGY STAR Compliant (continued)*

Brand	Model	Chip	Sleep Mode (Watts)
IBM	ThinkPad i Series 1200, 1161-27x	Intel Celeron	18
IBM	ThinkPad i Series 1200, 1161-42x	Intel Celeron	18
IBM	ThinkPad i Series 1200, 1161-62x	Intel Celeron	18
IBM	ThinkPad i Series 1200, 1161-62x	Intel Celeron	18
IBM	ThinkPad i Series 1200, 1161-92x	Intel Celeron	18
IBM	ThinkPad i Series 1200,1161-93x	Intel Pentium III	10
IBM	ThinkPad i series 1200,1161-94x	Intel Pentium III	10
IBM	ThinkPad i Series 1300 1171-31x/32x	Intel Celeron	17
IBM	ThinkPad i Series 1300 1171-33x	Intel Celeron	18
IBM	ThinkPad i Series 1300 1171-34x	Intel Celeron	18
IBM	ThinkPad i Series 1300 1171-37x	Intel Celeron	18
IBM	ThinkPad i Series 1300 1171-5Wx/5Bx	Intel Celeron	18
IBM	ThinkPad i Series 1300 1171-61x	Intel Celeron	16
IBM	ThinkPad i Series 1300 1171-91x	Intel Pentium III	16
IBM	ThinkPad i Series 1300 1171-9Mx	Intel Pentium III	10
IBM	THinkPad i Series 1300, 1171-5Xx, 5Cx	Intel Celeron	10
IBM	ThinkPad i Series 1300, 1171-5Xx, 5Cx	Intel Celeron	10
IBM	ThinkPad i Series 1300, 1171-6Lx	Intel Celeron	18
IBM	ThinkPad i Series 1300, 1171-6Mx	Intel Pentium III	10
IBM	ThinkPad i Series 1300, 1171-7Wx	Intel Celeron	18
IBM	ThinkPad i Series 1300, 1171-9Lx	Intel Celeron	18
IBM	ThinkPad i Series 1300, 1171-9Xx	Intel Pentium III	10
IBM	ThinkPad i Series 1400 2621-xxx	Intel Pentium III	6
IBM	ThinkPad i Series 1500 2651-xxx	Intel Pentium III	6
IBM	ThinkPad i Series 1800, 2632-lxx	Intel Celeron	5
IBM	ThinkPad i Series 2611-472	Intel Pentium II	3

Table 9.6   *Popular Computers that Are ENERGY STAR Compliant (continued)*

Brand	Model	Chip	Sleep Mode (Watts)
IBM	ThinkPad i Series 2621-42x	Intel Celeron	6
IBM	ThinkPad i Series 2621-44x	Intel Celeron	6
IBM	ThinkPad i Series 2621-46x	Intel Celeron	6
IBM	ThinkPad i Series 2621-48x	Intel Celeron	6
IBM	ThinkPad i Series 2621-54x	Intel Celeron	6
IBM	ThinkPad i Series 2621-56x	Intel Celeron	6
IBM	ThinkPad i series 2627-721	Intel Pentium II	6
IBM	ThinkPad i series 2627-781	Intel Pentium III	19
IBM	ThinkPad i Series s30, 2639-43x	Intel Pentium III	5
IBM	ThinkPad i Series s30, 2639-4Ax	Intel Pentium III	5
IBM	ThinkPad i Series, 2611-410	Intel Pentium II w/ MMX	3
IBM	ThinkPad i Series, 2611-412	Intel Celeron	3
IBM	ThinkPad i Series, 2611-434	Intel Pentium II w/ MMX	3
IBM	ThinkPad i Series, 2611-450	Intel Pentium II w/ MMX	3
IBM	ThinkPad i Series, 2611-452	Intel Celeron	3
IBM	ThinkPad i Series, 2627-720	Intel Pentium II	6
IBM	ThinkPad i-series s30,2639-R3x/R5x/45x	Intel Pentium III	6
IBM	ThinkPad i-series s30,2639-RAx/RRx/4Rx	Intel Pentium III	6
IBM	ThinkPad R30 2656-4Ax/4Bx/CAx	Intel Pentium III	12
IBM	ThinkPad R30,2656-19x/21x/A2x	Intel Celeron	12
IBM	ThinkPad R30,2656-20x	Intel Celeron	12
IBM	ThinkPad R30,2656-22x/A0x/A3x	Intel Celeron	12
IBM	ThinkPad R30,2656-2Ax	Intel Celeron	12
IBM	ThinkPad R30,2656-2Bx/A1x	Intel Celeron	12

Table 9.6   *Popular Computers that Are ENERGY STAR Compliant (continued)*

Brand	Model	Chip	Sleep Mode (Watts)
IBM	ThinkPad R30,2656-30x/32x/B0x	Intel Pentium III	12
IBM	ThinkPad R30,2656-5Ax/5Bx/DAx	Intel Pentium III	12
IBM	ThinkPad R30,2656-60x/61x/62x/E0x,2657-20U,2676-20	Intel Pentium III	12
IBM	ThinkPad R30,2656-6Ax/6Bx/7Bx/EAx	Intel Pentium III	12
IBM	ThinkPad R31, 2656-25x/A5x/AKx/A4x	Intel Celeron	9.4
IBM	ThinkPad R31, 2656-3Fx/BEx/BFx	Intel Pentium III	9.4
IBM	ThinkPad R31, 2656-AEx/AFx	Intel Celeron	9.4
IBM	ThinkPad R31, 2656-E5x/E4x	Intel Pentium III	9.8
IBM	ThinkPad R31, 2656-E6x/E7x	Intel Pentium III	9.4
IBM	ThinkPad R31, 2656-EEx/EFx/EHx	Intel Pentium III	9.4
IBM	ThinkPad R31, 2656-HEx/HFx/HGx	Intel Pentium III	9.4
IBM	ThinkPad R31, 2656-J2x/J1x	Intel Pentium III	9.4
IBM	ThinkPad R31,2656-2Hx/2Gx/2Vx/1Cx/1Gx/1Fx	Intel Celeron	9.2
IBM	ThinkPad R31,2656-3Cx/KCx/KDx/KEx/KFx	Intel Celeron	9.2
IBM	ThinkPad s30, 2639-42x	Intel Pentium III	5
IBM	ThinkPad s30, 2639-4Wx	Intel Pentium III	5
IBM	ThinkPad s30,2639-53x	Intel Pentium III	6
IBM	ThinkPad s30,2639-54x	Intel Pentium III	6
IBM	ThinkPad s30,2639-5Ax	Intel Pentium III	6
IBM	ThinkPad T20, 2647-2xx/6xx	Intel Pentium III	8
IBM	ThinkPad T20, 2647-31x	Intel Pentium III	8
IBM	ThinkPad T20, 2647-4xx/8xx	Intel Pentium III	8
IBM	ThinkPad T21, 2647-2xx/6xx	Intel Pentium III	10.6
IBM	ThinkPad T21, 2647-4xx/8xx	Intel Pentium III	10.6
IBM	ThinkPad T21, 2647-5xx/9xx	Intel Pentium III	10.6
IBM	ThinkPad T22, 2647-3Cx/7Cx	Intel Pentium III	8.6

Table 9.6   *Popular Computers that Are ENERGY STAR Compliant (continued)*

Brand	Model	Chip	Sleep Mode (Watts)
IBM	ThinkPad T22, 2647-3Ex/7Ex	Intel Pentium III	9.2
IBM	ThinkPad T22, 2647-3xx/7xx	Intel Pentium III	8.9
IBM	ThinkPad T22, 2647-4Cx/8Cx	Intel Pentium III	9.5
IBM	ThinkPad T22, 2647-4xx/8xx	Intel Pentium III	8.9
IBM	ThinkPad T22, 2647-5Cx/9Cx	Intel Pentium III	10.5
IBM	ThinkPad T22, 2647-5Ex/9Ex	Intel Pentium III	11.8
IBM	ThinkPad T22, 2647-5xx/9xx	Intel Pentium III	8.9
IBM	ThinkPad T23, 2647-2Kx/6Kx	Intel Pentium III	10
IBM	ThinkPad T23, 2647-2Rx/6Rx	Intel Pentium III	10.5
IBM	ThinkPad T23, 2647-2Ux/6Ux	Intel Pentium III	10.5
IBM	ThinkPad T23, 2647-3Tx/7Tx	Intel Pentium III	10.5
IBM	ThinkPad T23, 2647-5Kx/9Kx	Intel Pentium III	11
IBM	ThinkPad T23, 2647-5Lx/9Lx	Intel Pentium III	12
IBM	ThinkPad T23, 2647-5Sx/9Sx	Intel Pentium III	12.5
IBM	ThinkPad T23, 2647-5Ux/9Ux	Intel Pentium III	12
IBM	ThinkPad T23,2647-4Rx/8Rx	Intel Pentium III	9.5
IBM	ThinkPad T23,2647-BSx/4Sx/8Sx	Intel Pentium III	9.8
IBM	ThinkPad T23,2648-4Rx/8Rx	Intel Pentium III	9.5
IBM	ThinkPad T30,2366-2xx/6xx	Intel Pentium IV	12
IBM	ThinkPad T30,2366-4xx/5xx/8xx/9xx	Intel Pentium IV	13
IBM	ThinkPad T30,2367-2xx/6xx	Intel Pentium IV	12
IBM	ThinkPad T30,2367-4xx/8xx	Intel Pentium IV	13
IBM	ThinkPad X20 266x-11U/12U	Intel Celeron	14.3
IBM	ThinkPad X20 266-x31U/32U	Intel Pentium III	14.3
IBM	ThinkPad X20 266-x34U/35U/36U/37U	Intel Pentium III	14.3
IBM	ThinkPad X20 266x-38U/39U	Intel Pentium III	14.3

Table 9.6   *Popular Computers that Are ENERGY STAR Compliant (continued)*

Brand	Model	Chip	Sleep Mode (Watts)
IBM	ThinkPad X21,266-41U,42U	Intel Pentium III	14.8
IBM	ThinkPad X21,266x,61U,62U,68U,69U	Intel Pentium III	14.8
IBM	ThinkPad X21,266x-64U,65U,66U,67U	Intel Pentium III	14.8
IBM	ThinkPad X22,266x-93J,8Bx,85x,7BJ,75J	Intel Pentium III	9.2
IBM	ThinkPad X22,266x-9Ax,92x,9Bx,95x,9Ex,90x	Intel Pentium III	9.2
IBM	ThinkPad X23,266x-DBx,D5x,D1x	Intel Pentium III	10.3
IBM	ThinkPad X23,266x-EBx,E5x	Intel Pentium III	10.2
IBM	ThinkPad X23,266x-EGx,E7x,ECx,EEx,EDx	Intel Pentium III	11.3
IBM	ThinkPad X23,266x-ELx,E6x,E4x	Intel Pentium III	10
IBM	ThinkPad X24,266x-FBx,F5x,F1x	Intel Pentium III	10.5
IBM	ThinkPad X24,266x-MLx,M6x,M4x	Intel Pentium III	13.6
IBM	ThinkPad X24,266x-MQx,MPx,MBx,M5x,M1x	Intel Pentium III	11.4
IBM	ThinkPad X24,266x-MWx,MXx,MGx,M7x,MCx	Intel Pentium III	12.2
IBM	ThinkPad T22, 2647-4Ex/8Ex, 4Gx/8Gx	Intel Pentium III	10.4
IBM	ThinkPad T23, 2647-5Rx/9Rx	Intel Pentium III	12
IBM	WorkPad Z50 2608-1Ax	Power PC	0.25
IBM	xxx	Intel Celeron	2.9
IBM	z179	Intel Celeron	2.9
Micron	Client Pro	Intel Pentium	28.8
Micron	Client Pro (CP)	Intel Pentium II	29.6
Micron	Client Pro (CS)	Intel Pentium II	26
Micron	Client Pro 350	Intel Pentium II	27.2
Micron	Client Pro 400	Intel Pentium II	27.2
Micron	Client Pro 766 xi	Intel Pentium II	29.6
Micron	Client Pro CP	Intel Pentium	29.6
Micron	Client Pro CP 400	Intel Pentium II	29.6

Table 9.6   *Popular Computers that Are ENERGY STAR Compliant (continued)*

Brand	Model	Chip	Sleep Mode (Watts)
Micron	Client Pro CX	Intel Celeron	25.5
Micron	Client Pro Dx5000	Intel Pentium III	3.3
Micron	Client Pro MRE	Intel	22.5
Micron	Client Pro MTE	Intel Pentium	23
Micron	Client Pro VXE	P55	29.6
Micron	Client Pro XLU	Intel Pentium II	23.4
Micron	Client Pro Cf	Intel Pentium III	26.5
Micron	Client Pro CG2	Intel Pentium IV	10
Micron	Client Pro CH	Intel Pentium III	3
Micron	Client Pro Cn	Intel Pentium III	3.9
Micron	Client Pro CR		6.5
Micron	Client Pro CR	Intel Pentium IV	11
Micron	Client Pro Ct	Intel Pentium III	3.5
Micron	GoBook2	Intel Pentium II	24.6
Micron	HOME MPC P166hx	Intel Pentium	28.8
Micron	M400	486	9.2
Micron	Millennia B602-E300		3.4
Micron	Millennia Max XP	AMD	14.6
Micron	Millennia (P)	Intel Pentium II	29.6
Micron	Millennia 350	Intel Pentium II	26.5
Micron	Millennia 400	Intel Pentium II	27.2
Micron	Millennia 400 (M400P-HE)	Intel Pentium II	29.6
Micron	Millennia 400 (M400P-SBE)	Intel Pentium II	29.6
Micron	Millennia 400C	Intel Pentium II	20
Micron	Millennia Max	Intel Pentium II	24
Micron	Millennia MAX GS	Intel Pentium III	24.6

Table 9.6   *Popular Computers that Are ENERGY STAR Compliant (continued)*

Brand	Model	Chip	Sleep Mode (Watts)
Micron	Millennia Max XP+	AMD Athlon	5
Micron	Millennia MME	Intel Pentium	25.1
Micron	Millennia P166hx	Intel Pentium	28.5
Micron	Millennia RS2150A	Intel Pentium III	2.6
Micron	Millennia Transport	Intel Pentium	20
Micron	Millennia TS	Intel Pentium IV	6
Micron	Millennia VX	Intel Celeron	25.2
Micron	Millennia XKU	Intel Pentium II	27.2
Micron	Millennia XRU	Intel Pentium II	23.4
Micron	Transport XPE	Intel	9.2
Micron	Trek2	Intel Pentium II	24.8
Micron	Trek2 AGP	Intel Pentium II	27.6
NEC	Power Mate 2000	Intel Pentium III	17.5
NEC	Versa Aptitude	Intel Pentium III	4
NEC	Versa AX	AMD	5
NEC	Versa DayLite	Crusoe	5
NEC	Versa E120 Daylite	Intel Pentium III	1.1
NEC	Versa L320	Intel Pentium III	0.94
NEC	Versa Lite FX	Intel Celeron	2.5
NEC	Versa Lite FX		2.5
NEC	Versa LX	Intel Pentium II	7
NEC	Versa LX	Intel Pentium II	2
NEC	Versa LXi	Intel Pentium III	7.18
NEC	Versa LXi	Intel Pentium III	7.18
NEC	Versa Note	Intel Pentium II	4
NEC	Versa Note	Intel Pentium II w/ MMX	5

Table 9.6 *Popular Computers that Are ENERGY STAR Compliant (continued)*

Brand	Model	Chip	Sleep Mode (Watts)
NEC	Versa Note	Intel Pentium II w/ MMX	4.13
NEC	Versa Note	Intel Celeron	5.72
NEC	Versa Note VXi	Intel Pentium III	4
NEC	Versa Premium	Intel Pentium III	2.8
NEC	Versa Pro R	AMD	5
NEC	Versa Rxi	Intel Pentium III	2
NEC	Versa SX	Intel Pentium II	4.5
NEC	Versa SX	Intel Pentium II	4.41
NEC	Versa SXi	Intel Pentium III	2.4
NEC	Versa TXi	Intel Pentium III	15
NEC	Versa UltraLite	Crusoe	5
NEC	Versa VX	Intel Celeron	4.75
NEC	Versa VX	Intel Celeron	4.77
NEC	Versa VX	Intel Celeron	5.31
NEC	Versa VX		5.56
Packard Bell	852	Cyrix	27
Packard Bell	925C	AMD	27
Packard Bell	Chrom@	Intel Pentium III	2
Packard Bell	Easy Note SC	Intel Pentium III	4
Packard Bell	Easy Note VX	Intel Pentium III	4
Packard Bell	Easy One DC	AMD	5
Packard Bell	Easy One Silver	AMD	11
Packard Bell	iBox 1100 A Combo	AMD K7	3.2
Packard Bell	iBox 800 C	Intel Celeron	3
Packard Bell	iBox 805 d	AMD Duron	3.2
Packard Bell	iBox Epson 680	AMD K7	3.2

Table 9.6   *Popular Computers that Are ENERGY STAR Compliant (continued)*

Brand	Model	Chip	Sleep Mode (Watts)
Packard Bell	iBox iXtreme	AMD K7	3.7
Packard Bell	iBox iXtreme 8145 A	AMD K7	3.7
Packard Bell	iMedia 4500	Intel Celeron	3
Packard Bell	iMedia 4600	Intel Celeron	3
Packard Bell	iMedia 4700	Intel Celeron	3
Packard Bell	iMedia 4800	AMD K7	3.2
Packard Bell	iMedia 4812 d	AMD Duron	3.2
Packard Bell	iMedia 4900	AMD K7	3.2
Packard Bell	iMedia 5105	Intel Pentium IV	5.7
Packard Bell	iMedia5205	Intel Pentium IV	5.7
Packard Bell	Pro Note VXi	Intel Pentium III	4
Packard Bell	ProLite NC	Intel Pentium III	15
Packard Bell NEC	Z1	Intel Pentium III	28
Panasonic	CF-17TR42AAM	Intel Celeron	5.5
Panasonic	CF-17TR42AAMCDP	Intel Celeron	5.5
Panasonic	CF-17TR42AAMRAM	Intel Celeron	5.5
Panasonic	CF-27EA6GCAM	Intel Pentium	8.5
Panasonic	CF-27EB6GCAM	Intel Pentium	8.5
Panasonic	CF-27LBAGHCM	Intel Pentium III	8.5
Panasonic	CF-27LBAGHDM	Intel Pentium III	8.5
Panasonic	CF-27LBAGHEM	Intel Pentium III	8.5
Panasonic	CF-27RA48BAM	Intel Pentium II w/ MMX	8.5
Panasonic	CF-27RG48AAM	Intel Pentium II w/ MMX	8.5
Panasonic	CF-27RJ48AAM	Intel Pentium II w/ MMX	8.5

Table 9.6   *Popular Computers that Are ENERGY STAR Compliant (continued)*

Brand	Model	Chip	Sleep Mode (Watts)
Panasonic	CF-27RJ48BAM	Intel Pentium II w/ MMX	8.5
Panasonic	CF-28MBFAZCM	Intel Pentium III	1.67
Panasonic	CF-28MBFAZDM	Intel Pentium III	1.67
Panasonic	CF-28MBFAZEM	Intel Pentium III	1.67
Panasonic	CF-28MCFAZCM	Intel Pentium III	1.67
Panasonic	CF-28MCFAZDM	Intel Pentium III	1.67
Panasonic	CF-28MCFAZEM	Intel Pentium III	1.67
Panasonic	CF-37LBA2BDMCB	Intel Pentium III	10
Panasonic	CF-37LBA2BEM	Intel Pentium III	10
Panasonic	CF-37MBA2CCM	Intel Pentium III	10
Panasonic	CF-37MBA2CDM	Intel Pentium III	10
Panasonic	CF-37MBA2CEM	Intel Pentium III	10
Panasonic	CF-37VB62AAM	Intel Celeron	7
Panasonic	CF-45DJ48AAM	Intel Pentium	9.5
Panasonic	CF-45DJ48JAM	Intel Pentium	9.5
Panasonic	CF-45EJ48AAM	Intel Pentium	9.5
Panasonic	CF-45EJ48JAM	Intel Pentium	9.5
Panasonic	CF-45RJ48AAM	Intel Pentium II w/ MMX	9.5
Panasonic	CF-47ET6GJEM	Intel Pentium II	9.5
Panasonic	CF-47ET6JEM	Intel Pentium II	9.5
Panasonic	CF-47G48AAM	Intel Pentium II	11
Panasonic	CF-47G48GGUHM	Intel Pentium II	12
Panasonic	CF-47GY6GUAM	Intel Pentium II	11
Panasonic	CF-47KY8GUMM	Intel Pentium II	12
Panasonic	CF-48M4AAUCM	Intel Pentium III	14

Table 9.6   *Popular Computers that Are ENERGY STAR Compliant (continued)*

Brand	Model	Chip	Sleep Mode (Watts)
Panasonic	CF-48P4AUEM	Intel Pentium III	14
Panasonic	CF-48P4CUEM	Intel Pentium III	14
Panasonic	CF-48P4CUPM	Intel Pentium III	14
Panasonic	CF-48P4FAUPM	Intel Pentium III	14
Panasonic	CF-48P4FGUPM	Intel Pentium III	14
Panasonic	CF-48P4RAUPM	Intel Pentium III	14
Panasonic	CF-48P4RGUPM	Intel Pentium III	14
Panasonic	CF-48R4GDUEM	Intel Pentium III	14
Panasonic	CF-48R4GDUPM	Intel Pentium III	14
Panasonic	CF-48R4GKUEM	Intel Pentium III	14
Panasonic	CF-48R4GKUPM	Intel Pentium III	14
Panasonic	CF-48R4GMUPM	Intel Pentium III	14
Panasonic	CF-48R4SDUPM	Intel Pentium III	14
Panasonic	CF-48R4SKUPM	Intel Pentium III	14
Panasonic	CF-71DJ48BAM	Intel Pentium II	8
Panasonic	CF-71EY6GBAM	Intel Pentium II	9
Panasonic	CF-71GYAGBAM	Intel Pentium II	9
Panasonic	CF-72N3FCZCM	Intel Pentium III	14
Panasonic	CF-72N3FCZDM	Intel Pentium III	14
Panasonic	CF-72N3FCZEM	Intel Pentium III	14
Panasonic	CF-M33W5M	Intel Pentium II w/ MMX	4
Panasonic	CF-M34JA2BCM	Intel Pentium III	12
Panasonic	CF-M34JA2BDM	Intel Pentium III	12
Panasonic	CF-M34JA2BEM	Intel Pentium III	12
Panasonic	CF-M34T42AAMADSM	Intel Celeron	5.5
Panasonic	CF-M34T42AAMCDPM	Intel Celeron	5.5

Table 9.6   *Popular Computers that Are ENERGY STAR Compliant (continued)*

Brand	Model	Chip	Sleep Mode (Watts)
Panasonic	CF-M34T42AAMM	Intel Celeron	5.5
Panasonic	CF-M34T42AAMRAMM	Intel Celeron	5.5
Power Mate	PM 5100	Intel Celeron	23
Power Mate	PM 5100	Intel Pentium II	24
Power Mate	PM ES5200	Intel Celeron	27
Power Mate	PM ES5200	Intel Pentium III	28
Power Mate	PM ES5200	Intel Pentium II	28
Power Mate	PM 8100	Intel Celeron	25
Power Mate	PM 8100	Intel Celeron	25
Power Mate	PM 8100	Intel Celeron	25
Power Mate	PM 8100	Intel Pentium II	28
Power Mate	PM 8100	Intel Pentium II	29
Power Mate	PM 8100	Intel Pentium II	29
Power Mate	PMS 100	Intel Celeron	27
Sharp	PC-3020	Intel Pentium	9
Sharp	PC-3030	Intel Pentium	3
Sharp	PC-3040	Intel Pentium	3
Sharp	PC-3060	Intel Pentium	9
Sharp	PC-3070	Intel Pentium	3
Sharp	PC-9020	Intel Pentium	8.4
Sharp	PC-9030	Intel Pentium	8.4
Sharp	PC-9050	Intel Pentium	8.4
Sharp	PC-9080	Intel Pentium	3.5
Sharp	PC-9300D	Intel Pentium	3
Sharp	PC-9300T	Intel Pentium	3
Sharp	PC-9320T	Intel Pentium	1.5

Table 9.6   *Popular Computers that Are ENERGY STAR Compliant (continued)*

Brand	Model	Chip	Sleep Mode (Watts)
Sharp	PC-9330T	Intel	3
Sharp	PC-9340T	Intel	3
Sharp	PC-9700T	Intel Pentium	3.5
Sharp	PC-9800T	Intel Pentium	7.1
Sharp	PC-9820-T	Intel	10.65
Sharp	PC-A100	Intel	3.4
Sharp	PC-A150	Intel Pentium II w/ MMX	3.4
Sharp	PC-A250	Intel Pentium II	7.5
Sharp	PC-A280	Intel Pentium II	30
Sharp	PC-A290	Intel Pentium II	30
Sharp	PC-A800		9.1
Sharp	PC-A810	Intel Pentium II	10.9
Sharp	PC-AR50	Intel Pentium III	1.6
Sharp	PC-M100	Intel	6.5
Sharp	PC-M200	Intel	6.5
Sharp	PC-UM10	Intel Pentium III	2.2
Sharp	PC-UM10M	Intel Pentium III	2.2
Sharp	PC-UM20	Intel Pentium III	4.3
Sharp	PC-W100D	Intel Pentium	0.5
Sharp	PC-W100T	Intel Pentium	0.5
Shuttle	Coretech II	Intel Celeron	12
Siemens	Activy 210	Cyrix GXm	27.4
Siemens	Mobile 800	Intel Pentium II	13.12
Siemens	SCENIC 320	Intel Pentium	20.8
Siemens	SCENIC 350	Intel Pentium II w/ MMX	23.6

→ **Table 9.6** *Popular Computers that Are ENERGY STAR Compliant (continued)*

Brand	Model	Chip	Sleep Mode (Watts)
Siemens	SCENIC 351	Intel Pentium II	24.9
Siemens	SCENIC 360	Intel Pentium III	25.22
Siemens	SCENIC 361	Intel Pentium II	24.9
Siemens	SCENIC 361	Intel Pentium III	25
Siemens	SCENIC 361	Intel Pentium III	27.94
Siemens	SCENIC 361	Intel Pentium III	27.35
Siemens	SCENIC 365	Intel Pentium III	27.15
Siemens	SCENIC 461	Intel Pentium III	28.54
Siemens	SCENIC 461	Intel Pentium III	27.94
Siemens	SCENIC 521	Intel Celeron	24
Siemens	SCENIC 560	Intel Pentium III	26.26
Siemens	SCENIC 560	Intel Pentium III	28.7
Siemens	SCENIC 560	Intel Pentium III	24.77
Siemens	SCENIC 560	Intel Pentium III	28.6
Siemens	SCENIC 562	Intel Pentium III	25.27
Siemens	SCENIC 600	Intel Pentium III	28.2
Siemens	SCENIC 600	Intel Pentium III	29.67
Siemens	SCENIC 621	Intel Celeron	26.5
Siemens	SCENIC 650	Intel Pentium III	29.7
Siemens	SCENIC 661	Intel Pentium III	29.67
Siemens	SCENIC 662	Intel Pentium III	22.76
Siemens	SCENIC 665	Intel Pentium III	26.73
Siemens	SCENIC 865	Intel Pentium III	28.23
Siemens	SCENIC 865	Intel Pentium III	25.6
Siemens	SCENIC eB	Intel Pentium III	29.2
Siemens	SCENIC eL	Intel Pentium III	29.2

Table 9.6   *Popular Computers that Are ENERGY STAR Compliant (continued)*

Brand	Model	Chip	Sleep Mode (Watts)
Siemens	SCENIC Mobile 750	Intel Pentium III	17.2
Sony	NTE-D101		12
Sony	NTE-D101	Power PC	11
Sony	PNC-D101		12
Sun	Java Station	SPARC 2	27
Sun	Java Station "Tower"	SPARC 2	14
Sun	SPARCStation 10	SUPRA-SPARC	5
Sun	SPARCStation 10SX	SUPRA-SPARC	5
Sun	SPARCStation 20	SUPRA-SPARC	3.5
Sun	Sun Blade 1000	ULTRA-SPARC-III	86
Sun	Sun Ray 1	SPARC 2	17
Sun	Sun Ray 100	SPARC 2	23.9
Sun	Sun Ray 150	SPARC 2	31.1
Sun	Ultra 1 Model 140	ULTRA-SPARC	4
Sun	Ultra 1 Model 170	ULTRA-SPARC	4
Sun	Ultra 10	ULTRA-SPARC	2
Sun	Ultra 10	ULTRA-SPARC	2.3
Sun	Ultra 10	ULTRA-SPARC	2.3
Sun	Ultra 10	ULTRA-SPARC	2.3
Sun	Ultra 10-B	ULTRA-SPARC	2.4
Sun	Ultra 10-C	ULTRA-SPARC	2.3
Sun	Ultra 2 Model 1170	ULTRA-SPARC	9.7
Sun	Ultra 2 Model 1200	ULTRA-SPARC	9.7
Sun	Ultra 2 Model 2170	ULTRA-SPARC	9.7
Sun	Ultra 2 Model 2200	ULTRA-SPARC	9.7
Sun	Ultra 5	ULTRA-SPARC	2

Table 9.6   *Popular Computers that Are ENERGY STAR Compliant (continued)*

Brand	Model	Chip	Sleep Mode (Watts)
Sun	Ultra 60	ULTRA-SPARC	2.2
Sun	Ultra 80	SPARC 2	11
Sun	Ultra 30-250	SPARC 2	12.4
Sun	Ultra 30-300	SPARC 2	12.4
Sun	Ultra 5	ULTRA-SPARC	2.6
Sun	Ultra 5	ULTRA-SPARC	2.6
Sun	Ultra 5	ULTRA-SPARC	2.6
Sun	Ultra 5	ULTRA-SPARC	2.5
Sun	Ultra 5-C	ULTRA-SPARC	2.5
Sun	Ultra 5-D	ULTRA-SPARC	2.6
Tatung	ADA1022	Cyrix	22.1
Tatung	Pavilion2100/2130/2150	Intel Celeron	2.9
Tatung	Pavilion2200/2230/2250	Intel Pentium III	2.87
Tatung	TCS-5170	Intel Pentium	18.4
Tatung	TCS-5290	Intel Pentium	24.3
Tatung	TCS-5480	Intel	27.6
Tatung	TCS-5590	Intel Pentium	22
Tatung	TCS-5610	Intel Pentium	20.5
Tatung	TCS-5900	Intel Pentium	27.7
Tatung	TCS-5960	Intel Pentium	22.5
Tatung	TCS-5970	Intel Pentium	18.4
Tatung	TCS-5980	Intel	27.7
Tatung	TCS-6610	Intel Pentium Pro	20.5
Tatung	TDA1022	Cyrix	21.5
Tatung	TDA1153	Intel Pentium	17.8
Tatung	TDB1153	Intel Pentium	18.4

Table 9.6   *Popular Computers that Are ENERGY STAR Compliant (continued)*

Brand	Model	Chip	Sleep Mode (Watts)
Tatung	TMP-5100	Intel Pentium	29.1
Tatung	TMP-6000	Intel Pentium II	23
Tatung	TNP-4453	Intel	16.1
Tatung	TTB3157	AMD K6	24.8
Tatung	TTC10222	Cyrix	16.5
Tatung	TTD2150	Intel	26.8
Tatung	TTD2261	Intel	27.6
Tatung	TTE3032	Cyrix	15.6
Tatung	TTE3156	Intel	26.8
Tatung	TTE3274	Intel Pentium	25.6
Tatung	TTF 2150	AMD K6	26.8
Tatung	TTF2280	Intel Pentium	29.5
Tatung	TTM2285, TTM 2286		23
Tatung	TTM2700	AMD	29.7
Toshiba	10XCS	P54	9
Toshiba	110CT	Intel Pentium	8.5
Toshiba	2800 Series	Intel Pentium III	17
Toshiba	420CDS	Intel Pentium	11.5
Toshiba	420CDT	Intel Pentium	9.7
Toshiba	425CDS	Intel Pentium	11.5
Toshiba	425CDT	Intel Pentium	9.7
Toshiba	500CDT	Intel Pentium	18.2
Toshiba	500CS	Intel Pentium	14.7
Toshiba	700 CT	Intel Pentium	9
Toshiba	710CDT	Intel Pentium	15
Toshiba	720CDT	Intel Pentium	15

Table 9.6   *Popular Computers that Are ENERGY STAR Compliant (continued)*

Brand	Model	Chip	Sleep Mode (Watts)
Toshiba	Protege 610 CT	P54	7.9
Toshiba	Satellite 1000	Intel Celeron	2.29
Toshiba	Satellite 1005	Intel Celeron	2.29
Toshiba	Satellite 1200	Intel Pentium III	2.63
Toshiba	Satellite 1200	Intel Pentium III	2.6
Toshiba	Satellite 1200	Intel Pentium III	2.65
Toshiba	Satellite 1200	Intel Celeron	2.6
Toshiba	Satellite 1200	Intel Celeron	2.62
Toshiba	Satellite 30 series	Intel Celeron	7.96
Toshiba	Satellite Pro 400	P54	6.9
Toshiba	T410CDT	P54	6.9
Toshiba	T41XCS	P54	6.7
Toshiba	V3300M	Intel Pentium III	22.9
Unisys	Aquanta LN Series	Intel Pentium	4
Unisys	CMT50073-ZA	Intel Pentium	26
Unisys	CMT50074	Intel Pentium	24
Unisys	CMT60061-ZA	Intel Pentium	26
Unisys	CMT60072-251	Intel Pentium Pro	27.2
Unisys	CMT60072-ZA	Intel Pentium	28
Unisys	CMT623371	Intel Pentium	25.8
Unisys	CMT623373	Intel Pentium	27.2
Unisys	CMT626673-FD	Intel Pentium	27.2
Unisys	CWD4001101-ZDL	486	15
Unisys	CWD5001101-ZDL	Intel Pentium	15
Unisys	CWD5001-ZA	Intel Pentium	15
Unisys	CWP 50073-ZA	Intel Pentium	26

Table 9.6   *Popular Computers that Are ENERGY STAR Compliant (continued)*

Brand	Model	Chip	Sleep Mode (Watts)
Unisys	CWP 513351	Intel Pentium	25.8
Unisys	CWP50021	P54	18
Unisys	CWP50033-Z	Intel Pentium	21.2
Unisys	CWP50033-ZA	Intel Pentium	21.2
Unisys	CWP513332	P54	20
Unisys	CWP513362	P54	24.7
Unisys	CWP516673	Intel Pentium	26
Unisys	CWV410021-35A	486	21
Unisys	CWV46621-35A	486	21
Unisys	ELI410035-35A	486	21
Unisys	ELI46635-35A	486	21
Unisys	FSD12041	Intel Pentium	25.2
Unisys	MPC520011-20	Intel Pentium	25.5
Unisys	NBC4734-D8/T8T	486	4
Unisys	NBF 5131131-10D/80D	Intel Pentium	4
Unisys	NBF 5151211-14T/20T	Intel Pentium	4
Unisys	NBF50022-ZT	Intel	3.08
Unisys	NBF5121042-12T	P54	3.7
Unisys	NBF5121042-12T	Intel Pentium	10
Unisys	NBF5131211-14T	Intel Pentium	4.9
Unisys	NBF5901041-80D/T	Intel Pentium	1.5
Unisys	NBV5131131-10D	Intel Pentium	4.9
Unisys	NF50021.ZAD	P54	3.7
Unisys	NPC516611-12	Intel Pentium	25.5
Unisys	WP3200	Cyrix	8
Unisys	WP3230	GX1	8

Table 9.6   *Popular Computers that Are ENERGY STAR Compliant (continued)*

Brand	Model	Chip	Sleep Mode (Watts)
Unisys	WP3235	GX1	9
Unisys	WP3320	Cyrix	10
Unisys	WP3360	Cyrix GXm	10
Unisys	WP3520	Cyrix	12.7
Unisys	WP8230	GX1	8
Unisys	WP8235	GX1	9
Unisys	WP8360		10
Wyse	WT1200LE	Cyrix	8
Wyse	WT3200LE	Cyrix	8
Wyse	WT3230LE	Cyrix	8
Wyse	WT3235LE	GX1	9
Wyse	WT3320SE	Cyrix	10
Wyse	WT3355SE	Cyrix GXm	13.3
Wyse	WT3360SE	Cyrix	10
Wyse	WT3530LE	GX1	12
Wyse	WT3630LE	Cyrix	29
Wyse	WT3720SE	Cyrix	12.7
Wyse	WT3730LE	Cyrix	13
Wyse	WT5357	Cyrix GXm	13.3
Wyse	WT8230LE	Cyrix	8
Wyse	WT8235LE	GX1	9
Wyse	WT8360SE	Cyrix GXm	10

Source: U.S. Environmental Protection Agency

10

Principle Nine: Properly Recycle Used Computer Equipment

> *Although electronic waste is less than 10 percent of the current solid waste stream, it is growing two to three times faster than any other waste stream. In 1998, of the 20 million computers taken out of service, only 2.3 million, which is slightly more than 10 percent, were recycled. Between 2000 and 2007, as many as 500 million personal computers will become obsolete.*

—U.S. Environmental Protection Agency

10.1   Why recycle?

There are several compelling reasons to recycle information technology. Environmental impact is certainly a key concern. Advances in information technology can quickly render systems obsolete. More than 100 million personal computers became obsolete from 1995 to 2000. Each year millions of pieces of computer equipment were disposed of in landfills. Data compiled by the EPA show how many computers are out of use, recycled, and landfilled:

- The average life span of a computer is two years (compared with five years in 1997).

- By 2004, there will be 325 million obsolete computers in the United States, according to the National Safety Council's Environmental Health Center.

- Between 2000 and 2007, 500 million personal computers will become obsolete, according to the National Recycling Coalition.

- Five percent of all computers ever bought in the United States are believed to be stored in closets, basements, and garages.

- In 1998, of the 20 million computers taken out of service, 2.3 million (slightly more than 10 percent) were recycled, according to the National Recycling Coalition.

- Electronics waste is less than 10 percent of the current solid waste stream but is growing two to three times faster than any other waste stream. Alameda County in California found that 1.25 percent of materials landfilled were electronic products, amounting to 19,000 tons in 1995.

- According to Carnegie Mellon University, by 2005 55 million personal computers (PCs) will be landfilled.

Discarded electronic equipment is a concern, because electronics are made with valuable resources, such as precious metals, engineered plastics, glass, and other materials, all of which require energy to manufacture. When equipment is thrown away, these resources cannot be recovered and additional pollution will be generated to manufacture new products out of virgin materials.

Users should be cautious of how old computers and peripherals are disposed of for security and privacy reasons as well. Old systems can store confidential information, user names, passwords, and other sensitive information. In addition, software for which an organization has purchased licenses could be on the systems, which may result in a violation of the software licensing agreement.

According to the Silicon Valley Toxics Coalition, electronic computer equipment is a complicated assembly of more than 1,000 materials, many of which are highly toxic, such as chlorinated and brominated substances, toxic gases, toxic metals, photoactive and biologically active materials, acids, plastics, and plastic additives. The comprehensive health impacts of the mixtures and material combinations in the products are often not known. The production of semiconductors, printed circuit boards, disk drives, and monitors uses particularly hazardous chemicals, and workers in chip manufacturing are reporting cancer clusters and birth defects. In addition, new evidence is revealing that computer recycling employees have high levels of dangerous chemicals in their blood.

Electronic equipment contains metals and other materials that can become hazardous to human health and the environment if they are not properly managed, including the following:

- Cadmium. The largest source of cadmium in municipal waste is rechargeable nickel-cadmium (NiCad) batteries, commonly found in laptop computers.

- Lead. Monitors and televisions contain a picture tube, known as a cathode ray tube, which contains leaded glass and is the largest source of lead in municipal waste.

- Mercury. Electronic waste is a leading source of mercury in municipal waste.

10.2   What to recycle

According to the International Association of Electronics Recyclers, electronics equipment is a product or apparatus that has its primary functions provided by electronics circuitry and components (semiconductor devices, integrated circuits, transistors, diodes), passive components (resistors, capacitors, inductors), electro-optical components (CRTs, LEDs, CCDs, lasers), and electronics packaging (printed circuit boards, connectors). Most information technology meets this definition, as is shown in Table 10.1.

10.3   Choosing a disposition method for information technology

There are several ways to recycle information technology. The method that is best for your organization will depend on numerous factors as well as the geographical location of the equipment. You should always consult corporate counsel about your disposal requirements.

In some cases you may find it necessary to actually have equipment destroyed for security or privacy protection reasons. If this is the case, you

Table 10.1   *Information Technologies that Require Recycling as Electronics Equipment*

ATMs	digital cameras	PDAs
bank teller machines	encryption systems	point-of-sale devices
calculators	fax machines	printing systems
cell phones	imaging systems	scanners
central processing units	monitoring/detection equipment	servers
computer monitors	networking equipment	storage devices
copiers	pagers	telephones
data entry devices	PBXs	workstations

need to contact a recycler that will provide you a certificate to show that the equipment was actually destroyed.

In other cases you may be able to have large amounts of equipment de-manufactured. This means that the equipment is broken down into usable components of recycleable material. The remains are usually sold to companies that will resell components or process material for use in other manufacturing situations.

If equipment is new enough to be of interest to used-equipment dealers or other end-user organizations, you may be able to dispose of the equipment on the used market. Note, however, that once equipment becomes five to six years old it has little if any resale value.

Information technology can also be donated to schools, nonprofit organizations that place equipment in schools or provide it to people that cannot afford to purchase it, or educational programs in which people are learning how to repair or refurbish information technology. There are also organizations that accept donated information technology that demanufacture the equipment and recycle basic materials.

In addition, there are numerous computer recyclers that will dispose of equipment for a fee. These companies use a variety of disposal approaches. Caution is urged in choosing a recycler. You should make sure that a recycling firm will certify that equipment has been disposed of in an agreed-on manner. Many of these companies ship equipment offshore and to China for demanufacturing, and many of those operations are severe polluters.

10.3.1   What it costs to dispose of information technology

Getting rid of used computer equipment, desktop systems, and monitors is becoming a challenge for most companies. Various plans have surfaced over the last few years, and most have gone out of style. There is such a large volume of equipment, especially monitors, that it is getting more difficult to dispose of it. In addition, many municipal trash services are refusing to haul away old equipment because of the cost of proper disposal.

The computer recycling business is booming in some places, and the charges are relatively high. The cost of having monitors properly disposed of ranges from $10 to $20 per monitor. To have obsolete printers, disks, or computers removed and disposed of ranges from $0.30 to $1 per pound. Disposal costs for various types of computer equipment are shown in Table 10.2.

Table 10.2   *Disposal Costs for Computer Equipment*

Computer Equipment	Disposal Cost ($)
½-inch tape drive	65
Circuit board	4
Color printer cartridge	5
Desktop printer	15
Desktop system	15
Floppy drive	15
Keyboard	5
Laser printer (large)	35
Laser printer (small)	15
Magnetic media	2
Minicomputer disk drive	50
Minicomputer double rack	150
Minicomputer single rack	125
Modem	10
Monitor	20
Monitor w/keyboard	25
PC hard drive	10
Power supply	9
Rack-mounted modems	25
Storage array (small)	125
Tape drive (small)	45
Workstation system	40

10.4   How recycling is evolving into product stewardship

Product stewardship is a product-centered approach to environmental protection that is supported by many interest groups in the United States. Also

known as extended product responsibility (EPR), product stewardship calls on those in the product life cycle, including manufacturers, retailers, users, and disposers, to share responsibility for reducing the environmental impacts of products. Product stewardship is different from the manufacturer-centered extended producer responsibility laws gaining prominence around the world. Product stewardship recognizes that product manufacturers can and must take on new responsibilities to reduce the environmental impact of their products.

However, as the sector with the closest ties to consumers, retailers are one of the gateways to product stewardship. From preferring product providers that offer greater environmental performance, to educating the consumer on how to choose environmentally preferable products, to enabling consumer return of products for recycling, retailers are an integral part of the product stewardship evolution.

In most cases, manufacturers have the greatest ability, and therefore the greatest responsibility, to reduce the environmental impacts of their products. Companies that are accepting the challenge are recognizing that product stewardship also represents a substantial business opportunity. By rethinking their products, their relationships with the supply chain, and the ultimate customer, some manufacturers are dramatically increasing their productivity, reducing costs, fostering product and market innovation, and providing customers with more value at less environmental impact. Reducing use of toxic substances, designing for reuse and recycleability, and creating takeback programs are just a few of the many opportunities for companies to become better environmental stewards of their products.

Solid waste programs in the United States are managed at the state and local level. Thus, state and local governments are essential to fostering product stewardship. A few progressive states have incorporated product stewardship objectives into their solid waste master plans and have launched cooperative efforts with industry to encourage recycling of their products. Some states have developed product stewardship–type legislation for selected products. In addition, state procurement activities can strongly encourage product stewardship innovations. In many cases, states need to work with their neighbors to develop cost-effective approaches to handling problem wastes.

Federal statutory authority to control the environmental impacts of product systems is limited. However, the EPA is actively facilitating coordination and collaboration among states, local governments, industry, and nongovernment organizations on these issues. As the nation's largest single consumer, federal agencies are using their market leverage to provide incentives for the development of products with stronger environmental attributes.

In addressing the life cycle of product systems, the EPA's Product Stewardship program has primarily focused on end-of-life considerations as a means of driving environmentally conscious design and resource conservation. To this end, the EPA's Product Stewardship program has supported projects in a number of product areas, ranging from electronics to carpet. To address the full range of life-cycle issues, the Product Stewardship program has also been working together with other EPA programs, as well as various public and private sector stakeholders across the country.

10.5 International initiatives in recycling

The European Commission is developing a Directive on Waste from Electronics and Electronic Equipment (WEEE) intended to bring some uniformity to the European Union member country requirements concerning electronics collection and recycling. The objectives of the directive are to encourage reuse, recycling, and other forms of recovery for electronics, and to minimize the risks and impacts to the environment associated with the treatment and disposal of WEEE. The most recent drafts of the WEEE Directive call for:

- Manufacturers to eliminate the use of lead, mercury, cadmium, hexavalent chromium, PBB, and PBDEs by 2008, unless their use is unavoidable.

- Governments to establish separate collection facilities for waste electrical equipment.

- Producers to take financial or physical responsibility for recycling, allowing households to return end-of-life equipment free of charge.

- Producer-paid systems to reuse or recycle waste electrical equipment according to specified targets.

- A labeling requirement for certain electrical and electronic equipment, informing users of their role in recycling, reuse, and other forms of recovery.

- Producers to be required to inform recyclers about certain aspects of the content of these equipment.

The Organization for Economic Cooperation and Development (OECD) is developing international guidelines for the environmentally sound management (ESM) of used and scrap personal computers. The

OECD plans to develop ESM guidelines for different recycelable wastes, with personal computers serving as the pilot case. The initial focus of the OECD ESM program is on waste recovery and recycling rather than product design and disposal issues.

ISO 14000 is an international standard for environmental management systems, applicable to any type and size of organization. ISO 14001 offers a common, harmonized approach for organizations to achieve and demonstrate sound environmental performance. The main objective of ISO 14001 is to help organizations manage the environmental aspects and impacts of their operations while always working toward continual improvement. The most active industries with ISO 14001 to date have been the electronics/computer group and automotive manufacturers and suppliers. Japanese companies are heavily registered to the standard, followed by a strong showing in Europe. North American companies are beginning to show strong interest.

In New South Wales, Australia, the government is helping to fund a pilot program for taking back and recycling computers in the Sydney metropolitan region. Companies involved in the pilot include Compaq and MRI, but the program will accept computers of all system types and from all manufacturers. In addition to computer recycling, the companies will develop a process for recycling CRTs from computer monitors. They will also support the development of the second-hand computer market by diverting goods collected to reuse before recycling.

The Recyle-IT! Austria (RITA) is an initiative to collect used computers from manufacturers and other companies, upgrade and repair the computers as necessary, and then sell them at reasonable prices to low-income households, schools, and voluntary organizations. The project is modeled after London-based Recycle-IT, which runs a similar scheme in the United Kingdom. The organizers of RITA hope to take back and resell 5,000 computers. Plans are also being made to replicate the project in other European countries.

Denmark's 1998 statutory order on the management of waste electrical and electronic equipment (WEEE) gave local authorities the responsibility for developing detailed regulations on the collection and recovery of end-of-life products. All parties—consumers, retailers, distributors, producers, and importers—must follow the rules established by each local council. Councils can also issue permits to manufacturers or importers, allowing them to take back, free of charge, their own products (and/or similar products) for reuse, recycling, or disposal, so long as the manufacturer or importer demonstrates that it is using processes that meet the local requirements. Consumers finance each local collection and recovery system through local taxes or collection fees. However, the Danish government has stated that it supports the idea, laid out in the European Commission's draft directive on WEEE, of having producers take financial responsibility for WEEE recycling in the future.

Germany is developing legislation that will require takeback and recycling of waste electrical products. Under the legislation, municipalities will be compelled to collect discarded electrical products, and producers will be required to treat, recover, and dispose of the products.

In Japan, starting in April 2001, manufacturers must recycle appliances, televisions, refrigerators, and air conditioners. Traditionally these products were collected by electronics shops or municipalities and crushed, landfilled, or exported. However, now there is little land left for landfill. Under the new law, manufacturers would charge a recycling fee to consumers ($20 for washing machines, $40 for refrigerators). Approximately 20 million used home appliances are disposed of annually.

The Disposal of White and Brown Goods Decree, passed in the Netherlands in 1998, requires manufacturers and importers of electrical and electronic equipment sold in the country to take back their end-of-life products for reuse or recycling. In response to the decree, the country's electronics industry has set up and financed a system for collecting and disposing of WEEE. Under the system, an official carrier transports WEEE from various collection sites to approved processing plants. There, the equipment is processed for reuse or recycling in an environmentally sound manner. Manufacturers and importers don't charge a visible fee for these services, but they can pass on the costs to consumers. The 1998 decree also sets out detailed requirements for all other parties, as follows:

- Consumers, either private or business, are given several options for disposing of end-of-life equipment, including returning it to a supplier when purchasing new equipment, offering it directly to the manufacturer (businesses only), or handing it in to the municipality (private consumers only).

- Suppliers (including dealers, retailers, and distributors) must accept used equipment free of charge when selling new equipment. Suppliers can resell this used equipment, arrange for free pick-up and transport via the official carrier, offer the equipment directly back to the manufacturer or importer, or hand it in to the municipality (provided that the WEEE came from private consumers).

■ Municipalities must accept WEEE from private consumers and suppliers, though they may charge a fee for this service. Some municipalities require that WEEE be brought to a designated collection site; others operate neighborhood collection programs. Accumulated equipment is picked up and transported for processing by the official carrier.

Sweden's ordinance on producer responsibility took effect on July 1, 2001. Dealers and manufacturers of electrical and electronic equipment are now required to take back free of charge a piece of old equipment when the customer buys a new product. They must also inform households about the takeback obligation and present a takeback plan to the municipalities. Sweden has established approximately 1,000 collection points throughout the country. The equipment must be treated at a certified facility before landfilling, shredding, or incineration. Swedish law requires these facilities to be certified according to ISO 9000, ISO 14000, or an equivalent system; further, they must separate all hazardous waste using the best available technology.

Recycling policies implemented in 1998 made Taiwan the first country to require the recycling of used computer hardware, including central processing units, monitors, and notebook computers. Consumers can return used hardware to one of 600 takeback stations operated around the country, or to a recycling company or municipal recycling facility, where the hardware is disassembled and separated for reuse or recycling. As of October 2000, roughly 1.4 million used computers had been recycled, and officials of Taiwan's Environmental Protection Administration said that they were achieving a recycling rate of about 75 percent of all used computers. In 2001, Taiwan added printers to the list of equipment that must be recycled.

10.6 Manufacturers' initiatives in recycling

The Electronics Industries Alliance (EIA) announced a pilot electronics recycling project in June 2001. Collaborating manufacturers include Canon, Hewlett-Packard, JVC, Kodak, Panasonic, Philips Electronics, Sharp, Sony, and Thomson. The EIA is now testing three different models of electronics collection and recycling:

■ Municipal collection model. The consortium of companies will contract private companies to recycle products they manufacture. The contracts will cover transportation from consolidation points to the recycling facilities. Municipalities will be responsible for collecting and consolidating used electronics.

- Retailer collection model. A selected number of retailers will hold collection events and direct returned equipment to private recyclers with whom the industry group has made arrangements. Collaborating manufacturers will reimburse the participating retailer for recycling costs based on the number of units sold. This model is intended to simulate and evaluate an advance disposal fee, which in reality (although not the case in the pilot) would be paid by the purchaser at the point of sale.

- Consumer drop-off model. The collaborating manufacturers will partner with any retailer willing to host a collection event. The retailer would contract with a recycler and charge consumers a drop-off fee for all products collected. Industry will supply funds for promotion, education, coupons, and/or rebates.

Apple Computer designs its products for ease of assembly and disassembly, using latches, snap-in connections, and single screw types requiring no specialized tools. Apple is also taking steps to increase recycleability by using materials that can be easily recycled, marking materials with international recycling codes, standardizing designs and components to facilitate materials use along product lines, and reducing the weight and amount of material used in products.

Compaq focuses on environmental stewardship during every phase of the product life cycle. For example, when Compaq engineers begin the design of a computer, they consider the environmental impact of its component parts and their readiness to be recycled when the computer is no longer useful. Design for the Environment guidelines have been developed for use across Compaq product lines on a worldwide scale.

In June 2001, Compaq and a Midwestern electronics recycling firm launched the United Recycling Industries' (URI) Electronics Take-Back Program. This program offers participating customers a 6 percent to 9 percent discount on Compaq products if consumers return used electronics equipment. URI provides shipping boxes and labels, while customers pay URI $27.99 to process up to 70 pounds of returned computers, monitors, and peripherals. URI's pilot program is currently open to residents and small businesses in seven Midwestern states.

Dell Computer, as part of a move toward an entirely green product range, is manufacturing a line of professional-level computers that are completely recycleable. Dell's OptiPlex PCs meet the stringent standards for Germany's Blue Angel environmental label, which is awarded to those products that combine improved longevity of the system and its components with a recyclable design and the opportunity to reuse and recycle used products or product components. The OptiPlex range incorporates Dell's Optiframe chassis, which uses few screws and opens with ease, making upgrades and dismantling simpler and less expensive. All of the materials in the PCs are labeled for easy recycling.

Dell has also launched DellExchange, an on-line system that provides consumers with three options for dealing with end-of-life computers, as follows:

- Trade in to receive a discount on a new computer based on fair market value

- Donation through the National Cristina Foundation

- Auction through www.dellauction.com

Gateway has offered customers a $50 rebate after they purchase a new Gateway computer and then donate or recycle their old system. Customers are responsible for finding a recycler or receiving organization for their computers, after which they submit confirmation forms to Gateway to receive the rebate.

Hewlett-Packard (HP) has incorporated design improvements that facilitate disassembly and has initiated a computer hardware takeback program. This involves using a foam chassis, which reduces the parts needed for some products, simplifies disassembly, and reduces the amount of protective packaging required during shipping. It further involves identifying the resin content of plastic parts by marking the plastic instead of using a paper label to facilitate recycling.

HP announced in May 2001 that it will take back computer hardware from any manufacturer. The cost of this service ranges from $13 to $34 per item, depending upon the type and quantity of hardware to be returned. HP will assess all returned hardware to determine whether it meets minimum criteria for donating to nonprofit organizations. If the computer has no value as a whole product, HP and its recycling partner, Noranda, will disassemble and separate products into their key commodities, such as steel, aluminum, copper, and plastics, and sell the raw materials to manufacturers, who will use the recycled materials to make new products.

IBM's PC Recycling Service allows consumers and small businesses to recycle any manufacturer's PCs, including peripherals. For a fee of $29.99, the customer receives a prepaid mailing label and ships the computer equipment via UPS to Envirocycle, an electronics recycler in Pennsylvania. Depending on its age and performance capability, the computer will either be recycled in an environmentally responsible manner or refurbished for donation through Gifts in Kind International. If the computer can be donated, the donor receives a receipt, which can be used for tax deduction purposes.

Intel has a number of product stewardship initiatives underway, including one design project involving an industry group to standardize server building blocks, such as the chassis, power supplies, and boards. This standardization allows consumers to upgrade, add, or remove components without having to purchase an entirely new system. In addition, all motherboards, PCs, workstations, and server major subassemblies can be disassembled and upgraded with only a screwdriver. Intel has prevented packaging waste by moving to lightweight shipping trays and tray caps, maximizing the number of CPUs that can be shipped in a box, and replacing foam padding with paper. To keep track of packaging use, the company established a database that can track the amount of packaging material shipped into each country.

Panasonic's High Vision television model, offered in Japan, uses a screwless locking structure that reduces the number of parts by 80 percent compared with previous models. The company also has reduced the number of polystyrene resin grades used in its televisions from 20 to 4, greatly improving the recycleability of parts. Panasonic is also working with the states of New Jersey and Connecticut, along with manufacturers Sharp and Sony, in a Recycling Infrastructure Development Pilot Program. The goal of this project is to stimulate the development of collection infrastructure, recycling technology, and end markets for household electronics in New Jersey and Connecticut.

Philips Electronics has a strong global EcoDesign program, supported by the Delft University of Technology in the Netherlands. Philips believes that EcoDesign principles can be a strong basis to enhance business and that EcoDesign is not chiefly a technical activity anymore but a concept to be embedded in the business value chain. The company's EcoVision program aims to integrate EcoDesign into every aspect of product development across all product divisions, focusing on five key areas: weight, hazardous substances, energy use, recycling, and packaging. Within Philips, business divisions are being challenged to develop and market Green Flagship products.

Sharp Electronics is significantly reducing material usage in the design of its televisions. The company is reducing the types of plastics used by one-half and the number of parts by one-third. Similarly, the company has reduced the weight of its VCRs by 27 percent and the number of parts by 15 percent. Sharp is also working with the states of New Jersey and Connecticut, along with manufacturers Panasonic and Sony, in a Recycling Infrastructure Development Pilot Program. The goal of this project is to stimulate the development of collection infrastructure, recycling technology, and end markets for household electronics in New Jersey and Connecticut.

Sony Electronics aims to reduce its products' power consumption by 30 percent by 2005, compared with average energy consumption of products manufactured in 2000. Many of the company's products have other environmental features as well. For example, the body and mounting brackets of one of its computer lines are aluminum for ease of recycling. This product is packaged only in cardboard. Another laptop computer is constructed with a rigid magnesium alloy for all four sides, which reduces the use of plastic and makes the product easier to recycle. Sony has also teamed with the Minnesota Office of Environmental Assistance and Waste Management, Inc., to establish a takeback and recycling program for Sony electronics products in Minnesota.

Xerox is taking more responsibility for its products at end of life by increasing takeback and remanufacturing its durable as well as consumable products. Xerox's asset recycling program is encouraging customers to return a wide range of products, including printers and toner bottles. Employees disassemble and sort parts from returned equipment that meet internal criteria for remanufacturing. Remanufactured parts are incorporated into new products. Parts that do not meet remanufacturing criteria and cannot be repaired are ground, melted, or otherwise converted into basic raw materials. The company integrates remanufacturing into the same assembly lines that produce new products. To achieve the company's zero waste goal, the eventual recycling of products is anticipated in product design.

10.7 Purchasing environmentally preferable products

Environmentally preferable purchasing (EPP) is the purchase of products and services that have a lesser or reduced effect on human health and the environment as compared with other products and services that serve the same purpose.

The U.S. federal government is committed to minimizing the adverse environmental impacts of its purchases. Spending more than $200 billion annually on the purchase of products and services, the federal government's commitment to EPP is helping increase the availability of products and services with improved environmental performance. EPP outlines the federal government's approach for incorporating environmental considerations into its purchasing decisions by establishing five guiding principles.

10.7.1 Principle one: Include environmental considerations as part of the normal purchasing process

The EPA encourages all purchasers to examine environmental considerations along with traditional factors such as product safety, price, performance, and availability when making purchasing decisions. Each of these factors, including environmental performance, provides important information about a product's or a service's overall value and quality, which are the ultimate criteria for all government purchasing decisions. As a result, environmental considerations should be a regular part of the normal purchasing process.

10.7.2 Principle two: Emphasize pollution prevention early in the purchasing process

Preventing pollution is far less costly and more effective than correcting a problem after it has occurred. EPP can be an important part of any pollution prevention effort by identifying environmental implications before purchase of a product or service. Emphasizing pollution prevention throughout the purchasing process can lead to significant savings (such as avoided disposal costs) and to improvements in product performance.

10.7.3 Principle three: Examine multiple environmental attributes throughout a product's or service's life cycle

The EPA encourages purchasers to select products and services with as few adverse environmental impacts in as many life-cycle stages as possible. A product's life cycle includes activities associated with raw material acquisition, manufacturing, packaging and transportation, product use, and ultimate disposal. When examining the life cycle of a service, particular emphasis is placed on the use phase of the products required to provide the service, although the entire life cycle of the products being used should be examined carefully. To determine environmental preferability, the EPA suggests purchasers compare the severity of environmental impacts throughout the life cycle of the product or service with those of competing products and services.

Environmental preferability should also reflect the consideration of multiple environmental attributes, such as increased energy efficiency, reduced toxicity, or reduced impacts on fragile ecosystems at each phase in the life cycle. Although the determination of environmental preferability should be based on multiple environmental attributes examined from a life-cycle perspective, purchasing decisions can be made based on a single environmental attribute, such as recycled content or energy efficiency, when that attribute is the strongest distinguishing characteristic of a product's or service's environmental preferability. Positive attributes of products include:

- Manufactured with recycled content

- Has easy recycleability

- High product disassembly potential

- Has high durability

- Has high reusability

- Is reconditioned or remanufactured

- There is a takeback program in place

- Bio-based materials are used to manufacture the product

- Favorable energy-efficiency ratings

- Manufacturing process is high in water efficiency

10.7.4   Principle four: Compare relevant environmental impacts when selecting products and services

The EPA recognizes that competing products might have different environmental impacts. For example, one product might consume significantly less energy while another might be less water polluting. While the ideal solution would be to find a product that maximizes both of these environmental attributes, sometimes purchasers must choose between them, which can be a challenging endeavor. To compare the environmental impacts of products or services, EPA recommends considering the following:

- Choose products and services with easily reversible environmental impacts or impacts with short durations. Impacts that can be reversed in years are preferable to those requiring centuries.

- Choose products and services with local rather than global environmental impacts. An increase in local toxicity, while undesirable, generally is preferable to global impacts, such as those caused by the release of ozone-depleting substances.

- Choose products and services with the greatest improvement in environmental performance. For example, a product that significantly reduces toxicity might be preferable to one that makes only a minimal reduction in solid waste generation.

- Choose products and services that are at least equivalent to traditional products and services in protecting human health. A product cannot be considered environmentally preferable if it increases risks to human health.

10.7.5   Principle five: Collect and base purchasing decisions on accurate and meaningful information about environmental performance

Making an environmentally preferable purchasing decision requires accurate and meaningful environmental attribute information for each stage in a product's life cycle. EPA encourages purchasers to seek out this information from manufacturers or suppliers when researching products and services and to base their decisions on this information.

10.8   Nonprofit organizations that accept technology

There are numerous organizations and programs across the country that accept donations of information technology. The organizations listed in Table 10.3 are geared to help educational organizations as well as provide computers to those who cannot afford to purchase them. The list is organized by state. It is advisable to check your local telephone directory for current telephone numbers, additional organizations, and updated contact information.

Table 10.3   *Nonprofit Organizations that Accept Information Technology*

State/Organization	City
Arizona	
Southwest Public Recycling Association	Tucson
Tucson Metropolitan Ministry Community Closet	Tucson
California	
Computer Recycling Project	San Francisco

Table 10.3   *Nonprofit Organizations that Accept Information Technology (continued)*

State/Organization	City
Computers & Education	Santa Rosa
Detwiler Foundation	La Jolla
DigiQuest Learning Center	San Rafael
Goodwill Industries of Orange County	Santa Anna
Kidsource Online	San Jose
LA Shares	Los Angeles
Lazarus Foundation	Santa Barbara
Marin Computer Resource Center	San Rafael
NETI Initiative	Sherman Oaks
NICR	San Clemente
Nonprofit Services	Emeryville
Project Y.E.S.	San Francisco
Salvation Army	Oakland
Shelter Hill Computer Learning Center	Mill Valley
Youth For Service	San Francisco
Connecticut	
Bristol Resource Recovery Facility	Bristol
Computers 4 Kids	Waterbury
National Cristina Foundation	Greenwich
District of Columbia	
Davis Memorial Goodwill Industries	Washington, DC
Georgia	
Computers for Classrooms	East Point
Computers for Families	Hephzibah
Materials for the Arts	Atlanta
StRUT-Georgia	Sandersville
Zentech	Atlanta

Table 10.3   *Nonprofit Organizations that Accept Information Technology (continued)*

State/Organization	City
Illinois	
Educational Assistance Ltd.	Wheaton
Goodwill Industries	Chicago
Salvation Army	Chicago
Kentucky	
McConnell Technology & Training Center	Louisville
Maryland	
Lazarus Foundation	Columbia
Phoenix Project	Ellicott City
Massachusetts	
East West Education Development Foundation	Boston
Mindshare Collaborative	Brighton
Nonprofit Computer Connection	Boston
YouthBuild Boston	Boston
Minnesota	
Goodwill Industries of St. Paul	St. Paul
Missouri	
Yellow Bug Computers	Columbia
New Jersey	
La Casa de Don Pedro	Newark
Paterson Education Fund	Paterson
New York	
Computers for Africa Project	New York
Long Island Arts Council at Freeport	Freeport
Robin Hood Foundation	New York
Women's Environment and Development Organization	New York

Table 10.3   *Nonprofit Organizations that Accept Information Technology (continued)*

State/Organization	City
North Carolina	
IBM Credit Corporation	Raleigh
Ohio	
Community Resource Center	Cincinnati
MUSIC Computer Recycling Program	Lorain
Oregon	
FreeGeek	Portland
Oregon Public Networking	Eugene
STRUT (Student Recycling Used Technology)	Hillsboro
Pennsylvania	
Goodwill Computer Recycling Center	Pittsburgh
Philadelphia Area Computer Society (PACS)	Philadelphia
South Carolina	
Computer Re-Use Network (CoRN)	Hollywood
Tennessee	
Jericho Road/Cooperative Computer Ministry	Memphis
Texas	
Computer Recycling for Education and Community Enhancement	San Antonio
Dallas Computer Literacy Program	Dallas
Houston Area League of PC Users	Houston
Virginia	
Gifts In Kind America	Alexandria
Second Chance Program	Fairfax
Wisconsin	
Tech Corps Wisconsin	Racine

10.9　What a donation is worth

When donating equipment to a nonprofit organization or to a school, it is likely that you will be eligible for a tax deduction. Computer Economics has provided market price analysis on information technology for over 20 years and researches fair market value (FMV) and makes residual value forecasts. This service helps you determine the amount you can deduct for making a donation.

The amount you can deduct is known as fair market value (FMV), which is defined as the estimated amount, expressed in terms of money, that may reasonably be expected for the equipment, in exchange, between a willing buyer and a willing seller, neither under any compulsion to buy or sell, with both parties reasonably cognizant of all relevant facts and circumstances. Table 10.4 shows the FMV and RVF for a wide variety of information technology.

A residual value forecast (RVF) is a projected FMV, which is derived by evaluating the age of the equipment, replacement equipment available through upgrade paths or new models, new chip technologies, initial cost, maintenance, population, age, method of sale, and other factors that may impact the future value of equipment.

Another method of valuing equipment is orderly liquidation value (OLV), which is defined as the estimated gross amount expressed in terms of money that typically could be realized from a liquidation sale, given a reasonable period of time to find a purchaser, with the seller being compelled to sell on an as-is where-is basis, as of a specific date. No freight, installation, or software charges are included in the values quoted for the equipment.

Table 10.4　*Information Technology Value*

Manufacturer	Description	Equipment Values (U.S. $)		
		FMV 2002	RVF 2003	RVF 2003
ACER	ACER 15" COLOR DISP .28DP 1024X768	79	61	44
ACER	ACERVIEW76IE 17" .27 SVGA NI. 1280X1024	54	43	33
ACER	ALTOS9000 P/166 32MB NOHD TWR 4XCD	100	75	53
Alps	ALLEGRO 500 Printer	41	33	25

Table 10.4   *Information Technology Value (continued)*

Manufacturer	Description	Equipment Values (U.S. $)		
		FMV 2002	RVF 2003	RVF 2003
Alps	ALQ 224E Printer	41	33	25
Andrew	400 Twinax Active Hub – 14 RJ45 Ports	49	40	30
Apollo	DN5500, 8 MB/380 MB	152	113	79
Apollo	Vision Q2 LCD panel 16M color active	105	79	56
AST	Ascentia 100	115	85	60
AST	Ascentia 133	94	70	50
AST	Ascentia 910N	44	35	26
AST	Ascentia J30	96	72	51
AST	Ascentia P90	87	66	47
AST	Bravo MS, 16 MB/1.2 GB	56	45	34
AT&T	33.6 KBPS Modem	71	55	40
AT&T	444 Printer	147	109	76
AT&T	Globalyst 630	71	55	40
Brother	INTELLIFAX 3750 PPFAX 4MB 600DPI	104	78	55
Brother	MFC 7650 MULTIFUNCTION 6PPM 600DPI IM	95	71	50
C.Itoh	C.ITOH-1000	354	255	173
C.Itoh	C.ITOH-1000/800	99	74	53
C.Itoh	C.ITOH-215	44	35	26
C.Itoh	C.ITOH-300	79	61	44
C.Itoh	C.ITOH-3500/4000	42	34	25
C.Itoh	C.ITOH-400/Q	99	74	53
C.Itoh	C.ITOH-5000	105	79	56
C.Itoh	C.ITOH-600	113	84	59
C.Itoh	C.ITOH-61011	47	38	28
C.Itoh	C.ITOH-LIPS 10+	42	34	25
C.Itoh	CI 5000 DOT MATRIX SERIAL PRINTER	169	125	88

Table 10.4   *Information Technology Value (continued)*

Manufacturer	Description	Equipment Values (U.S. $)		
		FMV 2002	RVF 2003	RVF 2003
Canon	BJC7000 Printer	42	34	25
Canon	BJC-80 COL BUBJETPR PRTBL 5PPM 720X360DP	52	41	31
Canon	Innovabook 360CD Laptop	66	51	36
Cipher	F880 9-Track tape drive	71	55	40
Cipher	M891 9-Track tape drive	95	71	50
Cipher	M891-I 9 TRK PERTEC 1600BPI	42	34	25
Cipher	M891-II 9 TRK PERTEC 1600/3200BPI	54	43	33
Cipher	M990 9 TRK PERTEC 800/1600/6250BPI	115	85	60
Cipher	M990 9-Track tape drive	105	79	56
Cipher	M990-S 9 TRK SCSI 800/1600/6250BPI	155	115	80
Cipher	M995 9-Track tape drive	404	291	198
Cipher	M995C 9 TRK PERTEC 800/1600/6250BPI	268	193	131
Cipher	M995S 9 TRK SCSI 800/1600/6250BPI	268	193	131
CTX	17" COLOR MONITOR	45	36	27
CTX	17"/16.0v 25mm 1600x1200 Monitor	49	40	30
CTX	19"/18.0v 26mm 1600x1200 Monitor	63	49	35
Daewoo	17"/16.1v 28mm 1280x1024 Monitor	41	33	25
Daewoo	17"/16.2v 26mm 1600x1280 Monitor	54	43	33
Daewoo	17"/16.2v 28mm 1280x1024 Monitor	47	38	28
Data General	61005 1GB Disk Drive	204	151	106
Data General	61006 2GB Disk Drive	227	168	117
Data General	61007 4GB Disk Drive	272	196	133
Data General	6125 1600 BPI Tape Drive	181	134	94
Data General	6328 70MB DISK FOR MV2000	136	101	70
Data General	6329 120MB DISK	181	134	94

Table 10.4   *Information Technology Value (continued)*

		Equipment Values (U.S. $)		
Manufacturer	Description	FMV 2002	RVF 2003	RVF 2003
Data General	6492 727MB DISK	227	168	117
Data General	6554 662MB SCSI S.E.	227	168	117
Data General	6577 150MB QIC TAPE FOR AVIION	159	117	82
Data General	6589 6250 BPI 125IPS 9 TRACK	1,497	928	538
Data General	6676 525MB QIC TAPE DRIVE	249	185	129
Data General	6762 4MM DAT TAPE CARTRIDGE	318	229	155
Data General	6841 2GB AVIION DISK DRIVE	363	261	178
Data General	6842 2GB SCSI DIFF	590	413	268
Data General	6855 1600 BPI TAPE DRIVE	386	278	189
Data General	6885-A 4/8GB SE SCSI 4MM TAPE	363	261	178
Data General	6888-A 4/8GB DIFF. 4MM	544	381	248
Data General	79010 1GB CLARIION	272	196	133
Data General	79011 2GB CLARIION	295	212	144
Data General	79012 4GB CLARIION	363	261	178
Data General	79013 9GB CLARIION	590	413	268
Data General	AViiON AV1600	343	247	168
Data General	AViiON AV2600	615	431	280
Data General	AViiON AV300	115	85	60
Data General	AViiON AV3600	805	556	339
Data General	AViiOn AV3700R 400Mhz	917	633	386
Data General	AViiON AV4100	309	222	151
Data General	AViiON AV412	151	112	78
Data General	AViiON AV4120	447	313	203
Data General	AViiON AV4300	468	327	213
Data General	AViiON AV4320	698	482	294
Data General	AViiON AV4600	522	366	238

Table 10.4   *Information Technology Value (continued)*

		Equipment Values (U.S. $)		
Manufacturer	Description	FMV 2002	RVF 2003	RVF 2003
Data General	AViiON AV4605	605	424	275
Data General	AViiON AV4620	649	448	273
Data General	AViiON AV4625	536	375	244
Data General	AViiON AV4700	839	579	353
Data General	AViiON AV5200	302	217	148
Data General	AViiON AV5240	816	563	343
Data General	AViiON AV6200	442	309	201
Data General	AViiON AV6240	705	486	297
Data General	AViiON AV85/9500+	839	579	353
Data General	AViiON AV8500+	1,398	909	545
Data General	AViiON AV9500	447	313	203
Data General	ECLIPSE MV1000, 4MB	151	112	78
Data General	ECLIPSE MV15000	115	85	60
Data General	ECLIPSE MV2000, 4MB	159	118	82
Data General	ECLIPSE MV20000	138	102	71
Data General	ECLIPSE MV30000	3,132	1,723	844
Data General	ECLIPSE MV40000	1,062	691	414
Data General	ECLIPSE MV5500, 8MB	698	482	294
Data General	ECLIPSE MV5600, 8MB	1,343	873	524
Data General	ECLIPSE MV9300	468	327	213
Data General	ECLIPSE MV9500	385	277	189
Data General	ECLIPSE MV9800	3,356	1,846	904
Dataproducts	8500 Printer	147	109	76
Dataproducts	B1000 Printer	218	162	113
Dataproducts	B610 Printer	181	134	94
Dataproducts	LM-415 7640 3000 Printer	92	69	49

Table 10.4   *Information Technology Value (continued)*

Manufacturer	Description	Equipment Values (U.S. $)		
		FMV 2002	RVF 2003	RVF 2003
Dataproducts	LX455 Printer	246	182	127
Dataproducts	LZR 1580 POSTCRIPT L2 LASER PRINTER	87	66	47
Dataproducts	LZR-960 Printer	95	71	50
Dataproducts	M120 Printer	61	47	34
Dataproducts	MODEL 9030D 300CPS 80COL 9PIN PRINTER	44	35	26
Datasouth	CX3180 Printer	115	85	60
Datasouth	CX3220 Printer	99	74	53
Datasouth	TX5180 Printer	81	61	43
Daytek	17" EVGA Color Monitor	44	35	26
Daytek	20" EVGA Color Monitor	70	54	39
Daytek	21" EVGA Color Monitor	79	61	44
DEC	4100	2,783	1,531	750
DEC	10000/7000 128MB	140	104	73
DEC	10000/7000 256MB	420	303	206
DEC	10000/7000 2GB	1,721	1,067	619
DEC	10000/7000 512MB	534	374	243
DEC	10000/7000 64MB	140	104	73
DEC	1000A 4/233	326	235	160
DEC	1000A 4/266	365	263	179
DEC	1000A 5/500 (AA)	711	491	299
DEC	1000A 5/500 (FA)	544	381	248
DEC	1200 5/400	648	447	273
DEC	2100A 4/275	538	377	245
DEC	2100A 5/250	813	561	342
DEC	2100A 5/300	825	569	347
DEC	4000 5/533	1,395	907	544

Table 10.4   *Information Technology Value (continued)*

Manufacturer	Description	Equipment Values (U.S. $)		
		FMV 2002	RVF 2003	RVF 2003
DEC	4000 5/600	2,940	1,617	792
DEC	4000-96	423	304	207
DEC	4100 5/300	775	535	326
DEC	4100 5/466	1,268	824	495
DEC	4100 5/533	1,268	824	495
DEC	500/266	488	341	222
DEC	500/333	236	175	122
DEC	500/400	488	341	222
DEC	500/500	614	430	279
DEC	600 5/333	336	242	164
DEC	600A 5/500	670	462	282
DEC	7000-610 256MB	2,328	1,280	627
DEC	7000-610 OSF/1 512MB	2,732	1,503	736
DEC	7810 OVMS BASE, 256MB,	4,780	2,486	1,119
DEC	800 5/333 (AA)	220	163	114
DEC	800 5/333 (FA)	406	292	199
DEC	800 5/400 Alpha Srvr	868	599	365
DEC	8200 5/350	3,103	1,707	836
DEC	8400 5/350	5,267	2,739	1,232
DEC	8400 5/440	4,466	2,322	1,045
DEC	ARRAY 10000	1,583	981	569
DEC	AXP 3000 32MB Memory	51	41	30
DEC	AXP 3000 64MB Memory	111	82	58
DEC	AXP 3000/800	950	656	400
DEC	AXP 3000/900	998	688	420
DEC	AXP2100 A500	855	590	360

Table 10.4   *Information Technology Value (continued)*

Manufacturer	Description	Equipment Values (U.S. $)		
		FMV 2002	RVF 2003	RVF 2003
DEC	DEC SYSTEM 5400	618	432	281
DEC	DECstation 200	86	64	46
DEC	DECstation 2100	95	71	51
DEC	DECstation 240	123	91	64
DEC	DECsystem 5400	155	115	80
DEC	DECsystem 5500	173	128	90
DEC	DEMSB-AA Cable	84	63	45
DEC	DETLX-SA Cable	61	47	34
DEC	DS 20 Alpha Srvr	2,275	1,251	613
DEC	LA400-CA Printer	127	94	66
DEC	LN03R-A2 Printer	73	56	41
DEC	LN05-A2 Printer	48	39	29
DEC	LP29-A2 Printer	280	202	137
DEC	LP37-A2 Printer	140	104	73
DEC	MICRO VAX 3500	190	141	98
DEC	MICRO VAX 3600	214	158	111
DEC	MicroVAX II	90	67	48
DEC	RA70-RK Disk Drive	90	67	48
DEC	RA71-AK Disk Drive	57	46	34
DEC	RA72-AF Disk Drive	67	52	37
DEC	RA73-AF Disk Drive	101	76	54
DEC	RAID Array 3000	434	313	213
DEC	RAID ARRAY 410 (SWXRA-YA)	504	353	230
DEC	RZ56-E Disk Drive	109	82	58
DEC	SC-4200 Storage Controller	104	78	55
DEC	VAX 4000-300 Processor	56	45	33

Table 10.4   *Information Technology Value (continued)*

Manufacturer	Description	Equipment Values (U.S. $)		
		FMV 2002	**RVF 2003**	**RVF 2003**
DEC	VAX 4000-500	660	456	278
DEC	VAX 4000-500 Processor	56	45	33
DEC	VAX 6310 CPU MODULE	523	366	238
DEC	VAX 6310 Processor	90	67	48
DEC	VAX 8200 CPU MODULE	190	141	98
DEC	VAXSTATION 3100	143	105	74
DEC	VAXSTATION 3500	238	176	123
DEC	VAXstation 3500 Processor	108	81	57
DEC	VAXstation 4000-VLC Processor	73	56	41
DEC	VRT19-HA 19" Monitor	90	67	48
DEC	VT220	71	55	40
DEC	VT320	81	61	43
DEC	VT330	333	239	163
DEC	VT340	333	239	163
DEC	VT420	119	88	62
DEC	VT510	143	105	74
DEC	VT520	238	176	123
DEC	VT525-AA	143	105	74
DEC	VXT2000	808	557	340
Decision Data	6530 Printer	111	82	58
Decision Data	6531 Printer	144	106	74
Decision Data	6540-03 Printer	171	127	89
Decision Data	6540-05 Printer	242	179	126
Decision Data	6570-03 Printer	273	197	134
Decision Data	6570-05 Printer	367	264	180
Decision Data	6605-AOO Printer	354	255	173

Table 10.4   *Information Technology Value (continued)*

Manufacturer	Description	Equipment Values (U.S. $)		
		FMV 2002	RVF 2003	RVF 2003
Decision Data	6605-AOOP Printer	294	212	144
Decision Data	6605-CTA Printer	404	291	198
Decision Data	6605-CTAP Printer	330	237	161
Decision Data	6605-TIA Printer	471	330	214
Decision Data	6605-TIAP Printer	411	296	201
Decision Data	6608-AOO Printer	467	327	213
Decision Data	6608-AOOP Printer	393	283	192
Decision Data	6608-CTA Printer	529	370	241
Decision Data	6608-CTAP Printer	480	336	218
Decision Data	6608-TIA Printer	571	400	260
Decision Data	6608-TIAP Printer	521	364	237
Decision Data	6614-AOO Printer	505	354	230
Decision Data	6614-CTA Printer	487	341	221
Fujitsu	RX7300E 7150 Printer	71	55	40
Hitachi	20" color monitor	49	40	30
Hitachi	21" HITACHI SUPERSCAN ELITE MONITOR	132	98	68
Hitachi	5GB 12MM NOTEBOOK HARD DRIVE	54	43	33
Hitachi	OD301-A-1 12" WORM rack mount	231	171	120
Hitachi	SUPERSCAN 813 21" .22MM 18X1	152	113	79
Hitachi	SUPERSCAN ELITE 802 PLUS 21" 20VIS .22	161	119	83
Hitachi	SUPERSCAN SUPREME 803 21" 20VIS .22MM1	169	125	88
Kennedy	9600 9-Track tape drive	92	69	49
Kennedy	9610 9-Track tape drive	113	84	59
Kennedy	9612 9-Track tape drive	150	111	78
Lantronix	EPS4UF Printer/Terminal Server	105	79	56
Lantronix	ETS16P Terminal/Print Servers	128	95	66

Table 10.4   *Information Technology Value (continued)*

Manufacturer	Description	Equipment Values (U.S. $)		
		FMV 2002	RVF 2003	RVF 2003
Lantronix	ETS16U Printer/Terminal Server	138	102	71
Lantronix	ETS4P4-018 Port Terminal/Print Servers	108	81	57
Lantronix	ETS8P Terminal/Print Servers	103	77	55
Lantronix	LB2 2 Port Bridge	114	85	59
Lantronix	LFR12-S Fast Ethernet hub	63	49	35
Lantronix	LFR8-S Fast Ethernet hub	42	34	25
Lee Data	1360 Printer	87	66	47
Lee Data	1361 Printer	87	66	47
Lee Data	1363 Printer	105	79	56
Lucent	7406D Display Telephone	47	38	28
Lucent	7407D Display Telephone	115	85	60
Lucent	7444D Telephone with Display, Speaker, and Power Supply	115	85	60
Lucent	8410D Telephone with Speaker and Display	47	38	28
Lucent	8434D Display Telephone with Speaker	81	61	43
Lucent	TN2181 16-Port Digital Pack	236	175	122
Lucent	TN464F T1/ISDN Pack	242	179	126
Lucent	TN746 16-Port Analog Pack (Old Style)	115	85	60
Lucent	TN746B 16-Port Analog Pack (New Style)	186	138	96
Lucent	TN754A Digital Line Circuit Pack (4-Wire)	56	45	34
Lucent	TN754B Digital Pack	81	61	43
Lucent	TN767E DSI/DMI Interface Pack	231	171	120
MAG InnoVision	17IN 15.8VIS .28MM 12X10 Color Monitor	45	36	27
MAG InnoVision	DJ 707, 17" Monitor	49	40	30
MAG InnoVision	DJ 800, 19" Monitor	74	57	41
MAG InnoVision	DJ 920, 21" Monitor	96	72	51

Table 10.4   *Information Technology Value (continued)*

Manufacturer	Description	Equipment Values (U.S. $)		
		FMV 2002	RVF 2003	RVF 2003
MAG InnoVision	DX715T, 17" Monitor	56	45	34
Meditech	5220 Terminal	63	49	35
Meditech	5222 Terminal	47	38	28
Meditech	5235 Terminal	63	49	35
Mitsubishi	DIAMOND PLUS 70 17" 16VIS .25MM 12X10 Monitor	45	36	27
Mitsubishi	DIAMOND PLUS 72 17" 16VIS .25 16X12 66H	61	47	34
Mitsubishi	DIAMOND PRO 67TXV 17" Monitor	81	61	43
Mitsubishi	DIAMOND PRO 91TXM 21" Monitor	99	74	53
Mitsubishi	DIAMOND PRO 91TXM-21" 1200 X 1600	135	100	70
Mitsubishi	MEGAVIEW 29 - .79 640X480	105	79	56
NEC	15" MULTIMEDIA MONITOR	38	30	23
NEC	17" VISTA SCAN MONITOR	63	49	35
NEC	21" E1100 MULTISCAN MONITOR	111	82	58
NEC	386DX/33, 4 MB memory	42	34	25
NEC	6FG 21" Monitor	125	92	65
NEC	COLORMATE P.S. 8MB 8PPM LASER	45	36	27
NEC	Docking Station 4000	91	68	48
NEC	DOCKING STATION 6000	100	75	53
NEC	E700 17" Monitor	71	55	40
NEC	LC890 Printer	61	47	34
NEC	LCD1810 18" TFT FLAT PANEL MONITOR	442	309	201
NEC	M500 15" 13.8VIS.25MM 12X10 NI WHITE	45	36	27
NEC	MULTISYNC A700 17" 15.6 VIS .28MM 12X1	100	75	53
NEC	MULTISYNC A700+ 17" 16VIS .28MM 12X10 C	56	45	34
NEC	MULTISYNC E700 17" 15.6 VIS .25MM 16X1	71	55	40

Table 10.4   *Information Technology Value (continued)*

		Equipment Values (U.S. $)		
Manufacturer	Description	FMV 2002	RVF 2003	RVF 2003
NEC	MULTISYNC E750 17" COLOR MONITOR	83	63	44
NEC	MULTISYNC E900+ 18VIS .26MM 16X12NI	96	72	51
NEC	MULTISYNC LCD2000 FLAT PANEL 20.1VIS 12X	463	324	211
NEC	MULTISYNC M700 17".25MM 12X10 MIST WHITE	87	66	47
NEC	MULTISYNC P1150 21".28MM 19.6VIS 16X12	142	105	73
NEC	MULTISYNC P1250+ 21" 19.6VIS 18X14.4 .2	147	109	76
NEC	MULTISYNC XV17+ 17 .28MM 12X10 NI FST Monitor	71	55	40
NEC	NEC MULTISPIN 6XI I	49	40	30
NEC	NEC XV15+ .28 1280X1024 MONITOR	52	41	31
NEC	NEC XV15+1280X1024 .28 15" MONITOR	61	47	34
NEC	P1150 21" Monitor	128	95	66
NEC	P750 17" COLOR MONITOR	85	64	45
NEC	P9300 Printer	61	47	34
NEC	PowerMate 8100 6/350 MT 128M 8.4G 10/100	123	91	64
NEC	PROSERVA V PLUS P/120 16MB 2GB CD 10BT	111	82	58
NEC	SMP1 P/166 32MB 2GB CDR ENET	110	82	57
Nokia	17" MONITOR .25 PITCH 1280X1024 TRINITRON	92	69	49
Nokia	21" PREMIUM COLOR Monitor	115	85	60
Nokia	445XIPLUS 21" 19.69VIS .22MM 16X12	121	89	63
Nokia	447X PRO 17" 15.82VIS .25MM 16X12 Monitor	42	34	25
Nokia	447ZA 17" 16VIS .27MM SP KRS 100MHZ	61	47	34
Panasonic	2123 Printer	38	30	23
Panasonic	2624 Printer	42	34	25
Panasonic	4410 Printer	63	49	35

Table 10.4   *Information Technology Value (continued)*

Manufacturer	Description	Equipment Values (U.S. $)		
		FMV 2002	RVF 2003	RVF 2003
Panasonic	4420 Printer	79	61	44
Panasonic	4450 Printer	85	64	45
Panasonic	4450L Printer	103	77	55
Panasonic	KXP 2023 Printer	38	30	23
Panasonic	KXP 2123 Printer	44	35	26
Panasonic	KXP 2180 Printer	45	36	27
Panasonic	KXP 2624 Printer	47	38	28
Panasonic	KXP 4410 Printer	63	49	35
Panasonic	KXP 4420 Printer	81	61	43
Panasonic	KXP 4450 Printer	81	61	43
Panasonic	KXP 4450L Printer	99	74	53
Panasonic	KX-P1695 Printer	41	33	25
Printronix	6280L Printer	231	171	120
Printronix	9012 Printer	345	248	169
Printronix	P300 Printer	105	79	56
Printronix	P300XQ Printer	109	82	58
Printronix	P600 Printer	92	69	49
Printronix	P6080L Printer	222	164	115
Seagate	ST11200N 3.5" 1GB SCSI	44	35	26
Seagate	ST11200ND 3.5" 1GB SCSI-DIFF	44	35	26
Seagate	ST12400N 3.5" 2.1 GB SCSI	88	66	47
Seagate	ST12550N 3.5" 2.1GB SCSI	59	45	33
Seagate	ST12550ND 3.5" 2.1GB SCSI-DIFF	59	45	33
Seagate	ST12550W 3.5" 2.1GB WIDE-SCSI	59	45	33
Seagate	ST12550WD 3.5" 2.1GB WIDE-SCSI-DIFF	59	45	33
Seagate	ST15150N 3.5" 4.3GB SCSI	88	66	47

Table 10.4 *Information Technology Value (continued)*

Manufacturer	Description	Equipment Values (U.S. $)		
		FMV 2002	RVF 2003	RVF 2003
Seagate	ST15150W 3.5" 4.3GB WIDE-SCSI	88	66	47
Seagate	ST15150WC 3.5" 4.3GB WIDE-SCSI-SINGLE	88	66	47
Seagate	ST15150WD 3.5" 4.3GB WIDE-SCSI-DIFF	88	66	47
Seagate	ST15230N 3.5" 4.3GB SCSI	88	66	47
Seagate	ST15230W 3.5" 4.3GB WIDE-SCSI	88	66	47
Seagate	ST15230WC 3.5" 4.3GB WIDE-SCSI-SINGLE	88	66	47
Seagate	ST19171N 3.5" 9GB SCSI	176	130	91
Seagate	ST19171WC 3.5" 9GB WIDE-SCSI-SINGLE	176	130	91
Seagate	ST19171WD 3.5" 9GB WIDE-SCSI-DIFF	176	130	91
Seagate	ST31200N 3.5" 1GB SCSI	59	45	33
Seagate	ST31200W 3.5" 1GB WIDE-SCSI	59	45	33
Seagate	ST31200WC 3.5" 1GB WIDE-SCSI-SINGLE	59	45	33
Seagate	ST31230N 3.5" 1GB SCSI	59	45	33
Seagate	ST31230W 3.5" 1GB WIDE-SCSI	59	45	33
Seagate	ST32171N 3.5" 2.1GB SCSI	88	66	47
Seagate	ST32430N 3.5" 2.1GB SCSI	88	66	47
Seagate	ST32430W 3.5" 2.1GB WIDE-SCSI	88	66	47
Seagate	ST32550N 3.5" 2.1GB SCSI	53	42	32
Seagate	ST32550ND 3.5" 2.1GB SCSI-DIFF	53	42	32
Seagate	ST32550W 3.5" 2.1GB WIDE-SCSI	59	45	33
Seagate	ST32550WC 3.5" 2.1GB WIDE-SCSI-SINGLE	59	45	33
Seagate	ST34371N 3.5" 4GB SCSI	147	109	76
Seagate	ST34371W 3.5" 4GB WIDE-SCSI	147	109	76
Seagate	ST34371WC 3.5" 4GB WIDE-SCSI-SINGLE	147	109	76
Seagate	ST39173LC 3.5" 9GB SCSI DIFF	176	130	91
Seagate	ST410800N 5.25" 9GB SCSI	117	87	61

Table 10.4   *Information Technology Value (continued)*

Manufacturer	Description	Equipment Values (U.S. $)		
		FMV 2002	RVF 2003	RVF 2003
Seagate	ST41200ND 5.25" 1GB SCSI-DIFF	73	56	41
Seagate	ST41201J 5.25" 1.2GB SMD	147	109	76
Seagate	ST41600N 5.25" 1.3GB SCSI	53	42	32
Seagate	ST41600ND 5.25" 1.3GB SCSI-DIFF	53	42	32
Seagate	ST42400N 5.25" 2.1GB SCSI	88	66	47
Seagate	ST42400ND 5.25" 2.1GB SCSI-DIFF	53	42	32
Seagate	ST43400N 5.25" 2.8GB SCSI	117	87	61
Seagate	ST43400ND 5.25" 2.8GB SCSI-DIFF	117	87	61
Seagate	ST4766N 5.25" 676MB SCSI	44	35	26
Seagate	ST4767N 5.25" 665MB SCSI	53	42	32
Seagate	ST51080A 3.5" 1GB IDE	44	35	26
Seagate	ST51080N 3.5" 1GB SCSI	70	54	39
Seagate	ST81123J 8" 1.1GB SMD (9720-1123)	117	87	61
Seagate	ST81154K 8" 1.1GB IPI	88	66	47
Seagate	ST81236J 8" 1.2GB SMD (9720-1230)	117	87	61
Seagate	ST81236K 8" 1.2GB IPI	88	66	47
Seagate	ST82038J 8" 2GB SMD	117	87	61
Seagate	ST82500J 8" 2.5GB SMD	147	109	76
Seagate	ST8368J 8" 368MB SMD (9720-368)	147	109	76
Seagate	ST8471J 8" 740MB SMD (9720-736)	440	308	200
Seagate	ST8500J 8" 500MB SMD (9720-500)	147	109	76
Seagate	ST8851J 8" 850MB SMD (9720-850)	147	109	76
Sony	100GS 15" Monitor	44	35	26
Sony	200ES 17" Monitor	54	43	33
Sony	200GS 17" Monitor	70	54	39
Sony	21" 19.8VIS .25MM 16X12 Monitor	108	81	57

Table 10.4   *Information Technology Value (continued)*

Manufacturer	Description	Equipment Values (U.S. $)		
		FMV 2002	**RVF 2003**	**RVF 2003**
Sony	CPD-200ES 17" 16VIS .25MM AG 12X10 PNP Monitor	47	38	28
Sony	CPD-200GS 17" 16VIS .25MM AG 12X10 PNP Monitor	71	55	40
Sony	MULTISCAN 17SF II Monitor	52	41	31
Sony	PCV-230 P2, 64 MB/6.4 GB	150	111	78
Sony	SDK5000 External 4-8GB DDS-2 DAT	92	69	49
Sony	SDT2000 Internal DAT	44	35	26
Sony	SDT5200 Internal 4GB DDS-2 DAT	54	43	33
Sony	SDT7000 Internal 4-8GB DDS-2 DAT	76	59	42
Sony	SDTS5000 External 4-8GB DDS-2 DAT	92	69	49
Sony	SDTS5200 External 4GB DDS-2 DAT	70	54	39
Sony	SDTS7000 External 4-8GB DDS-2 DAT	92	69	49
Sony	TRINITRON 20 MULTIMEDIA Monitor	99	74	53
Tandem	530 Terminal	91	68	48
Tandem	5512 PRINTER	38	30	23
Tandem	5541A PRINTER	38	30	23
Tandem	M200A PRINTER	38	30	23
Televideo	14" 990 Green 80/132 Column Monitor	26	21	16
Televideo	14" 990 White 80/132 Column Monitor	26	21	16
Texas Inst.	5020SE Pentium-75 8/500 DS	49	40	30
Texas Inst.	560CS Pentium-75 8/560 CD	71	55	40
Unisys	LT300-2 Terminal - Amber	26	21	16
Unisys	LT300-2 Terminal - Green	26	21	16
Unisys	UT200-1 Terminal - Amber	26	21	16
Unisys	UT200-1 Terminal - Green	26	21	16
Unisys	UT200-2 Terminal - Amber	26	21	16

Table 10.4   *Information Technology Value (continued)*

Manufacturer	Description	Equipment Values (U.S. $)		
		FMV 2002	RVF 2003	RVF 2003
Unisys	UT200-2 Terminal - Green	26	21	16
Versatec	7236 Plotter	85	64	45
Versatec	7444 Plotter	110	82	57
Versatec	8224 Plotter	54	43	33
Versatec	8836 Plotter	130	96	67
View Magic	G771 17" Monitor	54	43	33
View Magic	PT813 21" Monitor	128	95	66
Wang	2200 2 PC DATA ENTRY WORKSTATION	35	28	21
Wang	2248V-2S 9 Track SCSI, Reel to Reel Tape	499	349	227
Wang	2249V-2 18" Track 3490 Tape SCSI	499	349	227
Wang	2268-4 454MB disk	35	28	21
Wang	2268V-3 314MB disk	35	28	21
Wang	2336DW DATA ENTRY WORKSTATION	35	28	21
Wang	LM400 400 LPM Shuttle Matrix Printer	144	106	74
Wang	LM700 700 LPM Shuttle Matrix Printer	218	162	113
Wang	LM900 900 LPM Shuttle Matrix Printer	367	264	180
Wang	MDSC Mini Data Storage Cabinet	56	45	34
Wyse	Max 700 Amber 80,132-Col 14" Monitor	41	32	24
Wyse	Max 700 Green 80 132-Col 14" Monitor	41	32	24
Wyse	Max 700 White 80,132-Col 14" Monitor	41	32	24
Wyse	Mc-5 Amber 80 132-Col 14" Monitor	42	34	25
Wyse	Mc-5 Green 80,132-Col 14" Monitor	42	34	25
Wyse	Mc-5 White 80, 132 Col 14" Monitor	42	34	25
Wyse	Wy-150 Amber 80,132-Column 14" Monitor	42	34	25
Wyse	Wy-150 Green 80,132-Column 14" Monitor	42	34	25
Wyse	Wy-160es White 80,132 Col 14" Monitor	56	45	34

Table 10.4   *Information Technology Value (continued)*

Manufacturer	Description	Equipment Values (U.S. $)		
		FMV 2002	RVF 2003	RVF 2003
Wyse	Wy-185es White 80,132 Col 14" Monitor	35	28	21
Wyse	Wy-370 Color 80 132column 14" Monitor	110	82	57
Wyse	Wy-55 Green 80,132 Column 14" Monitor	44	35	26
Wyse	Wy-55 White 80,132 Column 14" Monitor	44	35	26
Wyse	Wy-55es White 80,132 Column 14" Monitor	41	32	24
Wyse	Wy-60 Amber 80,132 Column 14" Monitor	49	40	30
Wyse	Wy-60 Green 80,132 Column 14" Monitor	49	40	30
Wyse	Wy-60 White 80,132 Column 14" Monitor	49	40	30
Xerox	4030II Printer, 11ppm Laser, ASCII, Ser/Parll	71	55	40
Xerox	4220-SCST Printer, 20ppm Laser, 5 Trays, Twinax, 20MB	324	234	159
Xerox	5705 Digital Color	1,989	1,233	715
Xerox	DC 265 Digital Copier	3,223	1,772	868
Xerox	DC 332ST Digital Copier	992	685	418
Xerox	DC 340ST Digital Copier	1,290	838	503
Xerox	Docuprint 4508 Laser 8ppm	49	40	30
Xerox	Docuprint 4512 Plus Laser 12ppm	99	74	53
Xerox	Docuprint 4517plus Laser 17ppm	91	68	48
Xerox	Docuprint C55 Color Laser 12ppm	237	176	123
Xerox	Docuprint N24 Laser 24ppm	166	123	86
Xerox	Docuprint N32 Laser 32ppm	196	145	102

Principle Ten: Support Efforts to Reduce the Digital Divide

Some people have called the twenty-first century the digital century. As with all of the new centuries of the past, the digital century comes with its own set of social problems. We now have the digital divide, which, unless dramatic steps are taken, will further widen the gap between the haves and the have nots.

—Brandon L. Harris

11.1 End-user organizations should be concerned

There are many compelling reasons why IT managers and companies that are dependent on IT should support efforts to decrease the digital divide. First and foremost, full participation in life in the information age requires computer literacy and Internet access. Computer-literate people are more likely to:

- Have an interest in IT-related careers

- Require less on-the-job training

- Contribute higher value to their employers

- Shop on-line

- Participate in e-government

- Raise computer-literate children

In 1993 the world was buzzing with the prospects of developing the information superhighway. The development of the information superhighway was to unleash an information revolution that would change forever the way people live, work, and interact with each other, including the following:

- People could live almost anywhere they wanted, without forgoing opportunities for useful and fulfilling employment, by telecommuting to their offices through an electronic highway.

- The best schools, teachers, and courses would be available to all students, without regard to geography, distance, resources, or disability.

- Services that improve America's health-care system and respond to other important social needs would be available on-line, without waiting in line, when and where they were needed.

- The vast resources of art, literature, and science would be available everywhere, not just in large institutions or big-city libraries and museums.

- Small manufacturers would get orders from all over the world electronically—with detailed specifications—in a form that the machines could use to produce the necessary items.

- Applications such as electronic commerce, electronic payment, brokering services, and collaborative engineering could dramatically reduce the time required to design, manufacture, and market new products as well as strengthen the relationships between manufacturers, suppliers, developers, and customers.

- You could see the latest movies, play the hottest video games, or bank and shop from the comfort of your home whenever you chose.

- You would obtain government information directly or through local organizations such as libraries, apply for and receive government benefits electronically, and get in touch with government officials easily.

- Individual government agencies, businesses, and other entities all would exchange information electronically—reducing paperwork and improving service.

11.2 Has the 1993 National Information Infrastructure Agenda for Action been achieved?

In the fall of 1993 the U.S. Department of Commerce released the National Information Infrastructure Agenda for Action (NIIAA), which was to guide the government's involvement in the development and growth of the information superhighway. This analysis addresses the question: Has the 1993 National Information Infrastructure Agenda for Action been achieved? The goal of the analysis is not to criticize the NIIAA but rather to determine whether it was realistic and how much of the agenda was actually achieved.

The central proposition of the NIIAA was that all Americans have a stake in the construction of an advanced national information infrastructure (NII). The NII was to be a seamless web of communications networks, computers, databases, and consumer electronics that would put vast amounts of information at users' fingertips.

The federal government's position was that private sector firms were already developing and deploying that infrastructure but there remained essential roles for government in the process. It was believed that carefully crafted government action would complement and enhance the efforts of the private sector and assure the growth of an information infrastructure available to all Americans at reasonable cost. The federal government's efforts were to be guided by the following principles and objectives:

- To promote private sector investment through appropriate tax and regulatory policies.

- To extend the universal service concept to ensure that information resources are available to all at affordable prices. Because information means empowerment—and employment—the government has a duty to ensure that all Americans have access to the resources and the process of job creation.

- To act as a catalyst to promote technological innovation and new applications by committing important government research programs and grants to help the private sector develop and demonstrate technologies needed for the NII and to develop the applications and services that will maximize its value to users.

- To promote seamless, interactive, user-driven operation of the NII. As the NII evolves into a network of networks, government would ensure that users can transfer information across networks easily and efficiently. To increase the likelihood that the NII will be both interactive and, to a large extent, user driven, government would reform regulations and policies that might inadvertently hamper the development of interactive applications.

- To ensure information security and network reliability by making the NII trustworthy and secure, protecting the privacy of its users. Government action would also ensure that the overall system remains reliable, quickly repairable in the event of a failure, and, perhaps most important, easy to use.

- To protect intellectual property rights by strengthening domestic copyright laws and international intellectual property treaties to prevent piracy and to protect the integrity of intellectual property.

- To coordinate with other levels of government and with other nations. Because information crosses state, regional, and national boundaries, coordination is critical to avoid needless obstacles and prevent unfair policies that handicap U.S. industry.

- To provide access to government information and improve government procurement by ensuring that federal agencies, in concert with state and local governments, use the NII to expand the information available to the public, ensuring that the immense reservoir of government information is available to the public easily and equitably.

11.2.1   To what extent have the projected benefits been realized?

Did the principles and the goals of the NIIAA, combined with private sector activity, actually unleash an information revolution that changed the way people live, work, and interact with each other? We examined the potential benefits put forth in the NIIAA to see how much the world may have changed since 1993. We rated realization of each benefit on a scale of 1 (low realization) to 10 (high realization).

Telecommuting has indeed grown considerably during the past several years, according to the thirteenth annual "Information Systems and E-Business Spending" study conducted by Computer Economics. In 2002, telecommuting support was in place or being implemented in 58.7 percent of the organizations studied; another 7.7 percent were in the piloting stages, and 10.2 percent were in the research stages. However, 23.4 percent of the organizations studied were not pursuing telecommuting support. (Realization rating: 7)

Education, or making the best schools, teachers, and courses available to all students without regard to geography, distance, resources, or disability has not gone very well. (Realization rating: 2) There are certainly many schools that offer Internet-based courses. However, there are many barriers to the realization of on-line education, including the following:

- The effectiveness of on-line education as a learning or a teaching tool has not been systematically evaluated.

- Many universities have become frustrated with the overhead associated with supporting Internet courses, while a few still tout the opportunity as a marketing point.

- In early 2002 the much-publicized Einstein Academy Charter School, a cyber school in Pennsylvania, was out of money and under investigation for not providing students with promised resources, including computers and textbooks. Many other on-line schools had come and gone by 2002.

- Cyber education at the college level remains expensive; thus, the resource barrier to educational access remains.

- People with disabilities still face considerable hardships because computers are not very disabled–user friendly, and those systems that are specifically designed for disabled people are very expensive.

Efforts to bring services that improve America's health-care system and respond to other important social needs on-line have also met with little success. Many states have implemented some form of telemedicine support, but these efforts are in the very early stages. In addition, those people with the most severe social needs because of poverty, health, or disability remain grossly underserved with Internet-based applications. The expense of computers, the lack of training to use computers, and low literacy levels remain barriers to this effort. (Realization rating: 1)

The ability to access the vast resources of art, literature, and science from everywhere has been a rather dramatic achievement. The major museums and many literary works are now available on-line for those who can afford access and who are able to use computers. (Realization rating: 8)

The availability of applications such as electronic commerce, electronic payment, brokering services, and collaborative engineering to strengthen the relationships between manufacturers, suppliers, developers, and customers has grown rapidly. In spite of the dot-com bust, there are many companies that are pursuing such applications according to the "2002 Information Systems and E-Business Spending" study conducted by Computer Economics. In 2002, 96.2 percent of the organizations studied had implemented or were implementing Internet connectivity. E-commerce software was being used by 53.2 percent of the organizations, and another 27.4 percent were in some stage of implementation. (Realization rating: 8)

Access to the latest entertainment, such as movies and video games, has certainly been facilitated by the growth of the Internet. The financial success of these applications remains in doubt in 2002. However, the future still looks bright because of the potential convergence of wireless technology, television, and virtual reality. One business that has thrived on the Internet is pornography, much to the dismay of many conservative groups. (Realization rating: 5)

E-government, including access to services, getting in touch with government officials, and the electronic exchange of information between government agencies, businesses, and other entities is growing but seems to lack any solid direction. E-commerce software is in use in 56.3 percent of the state and local government organizations that participated in the "2002 Information Systems and E-Business Spending" study conducted by Computer Economics. However, 26.1 percent of the state and local government organizations reported that they were not involved in any e-commerce efforts. All of the organizations had Internet connectivity in 2002. (Realization rating: 5)

11.2.2 To what extent have the principles and objectives of the government been realized?

The NIIAA declared that the government had an essential role in the NII development process. The NIIAA presented several principles and objectives for the federal government. We examined the extent to which the principles and objectives put forth in the NIIAA have been realized. We rated realization of the each benefit on a scale of 1 (low realization) to 10 (high realization).

Private sector investment in the NII has certainly been realized. It is doubtful, however, that the sales tax moratorium or other regulatory positions of the federal government really had any significant impact. (Realization rating: 8)

The extension of the universal service concept to ensure that information resources are available to all at affordable prices has not been greatly realized. In February 2002, U.S. Department of Commerce released a report entitled "A NATION ONLINE: How Americans Are Expanding Their Use of the Internet." The study determined that there is a sizable segment of the U.S. population (as of September 2001, 46.1 percent of persons and 49.5 percent of households) that does not use the Internet. The nonusers include 75.0 percent of people who live in households where income is less than $15,000 and 66.6 percent of those in households with incomes between $15,000 and $35,000. Nonusers were also prevalent in groups with low education levels (87.2 percent of adults with less than a high school education), African Americans (60.2 percent), and Hispanics (68.4 percent). (Realization rating: 1)

As far as acting as a catalyst to promote technological innovation and new applications along with the promotion of seamless, interactive, user-driven operation of the NII, the federal government has provided a relatively good performance. There certainly has been a variety of funding efforts and the operation of the NII is largely user driven. (Realization rating: 7)

In regard to the reform regulations and policies that may inadvertently hamper the development of interactive applications, the federal government has provided a mixed performance. The U.S. Congress has repeatedly demonstrated, with numerous pieces of legislation, that it wants to regulate the use and content of the Internet. Most of the legislation has not been passed, and the Communications Decency Act was overturned in federal court. (Realization rating: 3)

When it comes to ensuring information security by making the NII trustworthy and secure and protecting the privacy of its users, there has been both failure and success. Secure the Internet is not. Cyber space is like a dark alley. Murder, rape, fraud, scams, privacy violations, spying, lurking, stalking, child pornography, and kidnapping have all been facilitated on the Internet. Technology is weak, hackable, crackable, and prone to virus attacks. The Clinton administration did make big pushes toward privacy protection, not only in the NII but also for citizens in general. The Bush administration prefers to backpedal on privacy initiatives every chance it gets. (Realization rating: 2)

Strengthening domestic copyright laws and international intellectual property treaties has certainly been pursued. However, piracy is at an all time high. Piracy losses exceeded $59 billion during the past five years, according to the Software and Information Industry Association (SIIA) and the Business Software Alliance (BSA). The Internet facilitates much of this piracy. A separate study by the SIIA and KPMG, which examined the acquisition and use of software and digital content via the Internet, found that nearly 30 percent of business people could be classified as pirating intellectual property through a variety of electronic methods. (Realization rating: 2)

Federal government coordination with other levels of government and with other countries to deal with issues of information crossing state, regional, and national boundaries to avoid needless obstacles has had mixed results. The U.S. Department of Commerce worked with the European Union (EU) for several years and succeeded in developing the safe-harbor

principles for protection of individual privacy. However, the Bush administration is standing back from such sticky Internet issues, with the exception
of security. It has also been realized that other countries will continue to
enforce their own laws regarding content on the Internet, as is illustrated
with the French judicial actions against Yahoo! for making Nazi memorabilia available on the Yahoo! auction service. (Realization rating: 3)

Providing access to government information and improving government
procurement by ensuring that federal agencies, along with state and local
governments, increase the availability and ease of public access to information looked promising for a while. Since the September 11, 2001 terrorist
attacks on the United States, governments at all levels are pulling information off the Internet as fast as possible. Nevertheless, there is a considerable
amount of information and data still available. (Realization rating: 7)

11.2.3   Conclusions on the achievement of the Agenda for Action

In some areas American society has rapidly accelerated into the Internet age.
In 2002 e-commerce is fairly healthy, with 34.8 percent of companies operating profitable B2C functions, according to the "2002 Information Systems and E-Business Spending" study conducted by Computer Economics.
There is certainly more entertainment, art, music, and information of all
types available to a larger number of people than there was in 1993. Private
sector investment and development of Internet applications has been
unprecedented.

In many other ways American society lags behind in realizing the benefits and behaving in accordance with the principles laid out in the NIIAA.
The Internet is certainly not secure. Universal access is far from being realized, and the digital divide becomes more serious every day. In addition,
since the September 11, 2001, terrorist attacks on the United States many
people view the Internet as a potentially great vulnerability rather than as a
national asset.

It is important, when taking stock, also to examine the validity of an
idea. The perceptions held by the drafters of the NIIAA of what the Internet could be may have been steeped in too much optimism. That does not
mean that the development of the Internet has been a failure. It does mean
that the Internet has likely taken on a life of its own that is quite different
from what the drafters of the NIIAA could have seen in 1993.

What the Internet has become is the greatest mirror of society that has
ever been created. The Internet is truly a citizens' medium. All people can

go to the Internet and use it to pursue their dreams, their desires, and even their perversions. When we look at the Internet and see things that we do not like, what we are really doing is looking at an image of our world and discovering how different it is from what we thought it was or what we want it to be.

11.3   Are we still moving ahead?

Many people comment that as a result of the failure of so many e-commerce companies at the turn of the century, the momentum of the information age has stalled. E-business practices are becoming rather widely adopted in most industry sectors according to the thirteenth annual "Information Systems and E-Business Spending" study conducted by Computer Economics.

Virtually all of the organizations that participated in the 2002 study have Web sites, and large percentages of companies in every sector are using B2B or B2C applications. There has also been a considerable increase in outsourcing Web site functions, and about 9 percent of the companies studied are outsourcing all of their Web site work. Table 11.1 shows the types of e-business practices used in various industry sectors. These data show that

Table 11.1   *E-business Activities in 2002*

E-Business Activity	Percent of Companies
Web site	97.2%
Web-based B2B transactions	47.8%
Profitable B2B e-commerce	26.6%
Web-based B2C transactions	48.3%
Profitable B2C e-commerce	32.1%
Outsource any Web site functions	47.4%
Outsource all Web site functions	8.6%
EDI via Web site	48.8%
EDI via direct dial connections with suppliers	47.7%
EDI via direct dial connections with consumers	34.3%

Source: Computer Economics 2002 Information Systems and E-Business Spending Report

the pursuit of e-commerce has not fallen by the wayside, and computer literacy remains an important issue.

11.4   Next-generation Internet grant program

In addition to the widespread implementation of e-commerce, there are also other efforts underway to maintain the attempt to move into the information age. Through a partnership with the California Technology, Trade, and Commerce Agency—Division of Science, Technology, and Innovation, CommerceNet is providing funding for the development of commercial Next-Generation Internet (NGI) applications. The NGI grant program nurtures the development of business applications that leverage the power, speed, and reliability of the Next-Generation Internet, as well as its pervasive and ubiquitous nature. These applications are expected to have a positive economic and social impact on individuals, companies, industries, regions, and communities.

The NGI grant program focuses on specific application areas that are critical to advancing e-business applications, business models, and startups, including:

- Collaborative design and product development
- Distributive workforce support
- Customer support with interactive video and intelligent agents
- Interactive selling and demonstrations
- Community interaction and real-time relationship support
- Real-time supply chain integration
- Manufacturing engineering
- Media and information services
- Training and technical support

Throughout the year, CommerceNet solicits proposals from interested California-based organizations, including nonprofit corporations, researchers, private companies, and public institutions. CommerceNet is looking for strategic, innovative applications that will drive the commercial success of the NGI.

To be eligible for the funding, the proposed NGI application must take advantage of the features and performance of the Next-Generation Internet, which requires one or more of the following:

- High-bandwidth infrastructure for the transmission of large data objects between a client and a server

- Deep interactivity and complexity between connected systems or servers

- Large numbers of interactive locations communicating with one another in almost real time

- Advanced security for sensitive e-business transactions or communications

- High reliability for running business-critical applications

- Quality of service of end-to-end connections coupled with the ability to distinguish between data types (e.g., audio, video, text, or other multimedia formats)

11.4.1   2001 grant recipients

The grant recipients for 2001 are discussed in the following paragraphs.

Internet seismic processing and collaboration for energy exploration

3DGeo's Internet seismic processing application promises to drastically improve the oil and gas exploration process by shortening analysis time, improving results, and reducing the strain on the environment. By using the Next-Generation Internet as a high-bandwidth communication medium, geologists and geophysicists in different locations can jointly carry out depth-imaging projects that require computation-intensive analyses on remote, large-scale parallel computers.

Effective implementation of QoS policy in real time

Aldea is developing a software tool that not only gathers information about network usage and provides possible network configuration solutions, but also allows the individuals responsible for setting human policy for an organization to realistically determine which applications and services should receive priority on the network itself.

Global Trading Web Catalog

Commerce One will pilot the first open, Internet-based virtual catalog. The Global Trading Web Catalog will provide real-time, uniform access to and search capability for information about products and services integrated from thousands of supplier catalogs.

Application Network

Kenamea's Application Network enables Next-Generation Internet applications and Web services with unprecedented reliability, security, and performance. Kenamea's CommerceNet grant will fund ground-breaking Internet application development projects that will use Kenamea's Application Network software to support distributed applications that provide a real-time interactive user interface, enterprise reliability and security, and off-line operation. These applications will enhance user productivity while reducing the cost of ownership and development time.

Abilities Networks

Pangea Foundation is developing Abilities Networks, a comprehensive program to research, design, and implement technologies that allow people with disabilities to participate fully in the digital economy. The network has a series of on-line information management tools and assisting technology applications that enhance Internet capabilities for people with disabilities.

Mobile Web Services Interoperability Test Bed

Sophica's project addresses Web service interoperability, a key requirement for mobile Web services that are delivered through the Next-Generation Internet (NGI). The development of a Mobile Web Services Interoperability Test Bed will provide project participants and sponsors with a working environment to test, demonstrate, and explore the potential applications, features, and requirements of mobile Web services.

NGI-based civil infrastructure monitoring systems

Strain Monitor Systems develops technologies that enable cost-effective solutions for remotely monitoring the "health" of civil structures. The company provides custom-engineered solutions that lower the growing risks associated with owning and managing aging buildings, bridges, dams, pipelines, stadiums, and the like.

Neighborhood Knowledge California (NKCA)

The UCLA's Advanced Policy Institute's project plans to build an on-line community platform that will help reduce California's economic divide by reducing the digital divide. By providing a geographically indexed database of local, regional, and statewide financial and development data, the project aims to provide Internet-based tools to spur community improvements; encourage new banking opportunities; have an effect on government, public policy, and neighborhood planning efforts; and contribute to new development projects and opportunities for local businesses.

Secure and scalable system logging for the Next-Generation Internet (NGI)

The San Diego Supercomputer Center will produce a robust implementation for a secure and scalable logging system. Message volume and speed of the Next-Generation Internet make it challenging to reliably record a network traffic log. This transaction log provides critical audit information for network security and management purposes.

11.5 How deep is the divide?

In February 2002, the U.S. Department of Commerce released a report entitled "A NATION ONLINE: How Americans Are Expanding Their Use of the Internet." This section presents a summary of the findings and selected data from the report. IT professionals need to be concerned about the digital divide, because this divide will likely reduce the number of people who will be interested in IT careers.

The report utilizes data from the Department of Commerce's U.S. Census Bureau, taken from the Census Bureau's September 2001 Current Population Survey (CPS) of approximately 57,000 sample households. The survey took place during the week of September 16–22, 2001, and generated response rates of 93.5 percent for the basic CPS and 92.1 percent for the Internet and Computer Use Supplement. The households surveyed were selected from the 1990 Decennial Census files with coverage in all 50 states and the District of Columbia. The sample is continually updated to account for new residential construction. The Census divided the United States into 2,007 geographic areas, each typically comprising a county or several contiguous counties. A total of 754 geographic areas were selected for the 2001 CPS survey.

The Census Bureau cross-tabulated the information gathered from the CPS according to specific variables, such as income, race, education level, household type, and age as well as by geographic categories, such as rural, urban, and central city, plus state and region. The Census Bureau determined that some of the data were statistically insignificant for meaningful analysis because the sample from which they were derived was too small.

The study determined that there is a sizable segment of the U.S. population (as of September 2001, 46.1 percent of persons and 49.5 percent of households), that does not use the Internet. This illustrates just how big the digital divide is and could be a predictor of how many people will grow up with little interest in entering the IT workforce. These nonusers include:

- People in households with low family incomes—75.0 percent of people who live in households where income is less than $15,000 and 66.6 percent of those in households with incomes between $15,000 and $35,000.

- Adults with low levels of overall education—60.2 percent of adults (age 25 and over) with only a high school degree and 87.2 percent of adults with less than a high school education.[1]

- Hispanics—68.4 percent of all Hispanics and 85.9 percent of Hispanic households where Spanish is the only language spoken.

- African Americans—60.2 percent of African Americans.

Consider the non-Internet-using population by educational attainment, for example. Among people at least 25 years old with a high school education, the share not using the Internet declined from 69.4 percent in August 2000 to 60.2 in September 2001. Over the same period and age level, the share of those with a college education who were not using the Internet shrank from 27.5 percent to 19.2 percent (see Figure 11.1).

Thus, high school graduates had a slightly larger point change (9.2 percentage points) than college graduates (8.3 percentage points). Because so many more high school graduates were not Internet users in August 2000, the 9.2 percentage point change over the next 13 months represented a 12 percent annual rate of decline in non-Internet users. On the other hand, so few college graduates were non-Internet users in 2000 that their 8.2 percent percentage point change reflected a 28 percent annual rate of decline in non-Internet users.

11.5.1 Cost to households and Internet connectivity

The cost of Internet access matters much more to households with lower incomes than to those with higher incomes. The September 2001 survey asked households without Internet subscriptions the question: What is the main reason that you don't have the Internet at home? Survey results indicated that the largest specific response was that the cost was "too expensive."

---

1.   A person's level of education is correlated to his or her income. People with low overall levels of education are more likely to live in households with lower family incomes. Levels of educational attainment have also increased over time; thus, age and education may be negatively correlated at the higher age levels.

Figure 11.1
*Individuals not
using the Internet,
by selected
educational
attainment level,
August 2000 and
September 2001.*

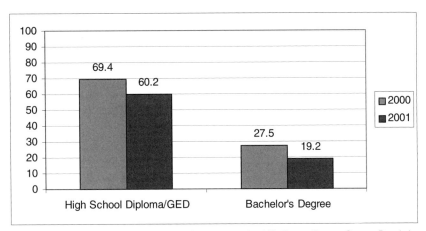

Figure 11.1
Individuals not using the Internet, by selected educational attainment level, August 2000 and September 2001.

Source: NTIA and ESA, U.S. Department of Commerce, using U.S. Census Bureau Current Population Survey Supplements

This response was volunteered by one-fourth of these households, but much more often by lower-income households than by higher-income households.

Households with annual incomes below $15,000 volunteered cost as the barrier to home Internet subscriptions 34.7 percent of the time. Among households in that income category, the share of the population without home Internet subscriptions declined by only 6 percent between August 2000 and September 2001. At the other end of the spectrum, only 9.6 percent of households with incomes of at least $75,000 said that they were deterred by cost. That income level saw a 34 percent reduction in the share of households without home Internet between August 2000 and September 2001.

Among specific responses, cost rated highly across a number of demographic groups of non-Internet households. In particular, respondents for married couples or single-parent families with children as well as heads of households that were younger than 45 years of age, less educated, or unemployed all identified "too expensive" as the most important reason for not being connected at a much higher level than the national figure of 25.3 percent.

Those households that have discontinued Internet access numbered 3.6 million, or 3.3 percent, of all U.S. households as of September 2001. Among this group of unconnected persons, cost was the most frequently cited reason for disconnecting. Households with incomes less than $50,000 identified "too expensive" as the primary reason for discontinuing their Internet connection (26.9 percent of such households).

Cost was more important in households with only high school degrees (24.6 percent) than in households with college degrees (13.7 percent). Those household heads younger than 45 rated cost (24.2 percent) more highly than household heads 45 years or older (19.0 percent). Geographic differentials existed: Households in rural areas cited cost less often (19.9 percent) than households in central cities (25.5 percent). Tables 11.2 and 11.3 show a breakdown of why people do not have Internet connectivity at home.

Table 11.2   *Main Reasons for No Internet Use at Home, by Selected Characteristics of Reference Person (Numbers in Thousands) Total USA, 2001*

	Total House-holds	Don't Want It		Too Expensive		Can Use Elsewhere		Concerned about Children Using It	
		No.	%	No.	%	No.	%	No.	%
All Households	49,197	26,100	53.05	12,443	25.29	2,010	4.09	456	0.93
Family Income									
Under $5,000	2,214	852	38.47	941	42.47	65	2.95	6	0.25
$5,000–$9,999	4,906	2,409	49.09	1,647	33.58	72	1.47	20	0.42
$10,000–$14,999	5,537	2,847	51.41	1,809	32.68	77	1.39	15	0.26
$15,000–$19,999	3,750	1,953	52.08	1,032	27.53	77	2.05	35	0.94
$20,000–$24,999	4,374	2,264	51.75	1,168	26.69	145	3.30	41	0.93
$25,000–$34,999	6,300	3,263	51.79	1,569	24.90	281	4.46	71	1.12
$35,000–$49,999	5,519	2,858	51.79	1,194	21.64	372	6.74	87	1.58
$50,000–$74,999	3,976	2,056	51.71	707	17.78	314	7.91	59	1.48
$75,000	2,293	1,236	53.88	219	9.55	330	14.41	50	2.17
Not reported	10,326	6,363	61.62	2,157	20.89	277	2.68	72	0.70
Age									
Under 25 years old	3,212	972	30.26	1,384	43.10	235	7.30	12	0.38
25–34 years old	6,970	2,262	32.46	2,803	40.21	497	7.13	109	1.56
35–44 years old	7,954	2,971	37.35	2,841	35.71	444	5.58	214	2.69
45–54 years old	7,815	3,752	48.00	2,263	28.96	414	5.30	89	1.13
55+ years old	23,246	16,143	69.44	3,152	13.56	421	1.81	33	0.14

Table 11.2   *Main Reasons for No Internet Use at Home, by Selected Characteristics of Reference Person (Numbers in Thousands) Total USA, 2001 (continued)*

	Total House-holds	Don't Want It		Too Expensive		Can Use Elsewhere		Concerned about Children Using It	
		No.	%	No.	%	No.	%	No.	%
Race									
White not Hispanic	32,586	19,276	59.15	6,105	18.74	1,476	4.53	288	0.88
Black not Hispanic	8,676	3,563	41.06	3,366	38.80	272	3.14	66	0.76
AIEA not Hispanic	455	180	39.52	158	34.85	20	4.37	5	1.01
API not Hispanic	1,023	470	45.90	274	26.78	70	6.88	12	1.18
Hispanic	6,456	2,611	40.45	2,539	39.33	172	2.66	85	1.32
Gender									
Male	23,620	13,022	55.13	5,244	22.20	1,021	4.32	249	1.06
Female	25,577	13,077	51.33	7,200	28.15	990	3.87	206	0.81
Educational Attainment									
Elementary: 0–8 years	5,985	3,468	57.95	1,505	25.15	67	1.11	24	0.40
Some high school: no diploma	7,579	4,052	53.46	2,241	29.58	135	1.78	73	0.97
High school diploma/GED	18,612	10,164	54.61	4,772	25.64	569	3.06	165	0.88
Some college	10,939	5,315	48.59	2,875	26.28	566	5.18	132	1.21
Bachelors degree or more	6,082	3,101	50.98	1,050	17.26	673	11.07	62	1.02
Household Type									
Married couple w/children <18 years old	6,556	2,331	35.56	2,388	36.43	285	4.35	319	4.87
Male householder w/children <18 years old	1,112	370	33.24	489	44.00	30	2.70	12	1.11
Female householder w/children <18 years old	5,030	1,176	23.38	2,766	55.00	177	3.53	76	1.51
Family household without children <18 years old	15,423	9,648	62.56	2,740	17.77	541	3.51	36	0.23
Non-family household	21,076	12,575	59.66	4,059	19.26	977	4.63	13	0.06

Table 11.2   *Main Reasons for No Internet Use at Home, by Selected Characteristics of Reference Person (Numbers in Thousands) Total USA, 2001 (continued)*

	Total House-holds	Don't Want It		Too Expensive		Can Use Elsewhere		Concerned about Children Using It	
		No.	%	No.	%	No.	%	No.	%
Employment									
Employed	25,078	11,040	44.02	7,459	29.74	1,699	6.77	356	1.42
Unemployed	1,406	412	29.28	668	47.47	42	2.99	24	1.73
Not in labor force	22,713	14,648	64.49	4,317	19.01	269	1.19	76	0.33
Region									
Northwest	9,088	5,116	56.29	2,094	23.05	321	3.53	72	0.80
Midwest	11,557	6,085	52.65	2,684	23.23	538	4.66	106	0.92
South	19,088	10,357	54.35	5,175	27.11	735	3.85	170	0.89
West	9,463	4,523	47.80	2,490	26.31	416	4.39	107	1.14

Source: A NATION ONLINE: How Americans Are Expanding Their Use of the Internet, U.S. Census Bureau

Table 11.3   *Main Reasons for No Internet Use at Home, by Selected Characteristics of Reference Person (Numbers in Thousands) Total USA, 2001*

	Computer Capability		No Computer in Household		Lack of Knowledge		Other	
	No.	%	No.	%	No.	%	No.	%
All Households	520	1.06	2,917	5.93	1,032	2.1	3,718	7.56
Family Income								
Under $5,000	12	0.53	156	7.03	42	1.89	142	6.42
$5,000–$9,999	12	0.26	250	5.09	204	4.16	291	5.94
$10,000–$14,999	51	0.93	346	6.26	127	2.29	265	4.79
$15,000–$19,999	36	0.96	265	7.07	122	3.26	230	6.12
$20,000–$24,999	62	1.41	312	7.13	100	2.29	284	6.48
$25,000–$34,999	67	1.07	474	7.52	124	1.97	451	7.16

Table 11.3   *Main Reasons for No Internet Use at Home, by Selected Characteristics of Reference Person (Numbers in Thousands) Total USA, 2001 (continued)*

	Computer Capability		No Computer in Household		Lack of Knowledge		Other	
	No.	%	No.	%	No.	%	No.	%
$35,000–$49,999	88	1.59	379	6.88	92	1.67	448	8.12
$50,000–$74,999	85	2.15	298	7.5	51	1.27	405	10.2
$75,000 and above	45	1.97	104	4.53	27	1.19	282	12.31
Not reported	62	0.6	333	3.23	143	1.38	920	8.9
Age								
Under 25 years old	39	1.23	317	9.85	21	0.67	232	7.21
25–34 years old	99	1.43	588	8.44	80	1.14	532	7.64
35–44 years old	146	1.84	570	7.16	104	1.31	664	8.35
45–54 years old	91	1.16	463	5.93	133	1.71	610	7.8
55+ years old	144	0.62	979	4.21	693	2.98	1,680	7.23
Race								
White	360	1.11	1,833	5.62	599	1.84	2,649	8.13
African American	57	0.66	585	6.74	173	2	594	6.84
AIEA ,not Hispanic	9	2.08	31	6.82	12	2.55	40	8.81
API, not Hispanic	16	1.59	44	4.3	43	4.18	94	9.19
Hispanic	77	1.2	424	6.57	206	3.19	342	5.29
Gender								
Male	268	1.14	1,334	5.65	516	2.18	1,966	8.32
Female	252	0.98	1,583	6.19	516	2.02	1,752	6.85
Education								
Elementary: 0–8 years	32	0.54	234	3.91	284	4.75	370	6.19
Some high school: no diploma	61	0.81	412	5.43	186	2.46	417	5.51
High school diploma/GED	156	0.84	1,160	6.23	347	1.87	1,280	6.88
Some college	151	1.38	806	7.37	130	1.19	964	8.82
Bachelor's degree or more	120	1.98	306	5.03	84	1.38	686	11.29

Table 11.3   *Main Reasons for No Internet Use at Home, by Selected Characteristics of Reference Person (Numbers in Thousands) Total USA, 2001 (continued)*

	Computer Capability		No Computer in Household		Lack of Knowledge		Other	
	No.	%	No.	%	No.	%	No.	%
Household Type								
Married couple w/children <18 years old	149	2.28	448	6.83	88	1.35	547	8.34
Male householder w/children <18 years old	30	2.66	101	9.08	22	2.01	58	5.2
Female householder w/children <18 years old	72	1.43	458	9.12	30	0.59	274	5.45
Family household without children <18 years old	127	0.82	734	4.76	355	2.3	1,242	8.05
Nonfamily household	143	0.68	1,176	5.58	537	2.55	1,598	7.58
Employment								
Employed	382	1.52	1,775	7.08	327	1.31	2,039	8.13
Unemployed	5	0.33	137	9.71	34	2.45	85	6.04
Not in labor force	133	0.59	1,006	4.43	670	2.95	1,594	7.02
Region								
Northwest	71	0.78	461	5.07	161	1.77	792	8.72
Midwest	133	1.15	768	6.65	259	2.24	983	8.51
South	160	0.84	951	4.98	395	2.07	1,127	5.9
West	156	1.64	738	7.8	218	2.3	816	8.62

Source: A NATION ONLINE: How Americans Are Expanding Their Use of the Internet,. U.S. Census Bureau

11.5.2   Confidentiality concerns

Some households may choose not to have a home Internet connection because of confidentiality concerns. The September 2001 survey asked respondents if they were more or less concerned about their confidentiality over the Internet as compared with the telephone. It is important to note that although respondents reported being more concerned about their confidentiality over the Internet, the question was phrased in such a way that respondents did not rate the degree of concern but rather whether they were more or less concerned.

About half (50.9 percent) of respondents were more concerned about their confidentiality over the Internet compared with the telephone. About one-third (41.4 percent) of respondents reported their concerns were the same for both media, and 7.7 percent of respondents reported feeling less concern about confidentiality over the Internet compared with a telephone.

In terms of age, persons under 25 years old were the least concerned about their confidentiality over the Internet (36.0 percent), compared with those 55 years of age or older who were the most concerned (54.8 percent). A majority of respondents in the two age groups under 35 reported that they were either neutral or more concerned about the telephone. In contrast, a majority of respondents over 35 were more concerned about the Internet than were either neutral or more concerned about the telephone.

Examining gender revealed that females and males shared a similar level of concern about confidentiality over the Internet: 51.8 percent compared with 50.1 percent, respectively. Looking at household types, male-led households were least likely to be concerned about confidentiality over the Internet (41.4 percent), while female-led households were most concerned (54.9 percent). Male-led households were also most likely to respond that there was no difference in confidentiality between the two media (52.5 percent), compared with 38.0 percent of female-led household that reported that there was no difference.

11.5.3   Content concerns

Some households, particularly those with children under the age of 18, may choose not to have a home Internet connection because of the concern that the children may access inappropriate material. The September 2001 survey found that among households with children, 68.3 percent responded that compared with material on television, they were more concerned about the kind of material children may be exposed to on the Internet. This concern, however, did not translate into lower rates of Internet access among this group. Among those who thought the Internet was a source of more concern than television, 51.8 percent had Internet in the home as compared with 48.2 percent who did not subscribe to the Internet. Those who were less concerned (5.6 percent) or had similar concerns (26.1 percent) actually constituted a lower proportion of Internet households.

11.6   What IT professionals have done and can do about the divide

There are many activities, organizations, and programs in which IT professionals have participated to address the digital divide. One of the most organized events that IT professionals have participated in is NetDay. The mission of NetDay is to connect every child to a brighter future by helping educators meet educational goals through the effective use of technology.

11.6.1   NetDay

NetDay began in 1995 as a grassroots volunteer effort by companies, educators, families, and communities to wire the nation's K–12 classrooms for Internet access. The organization, headquartered in Irvine, California, was founded by John Gage from Sun Microsystems and Michael Kaufman from KQED. The first national wiring event was NetDay 96, in which over 100,000 volunteers, including President Clinton and Vice President Gore, rolled up their sleeves to wire 4,000 schools across the state on March 9, 1996. Contributions of materials, time, and technical know-how from Sun Microsystems and partners such as 3Com and Pacific Bell poured in. The effort was hailed as an innovative success in getting the private sector motivated to bring schools into the twenty-first century. The NetDay event continued to prosper for several years. (Visit on-line at www.netday.org.)

Sun Microsystems played a key role in founding NetDay and making it succeed. The company donated the initial funding to help start the NetDay nonprofit organization and has made large contributions to help get schools wired. Sun's corporate affairs department is offering Sun employees grants of $500 to $1,000 if the employees can get five or more Sun employees involved in wiring a school. Sun also dedicated two full-time and several part-time staff members' time for NetDay California on March 9, 1996.

The NetDay concept and model also flourished outside the United Sates, with events taking place in South Africa, South Korea, Australia, New Zealand, Germany, Sweden, the United Kingdom, and Canada.

The NetDay AmeriCorps Bridge (NAB) Program is a strategic partnership between NetDay and national service programs to provide selected empowerment zone communities with facilitated access to technology resources. Through collaboration with selected schools, corporate partners, and community organizations, the NetDay AmeriCorps Bridge members serve as program facilitators and teach constructive and educational technology-based programs both during school hours and through after-school programs.

NetDay AmeriCorps Bridge members receive training and professional development from NetDay on education technology and best practices for working with children and teachers in a classroom environment. NetDay AmeriCorps Bridge members are assigned to particular schools and classrooms and work directly with the teachers on classroom-specific projects. In addition, NetDay AmeriCorps Bridge members participate in local community service projects with other National Service projects.

A NetDay project coordinator administers the program in each community and is responsible for supervising the NetDay AmeriCorps Bridge members. The project coordinator is responsible for the school and community relationships, local partner development, member development, and program paperwork.

Besides the Corporation for National Service, other significant partners for this program include Camp Yahoo (providing materials in Spanish and English), WebTeacher (curriculum in Spanish and English), Lightspan, AOL@School, PowerUp (NetDay PowerUp sites in each operating location), Connect America, Points of Light Foundation, and America's Promise.

NetDayCompass.org is a noncommercial, free service with over 1,700 high-quality educational technology resources. With this on-line initiative, NetDay aims to provide education technology decision makers in K–12 schools with a valuable tool to utilize when making decisions about technology and its impact in the classroom.

Resources are categorized into five sections: technology planning, infrastructure, funding, classroom support, and real stories–best practices. Each section includes resources from industry, nonprofit organizations, trade associations, government agencies, media, universities, and K–12 schools. Features include the following:

- NetDayCompass.org. This is an interactive site with several features that encourage educators to share knowledge and provide input for the benefit of the whole community.

- Research Desk. An easy-to-use help desk allows educators to submit questions about education technology. NetDay research experts search for the answers and recommend resources and information as appropriate. Questions and answers are displayed in the "Research Desk" area and an archive of these FAQs is hosted on the site.

- Information Source. Simple codes clearly identify what type of organization is responsible for the content of each link listed on NetDay-Compass.org. These codes provide educators with another method to screen and evaluate on-line content for authenticity, applicability, authorship, bias, and usability.

- Rate a Resource. Visitors are encouraged to share thoughts on the usefulness of resources currently listed in NetDayCompass.org. Evaluations and comments are posted under the description of each resource. Resources that receive positive feedback from educators receive the "Educators' Choice" designation.

- Recommend a Resource. Visitors can suggest useful Web sites they have found helpful when integrating or using technology in education. NetDay's editorial staff reviews all submissions and incorporates suggestions that meet editorial guidelines.

- NetDayCompass Newsletter. This subscription-based e-newsletter shares innovative best practices from educators and offers tips, guidance, and a list of new resources available on NetDayCompass.org.

- News. A weekly collection of the latest education technology headlines helps educators and technology decision makers stay updated on education technology trends.

On March 31, 2001, in conjunction with the fifth anniversary activities of NetDay, leaders from education, community, industry, and government gathered at NetDay's National Leadership Summit on Education and Technology to share experiences and expertise on how to use technology effectively to achieve educational goals.

At this National Leadership Summit, participants began identifying the challenges today's school leaders face when integrating technology. NetDay is committed to developing a national campaign to work toward solutions and technology support mechanisms for superintendents, principals, and school board members. Goals that were set include:

- Facilitating discussions at national, state, and local levels on education technology leadership.

- Sharing good models of effective leadership that can be emulated.

- Providing opportunities for community stakeholders to collaborate in support of effective school leadership.

- Developing support mechanisms at the national, state, and local levels for education technology leaders.

■   Bridging the "leadership divide" through the effective dissemination of information and knowledge so that all communities can benefit from the Leadership Campaign.

NetDay's Leadership Campaign for Education Technology promotes effective leadership models through national, regional, and local conferences and an on-line campaign, as well as by increasing the public's awareness about the need to support school leaders with technology integration. A key element of this public service campaign will be Leadership Summits—nationally, regionally, and locally.

NetDay will host several on-line activities to support the facilitation of ideas and information exchanged at the national- and state-level summits. As the campaign begins in the fall of 2001, some on-line activities to be supported by NetDay include:

■   Leadership for Education Technology listserv

■   Special on-line forums on the specific educational technology leadership issues

■   On-line reference materials for further study and research, including the NetDay library and defining leadership

■   Publication of profiles in education technology leadership from our nation's K–12 schools

■   Showcase of model schools or school districts that are integrating technology into learning activities

One of NetDay's goals is to increase the public's awareness of the need to support school leaders and their efforts to utilize technology. NetDay will provide support for public awareness efforts for each element of the Leadership Campaign. Beginning with the first state-level summit, NetDay will promote communication efforts through print public service advertisements, news releases announcing campaign activities, facilitation of press interviews on education technology, and creation and circulation of opinion articles by influential leaders.

11.6.2   TECH CORPS

TECH CORPS is a national nonprofit organization that is funded through corporate contributions and implemented through state chapters. A national staff oversees the TECH CORPS mission and agenda, assists in the formation and maintenance of effective state chapters, provides a national media focus, and ensures quality at all levels. The broader organization is based on a bottom-up philosophy and draws on the expertise and enthusiasm of technology-literate members of the local community.

In 1995, Gary J. Beach, senior vice president of International Data Group and publisher of *CIO* magazine founded TECH CORPS. The organization is dedicated to improving K–12 education at the grassroots level by helping educators effectively use technology in their schools. TECH CORPS supports the advancement of equal access to technology, technological resources, and skills development for students across the United States. National Sponsors include Cisco Systems, Inc.; Compaq Computer Corporation; and Intel Corporation.

TECH CORPS distinguishes itself through its people, programs, and partnerships. It recruits, places, and supports the highest-quality volunteers from the technology community to advise and assist schools in the introduction and integration of new technologies into the educational system. It also brings new technology resources to schools through national and local programs and brings education and industry leaders together to share a common commitment to helping schools integrate technology effectively into their teaching and learning.

TECH CORPS provides many national programs, including the following:

- CyberEd—A classroom on wheels bringing technology training to educators, parents, and community leaders in urban communities nationwide (MCI).

- WebTeacher—A free, on-line Web training tool for teachers (National Cable Television Association).

- techs4schools—On-line technical support for K–12 schools (Compaq Computer Corporation).

- Internet Safety Training—Internet safety guidelines, mousepads, screen savers, and curriculum materials (National Center for Missing and Exploited Children and Dr. Scholl Foundation).

- Living Legacy Virtual Community—A program to encourage high school students across the country to construct Web-based oral histories and digital documents that tell the story of their respective communities (Intel).

The national TECH CORPS organization assists motivated local leaders from business and education in forming state chapters that develop programs that address the unique needs of their own schools and communities. The state chapters have a great deal of latitude within the TECH CORPS framework, and the programs they develop are as different as the states themselves. These few examples are not meant to reflect the total amount of work being done at the state level, but its diversity:

- Wisconsin and Georgia volunteers refurbish donated equipment, then provide the equipment and teacher training to the schools.

- Washington, DC, volunteers hold weekly workshops on Internet and networking basics for area teachers.

- Ohio volunteers partner with teachers and students to train student technology assistants, create Web sites, and enhance curriculum with technology tools.

- Arizona volunteers hold wiring events, provide teacher training, and have modernized the schools' media centers.

- New Jersey volunteers, in collaboration with Prudential, conducted Y2K workshops in the schools.

11.6.3   SeniorNet

SeniorNet is a nonprofit organization of computer-using adults, age 50 and older. SeniorNet's mission is to provide older adults education for and access to computer technologies. The organization has over 39,000 members, publishes a quarterly newsletter and a variety of instructional materials, has over 220 learning centers throughout the United States and offers discounts on computer-related and other products and services, and holds regional conferences and collaborates in research on older adults and technology. Many retired IT professionals are members of the organization or volunteer in the learning centers.

SeniorNet grew out of a research project funded by the Markle Foundation in 1986 to determine whether computers and telecommunications could enhance the lives of older adults. Based in San Francisco, SeniorNet is funded by membership dues, learning center fees, the altruistic donations of individuals, and the sponsorship of many companies and foundations.

SeniorNet operates SeniorNet Online on America Online (keyword: SeniorNet) and on the World Wide Web at http://www.seniornet.org, where all individuals 50 and older, whether or not they are members of SeniorNet, can participate in the hundreds of discussion topics offered on these sites. *Yahoo! Internet Life* magazine named SeniorNet one of the "100 Best Sites for 2001" and the Best Senior Community, which is the third consecutive year that SeniorNet has received the Best Sites award.

SeniorNet members learn and teach others to use computers and communications technologies to accomplish a variety of tasks. They learn to desktop publish anything from a newsletter to an autobiography, to manage personal and financial records, and to communicate with others across the country.

The majority of the 50+ population still lacks Internet access, trailing other age groups in Web use by a factor of 2:1, while the 65+ population trails those under age 30 by a factor of 5:1. SeniorNet's Bridging the Digital Divide Enrichment Center was established in 2001 to serve as a nexus for the study and discussion of this troubling disparity.

Funding for the Bridging the Digital Divide Enrichment Center was provided by the eBay Foundation and the Charles Schwab Corporate Foundation, two of SeniorNet's closest strategic partners. Previously, eBay had named SeniorNet the cornerstone sponsor of its Digital Opportunity for Seniors initiative, through which the eBay Foundation committed up to $1 million to SeniorNet and pledged to work with SeniorNet to bring at least 1 million older adults on-line over the next five years.

SeniorNet's Enrichment Centers integrate the strengths of the organization's on-line community with the expertise of partners and sponsors. Other Enrichment Center topics include healthy aging, investment education, technology trends, the Golden Age of Entertainment, and consumer education.

SeniorNet worked with IBM to make the Internet more accessible. IBM launched a unique pilot program with SeniorNet to enable the organization's members to tailor how they view Web pages according to the personal preferences of each user.

The end result will enable individuals to increase the size of the text on the Web pages they access, quiet a distracting background, turn off flashing images, change the color for better contrast, adjust the keyboard to overlook typing errors, and avoid other features that now make the Internet difficult for many seniors or people with disabilities.

The software, created by IBM engineers and Web accessibility experts in IBM's Research Division, is now being piloted at select SeniorNet classrooms across the country. IBM hopes to expand the pilot nationally next year via SeniorNet and other nonprofit organizations in the United States and abroad through IBM grants that benefit seniors and people with disabilities.

Preliminary work by IBM scientists revealed that one set of solutions would not satisfy all users. Thus, creating a technology application that allows individuals to customize how they view Web pages according to their individual needs emerged as the best solution. The software enables users to set their preferences and then stores the information. When an individual enters the URL for a Web page, the request goes through a computer that includes the software. The computer calls up the page and automatically reformats a copy of it according to the preference settings of the user. When the Web page appears on the screen, it's displayed to the individual with the type size and other qualities that make it more legible and accessible to the viewer. No change is made to the Web page itself.

This means individuals can set the best type size for their eyes, eliminate the background if that makes viewing easier, increase or decrease the color contrast of Web sites, sharpen digital images, and even halt the animated images that blink on and off or move across the screen and can distract some viewers with vision problems. Users with tremors or other motor difficulties can have their keyboards filter out repeated key strokes and other typing errors.

11.6.4   Association of Personal Computer User Groups

The Association of Personal Computer User Groups (APCUG) is an organization dedicated to helping member computer user groups succeed. The APCUG helps to foster communications by operating as an informal network between user group organizations and also with companies that provide computer-related and Internet-related goods and services.

The APCUG also assists member groups in the fulfillment of their educational missions and activities by sharing with officers of member user groups the knowledge of what it takes for user groups to better serve their members. Many of the member user groups have IT professionals as members who provide a wide variety of community services. They also have cooperative relationships with SeniorNet.

The APCUG has member groups in Australia, Austria, Belgium, Canada, Costa Rica, Croatia, Denmark, France, Germany, Guam, Hong Kong, Ireland, Italy, Japan, Mexico, Nepal, Netherlands, New Zealand, Philippines, Romania, Russia, South Africa, Switzerland, Taiwan, the United Kingdom, and the United States.

The APCUG provides a variety of services for user groups, including the following:

- A collection of information, including sample Articles of Incorporation and Bylaws to help new user groups to form.

- A database, with contact information, of vendors willing to provide software for product reviews and door prizes for programs, or who are willing to give presentations at user group meetings.

- *APCUG Reports* are published four times a year and copies are mailed to all APCUG member groups. This publication contains many articles to help officers do their jobs better.

- The APCUG Editorial Committee sends one or more articles each month by e-mail to all editors in APCUG member groups. The APCUG BBS contains some newsletter articles from other groups that can be used in group newsletters.

- A user groups locator.

- Web space and other Web services for user groups.

- In association with Hal PC, APCUG provides a User Group National Ad Program, which benefits vendors by giving them a single point of contact to place ads in many different user group newsletters at the same time.

- The Video Tape Committee maintains a list of tapes available via APCUG and information APCUG has about vendors' presentations in a box (self-presentation kits) or videos.

- APCUG First Edition CD, which provides low-cost shareware/freeware CDs to member user groups for resale or promotional purposes.

11.7 Developing support for dealing with the digital divide

Thousands of companies and tens of thousands of IT professionals have volunteered their time and have made contributions to schools and associations working to promote connectivity to the Internet and improve computer literacy. A great deal has been accomplished, but there is still a considerable amount of work to be done.

The existence of the digital divide is clearly documented. However, how an organization may benefit from continued participation in efforts to overcome the digital divide may not be as apparent as the divide itself. In addition, different types of organizations will reap different benefits.

The most compelling argument can be made to those companies that see e-commerce as a key part of their future. The more people that are computer literate, the broader the potential customer base will be for e-commerce. Other compelling arguments are that employees would require less training and be able to provide more value to their employers. Both of these are long-term benefits but are, nevertheless, results that will benefit most organizations.

11.7.1   Taking steps to deal with the digital divide

There are many things that an organization can do to support the effort to overcome the digital divide. However, each organization must decide what works best for its specific situation and geographical location. Actions that have been successful for many organizations include:

- Contributing funds or equipment to local and regional programs

- Providing internships for local schools that have information technology programs

- Sponsoring career days for students attending local schools

- Supporting the efforts of employees to participate in outreach programs of local professional programs

- Developing incentives for employees to volunteer in hands-on local efforts

- Providing speakers for local events

It is important to recognize that every contribution is valuable. Each of these efforts requires different levels of commitment. Organizations that have the financial ability to contribute funds should do so. Those that do not have financial resources can concentrate their efforts on getting employees to participate in local efforts through their existing volunteer or community involvement programs.

Organizing for Socially Responsible Information Technology Management

Management by objective works—if you know the objectives.
Ninety percent of the time you don't.

—Peter F. Drucker

12.1 Departments responsible for establishing policies

It is critical to establish policies and the organizational areas of responsibility implementing the procedures. In many cases several departments in an organization will play a role in implementing the different principles. This chapter provides a high-level view of how to organize and assign responsibilities to achieve goals in each area of social responsibility.

Policy development procedures can be complicated and time consuming. The best way to streamline the process of policy development is to assign a knowledgeable staff person in each department to review any existing policies, draft a new policy if necessary, and submit the new policy to department managers for approval. The policies should be written in a straightforward manner and identify departments that have responsibility for implementing procedures to support the policies.

In all areas the IT department should play a key role in setting policies. The legal department or corporate counsel should be involved in privacy and intellectual property management issues. The human resources department (HR) will probably need to be involved in compensation for IT workers and setting policies on training computer users.

The public relations (PR) department should be involved in establishing corporate policies for support efforts to reduce the digital divide. The pur-

Table 12.1   *Departments Responsible for Establishing Policies*

Principle	IT	Legal	HR	PR	Purchasing	Facilities Management
Appropriately staff IT departments	X					
Fairly compensate IT workers	X		X			
Adequately train computer users	X		X			
Provide ergonomic user environments	X				X	X
Maintain secure and virus-free computer systems	X					
Safeguard the privacy of information	X	X				
Ethically manage intellectual property	X	X				
Utilize energy-efficient technology	X				X	X
Properly recycle used computer equipment	X					X
Support efforts to reduce the digital divide	X			X		

chasing department should be involved in policy making for ergonomic user environments and for utilizing energy-efficient technology. The facilities management department should be involved in policy making for ergonomic user environments, for utilizing energy-efficient technology, and for properly recycling used computer equipment. Table 12.1 shows which department should have a role in establishing policies to implement the ten principles of socially responsible IT management.

12.2   Departments responsible for implementing procedures

Once policies have been established, the process of implementing procedures to achieve socially responsible IT management will fall on a wide variety of departments. Table 12.2 shows which departments will be responsible for implementing procedures. The role of each department in implementing procedures is as follows:

- The IT department will bear the largest burden in appropriately staffing IT departments and fairly compensating IT workers, but support from the HR department will be critical to achieve success.

Table 12.2   *Departments Responsible for Implementing Procedures*

Principle	IT	Legal	HR	PR	Training	Purchasing	Facilities Management
Appropriately staff IT departments	X		X				
Fairly compensate IT workers	X		X				
Adequately train computer users	X		X	X			
Provide ergonomic user environments	X		X	X	X		X
Maintain secure and virus-free computer systems	X		X	X			
Safeguard the privacy of information	X	X	X	X			
Ethically manage intellectual property	X	X	X	X			
Utilize energy-efficient technology						X	X
Properly recycle used computer equipment			X		X		X
Support efforts to reduce the digital divide	X		X	X			

- To adequately train computer users the IT department will help identify training needs and develop training materials, the HR department will help monitor and track training that has occurred for each employee, and the training department will provide the training.

- To provide ergonomic user environments the IT department can help identify ergonomic solutions for information technology; the training department can work with IT, purchasing, and facilities management to develop training on ergonomics for all employees; the purchasing department will acquire ergonomic equipment; and the facilities management department will install and manage ergonomic office equipment.

- To maintain secure and virus-free computer systems the IT department will identify enabling technologies and practices and help develop training materials, the HR department will help monitor and track training that has occurred for each employee, and the training department will provide the training.

- To safeguard the privacy of information the IT department will identify enabling technologies and assist the legal department in developing training materials, the HR department will help monitor and track training that has occurred for each employee, and the training department will provide the training.

- To ethically manage intellectual property the IT department will identify enabling technologies and assist the legal department in developing training materials, the HR department will help monitor and track training that has occurred for each employee, and the training department will provide the training.

- To utilize energy-efficient technology the IT department will help to identify equipment that can be replaced with newer systems, the purchasing department will manage the acquisition of new equipment in accordance with enterprise policies, and the facilities management department will help install equipment and maintain or provide any necessary physical changes in office space to accommodate new equipment.

- To properly recycle used computer equipment the surplus property staff of the facilities management department will handle disposition of equipment and help to develop training materials, the HR department will help monitor and track training that has occurred for each employee, and the training department will provide the training.

To support efforts to reduce the digital divide the IT department will work with the HR and PR departments to develop corporate volunteer or contribution programs to support community or national efforts.

12.3 Achieving organization buy-in and beyond

All organizational development or change efforts face the challenge of achieving buy-in across the organization. Socially responsible information technology management programs will likely also face some challenges. However, the challenges will not be difficult to overcome if there is a strong internal and external PR effort to support the program. Socially responsible information technology management can be turned into a feel-good program. In addition, PR programs can gain almost automatic support because of several social trends, including the following:

- There is continued and growing concern about privacy in the United States and around the world. As a result, customers want to trust the organizations they do business with or have some sort of relationship with.

- There is growing concern about computer security and a perception that the Internet is causing many security problems. As a result, people, in general, feel good about things that they think will make them safer.

- Environmental protection through energy conservation and proper recycling is a popular movement, especially among younger people. As a result, people want to feel that they are making some effort to lessen their impact on the environment.

- The digital divide and ergonomics have become news items during the past three years, but most people do not really understand these issues or how to address them. However, they are recognized as problems, and people like to feel that they are socially good.

- Since the terrorist attacks of September 11, 2001, the population, in general, has become supportive of social responsibility and doing things that are good for people.

The most suitable PR effort to support a socially responsible information technology management program will be centered on the positive impact that the program can have inside the organization and in society at large.

It is important that the organization start building awareness of its socially responsible information technology management efforts early in the process. In-house media campaigns are helpful in achieving this goal, as is enterprise-wide training. Media campaigns can include articles in employee newsletters, postings on enterprise intranets, and posters on bulletin boards.

This is the type of work that public relations people are really good at. Because it can take a long time to get such campaigns rolling, awareness building should start during the early stages of the development and planning process. The major obstacles to implementing an effective awareness campaign are securing adequate funding and having an experienced communications staff to work on the campaign.

The funding required to accomplish an awareness campaign will, of course, depend on the size of an organization and its geographical characteristics. The goal of the awareness campaign is to reach all of the employees in an enterprise. If there are existing communications processes established, such as newsletters, annual or quarterly meetings, and intranets, it will be less expensive to launch the awareness campaign because the company can take advantage of the infrastructure already in place.

Regardless of whether an organization uses in-house or external staff it is important that the communications staff working on the campaign have experience in awareness-building efforts. If an organization is using in-house staff, it should send communications staff to training on awareness building if necessary. If the organization is using outside agencies, it should select an agency with demonstrated experience in awareness building.

12.4 Maintaining momentum in socially responsible information technology management

Developing an appropriate socially responsible information technology management program and successfully implementing it requires support from all departments in an organization. Executives need to bear in mind that the staff whose contribution to the project is absolutely essential will also have other tasks that need to be done. In some cases these critical contributions may run counter to the workload and departmental goals. This means that the process may often be pushed to the back burner or overridden by projects that team members feel are more important.

In some cases staff may not be able to meet all of their goals. If work on the socially responsible information technology management program impacts their ability to complete other tasks and that may impact their compensation, then it is likely that team members will pursue the work that they see as the most beneficial to them as individuals. This is basic human nature, and it is up to the organization's executives to keep the process moving and strike a balance between the various sources of pressure that employees may face.

Executives can play an important role in assuring that the planning and implementation process does not get ignored or slighted in the face of other organizational demands. Executives should take the following action steps to assure that the development of appropriate policies and procedures continues at an acceptable speed in their organization:

- Appoint an executive-level manager to oversee and to act as champion for the development of socially responsible information technology management programs.

- Schedule regular meetings with the directors of the various departments that have policy development or implementation responsibilities.

- Recognize the achievement of the staff who worked on the socially responsible information technology management programs at appropriate organizational events, retreats, or meetings.

12.5   The C-level emissaries

Executives are ultimately responsible for leading the development of policies and plans in their organizations. Middle -level managers will do most of
detailed and day-to-day work to analyze needs and develop procedures.
However, executive-level managers play an essential role in the communications process that no other person can perform—they serve as high-level
emissaries to boards of directors, investors, business partners, the general
public, and the media on behalf of the enterprise. This means that executives must understand and be able to readily articulate the philosophy and
policies of the socially responsible information technology management
efforts of an organization.

In many ways the executive is the embodiment of the enterprise. Executives represent their organizations in a way that no other employees can possibly accomplish. This is due in part to status and expectation, but it is
mostly due to the type of functions and events that executives attend and at
which they represent their organizations. They need to be able to serve as
high-level emissaries in a variety of public settings and do so in a manner
that helps to effectively position the organization in a positive light to each
of their audiences.

Organizations should take the following action steps to prepare the executive management team to discuss the socially responsible information
technology management efforts of their organization:

- Establish a briefing process for upper managers on the ongoing development of socially responsible information technology management
  policies and procedures.

- Develop appropriate statements on the organization's socially responsible information technology management policies and procedures
  for executives to deliver to different audiences, including the board of
  directors, investors, the media, business partners, and the general
  public.

- Determine the appropriate persons in their organizations to refer
  detailed questions to regarding socially responsible information technology management policies and procedures and assure that all executives know where they refer outside parties who have questions.

Much of this information will be made available to executives during the
training process that is an integral part of the implementation process. The
executive-level training sessions for socially responsible information technology management policies and procedures should take less than two

hours to conduct. The key points that executives should learn from training are as follows:

- The effort that has been put forth in developing socially responsible information technology management policies and procedures

- The ten principles of socially responsible information technology management

- The basics of socially responsible information technology management policies and procedures developed by the organization

- How to make decisions based on the enterprise philosophy toward socially responsible information technology management

- How to conduct business negotiations in accordance with socially responsible information technology management policies and procedures

- What employees should do when confronted with new situations

It is advisable that key public relations personnel and legal counsel attend the briefings to make sure that executives are aware of the issues they should address when discussing socially responsible information technology management policies and procedures with the board of directors, investors, the media, business partners, and the general public. Executives should be provided with a list of staff people they can call and discuss socially responsible information technology management issues with to help them prepare to addresses a specific audience about socially responsible information technology management issues.

As executives interact with representatives from other organizations during the course of business and even in social situations, they should convey a consistent and uniform message about enterprise socially responsible information technology management policies and procedures. The substance of these messages can surely be reinforced during the training process, but it is prudent to have agreed-on statements that executives should make. In general, any statement that executives make regarding socially responsible information technology management policies and procedures the organization is undertaking should be relatively short and to the point.

It is important to have at least one comeback to deal with likely questions. The most likely question is: Have you had any socially responsible information technology management problems? The response should be simple and to the point: We have not experienced any problems, but as our business model and the business climate evolve we want to make sure that we are taking appropriate steps to address our social responsibilities in information technology management.

An alternative question or sometimes a second question in such discussions often focuses on the general position of an organization toward the ten principles of socially responsible information technology management. Executives should respond: Of course we respect the ten principles of socially responsible information technology management and our efforts are focused on assuring that all of our operations are consistent in the way they deal with the ten principles.

12.6   Communicating with the board and investors

Executives are responsible for briefing the board of directors on the policies of an organization. During the development of socially responsible information technology management policies and procedures, executives should be prepared to inform the board of the status of the process. If the board does take an interest in the details, it is recommended that the director of the IT department prepare a brief, seven- to ten-minute presentation to the board that covers the high points of the implementation process.

The investor relations department and staff can work with executives to prepare a brief overview of socially responsible information technology management policies and procedures that can be made available to investors on the corporate Web page. In the event that there is an investor meeting that takes place on a scheduled basis, the investor relations staff should work with executives to determine the extent of information about socially responsible information technology management that should be included in information packets distributed to attendees. Investors should also be supplied with a telephone number to make further inquires. It is advisable that investors first speak with the investor relations staff, who can then collect information and make sure that investors are receiving consistent answers to their questions.

12.7   The message to take to the media and the general public

Executives are constantly confronted with questions from the media, and, as they attend various functions and meetings, they may need to deal with questions from the general public. Responses to media and public questions should be short and to the point, just as they are when executives deal with the board of directors, investors, and business partners. Detailed questions should be referred to appropriate public relations staff.

The purpose of this approach is not to obfuscate policies or positions but rather to avoid putting executives in a position where they attempt to convey details that they are not responsible for knowing right off the top of their head. This approach will make things easier for the executives as well as help to assure that the media and the public receive consistent answers to questions.

In the event that an organization decides to take a high profile about its socially responsible information technology management policies and procedures, a general press conference or briefing can be held, and all comments that are to be made by executives should be predetermined. Comments can be prepared and reviewed through the joint efforts of the public relations department and legal counsel.

Table 12.3   *Data on the Status of Socially Responsible Information Technology Management Efforts from the IT Department*

Principle	Data Provided
Appropriately staff IT departments	Changes in IT staffing and resulting improvements in operations and service delivery
Fairly compensate IT workers	Changes in IT staff compensation and resulting improvements in reduced turnover, changes in recruitment efforts, and improvements in employee morale
Adequately train computer users	Impact of training on help-desk requests and end-user problems reported
Provide ergonomic user environments	The types of new equipment reviewed and approved
Maintain secure and virus-free computer systems	The impact on security problems and the proliferation of viruses in the organization
Safeguard the privacy of information	Any problems that occurred with privacy protection and how the problems were addressed
Ethically manage intellectual property	Any problems that occurred with intellectual property management protection and how the problems were addressed
Utilize energy-efficient technology	Not applicable
Properly recycle used computer equipment	Not applicable
Support efforts to reduce the digital divide	Efforts in which IT staff have been involved and the results of those efforts

12.8   Periodic reviews of the status of socially responsible information technology management efforts

It is advisable to have a periodic review of the status of socially responsible information technology management efforts. The various departments involved in implementation can create their own status reports, and these reports can be compiled into an enterprise report by the PR department. In addition to compiling the enterprise report, the PR department should be responsible for compiling data on contributions made by the organization to community or national efforts to deal with the digital divide.

Data to be included in the IT department's report should include the impact of staffing and compensation changes, the new types of ergonomic

Table 12.4   *Data on the Status of Socially Responsible Information Technology Management Efforts from the HR and Training Departments*

Principle	HR	Training
Appropriately staff IT departments	Changes in policy on IT staffing within the central IT department or business units	Not applicable
Fairly compensate IT workers	Changes in compensation policies	Not applicable
Adequately train computer users	The number of employees trained during the reporting period	The type of training provided during the reporting period
Provide ergonomic user environments	Not applicable	The type of training provided during the reporting period
Maintain secure and virus-free computer systems	The number of employees trained during the reporting period	The type of training provided during the reporting period
Safeguard the privacy of information	The number of employees trained during the reporting period	The type of training provided during the reporting period
Ethically manage intellectual property	The number of employees trained during the reporting period	The type of training provided during the reporting period
Utilize energy-efficient technology	Not applicable	Not applicable
Properly recycle used computer equipment	The number of employees trained during the reporting period	The type of training provided during the reporting period
Support efforts to reduce the digital divide	The involvement of organizational staff in community or national efforts	Not applicable

equipment approved, and any problems that have occurred with privacy or intellectual property management protection and how the problems were addressed. Table 12.3 shows the data on the status of socially responsible information technology management efforts from the IT department.

Data that should be included in the HR and training departments' reports should include the number of employees trained during the reporting period and the type of training provided during the reporting period. Table 12.4 shows the data on the status of socially responsible information technology management efforts from the HR and training departments.

Data that should be included in the purchasing and facility management departments' reports should include the type of ergonomic equipment purchased and in use during the reporting period as well as the number of systems recycled during the reporting period. Table 12.5 shows the data on the status of socially responsible information technology management efforts of the purchasing and facilities management departments.

Table 12.5   *Data on the Status of Socially Responsible Information Technology Management Efforts from the Purchasing and Facilities Management Departments*

Principle	Purchasing	Facilities Management
Appropriately staff IT departments	Not applicable	Not applicable
Fairly compensate IT workers	Not applicable	Not applicable
Adequately train computer users	Not applicable	Not applicable
Provide ergonomic user environments	The type of equipment purchased and in use during the reporting period	The number of work areas reconfigured during the reporting period
Maintain secure and virus-free computer systems	Not applicable	Not applicable
Safeguard the privacy of information	Not applicable	Not applicable
Ethically manage intellectual property	Not applicable	Not applicable
Utilize energy-efficient technology	The type of equipment purchased and in use during the reporting period	The impact on energy costs during the reporting period
Properly recycle used computer equipment	Not applicable	The number of systems recycled during the reporting period
Support efforts to reduce the digital divide	Not applicable	Not applicable

13

The Future of Socially Responsible Information Technology Management

The illiterate of the twenty-first century will not be those who cannot read and write, but those who cannot learn, unlearn, and relearn.

—Alvin Toffler

13.1 Expected government and manufacturer action

The proposition that end-user organizations bear such a heavy burden in addressing the social responsibility issues of information technology management is very discouraging to many organizations. Although there are economic benefits to socially responsible information technology management, achieving that benefit requires time and resources and, more important, it requires that an organization focus on the effort. This in turn may distract from other things that could benefit an organization.

The question as to when there will be better products from technology producers is constantly asked. This is especially true when it comes to the production of more secure systems and software, which has been an international concern since the terrorist attacks of September 11, 2001. Another key question is: When will governments start taking action against technology manufacturers, requiring better products or imposing liability for poorly designed products with flaws that can be exploited by hackers or virus writers?

Government actions are certainly political. Opposing political parties usually have different views on how to deal with social issues and legal liabilities, as was demonstrated by the Bush administration's efforts to overturn the work of the Clinton administration on ergonomics. Table 13.1

Table 13.1   *Type of Government Action Expected to Address Socially Responsible Information Technology Management*

Principle	Type of Government Action Expected	When Action Is Expected
Appropriately staff IT departments	Owners of information technology will be held responsible for meeting minimum standards to protect security and privacy.	After 2010
Fairly compensate IT workers	Not applicable	—
Adequately train computer users	Not applicable	—
Provide ergonomic user environments	OSHA has implemented a new program to replace regulations proposed by Clinton administration.	2002–2003
Maintain secure and virus-free computer systems	Vendors will be required to meet minimum standards for security and start facing product liability.	2005
Safeguard the privacy of information	Continued privacy legislation will be enacted around the world.	In progress and ongoing
Ethically manage intellectual property	Increased investigation activity by law enforcement will occur.	In progress and ongoing
Utilize energy-efficient technology	Programs similar to ENERGY STAR are being replicated around the world.	In progress and ongoing
Properly recycle used computer equipment	Regulations on recycling are being imposed.	2004–2005
Support efforts to reduce the digital divide	Computer literacy programs are being improved around the world.	In progress and ongoing

shows the author's opinion about the type of government action expected to address socially responsible information technology management and when those actions will occur.

There are many socially responsible information technology management programs in place around the world. In addition, many countries are starting to replicate programs that have been successful in other countries. There have been numerous efforts to reduce the digital divide, utilize more energy-efficient technology, and better safeguard the privacy of information—efforts that have been successful and are still ongoing.

On the other hand, efforts to ethically manage intellectual property are strongly tied to the economic conditions in specific countries. There will be little if any progress in countries that have very low per-capita incomes in

Table 13.2   *Type of Manufacturer Action Expected to Address Socially Responsible Information Technology Management*

Principle	Type of Manufacturer Action Expected	When Action Is Expected
Appropriately staff IT departments	Develop better applications that require less staff to maintain and operate	In progress and ongoing
Fairly compensate IT workers	Not applicable	—
Adequately train computer users	Develop applications that require less training and have better help and tutorial systems	In progress and ongoing
Provide ergonomic user environments	Produce more ergonomic out-of-the-box technology and components	Slowly progressing
Maintain secure and virus-free computer systems	Develop more secure systems and software	Slowly progressing
Safeguard the privacy of information	Develop more secure systems and software	Slowly progressing
Ethically manage intellectual property	Create better protection for digital properties	In progress and ongoing
Utilize energy-efficient technology	Produce more energy-efficient out-of-the-box technology and components	In progress and ongoing
Properly recycle used computer equipment	Produce out-of-the-box technology and components that are easier to recycle	Slowly progressing
Support efforts to reduce the digital divide	Produce less expensive out-of-the-box technology and components	Slowly progressing

addressing piracy. In fact many of these countries will continue to openly support piracy as a means of improving economic conditions.

When it comes to technology manufacturers improving their products, there is considerable anger and disappointment on the part of technology managers. The process of maintaining patches to systems and applications is time consuming and costly. The necessity for add-on security and anti-virus products is also costly and time consuming. Table 13.2 shows the author's opinion about the actions manufacturers are expected to take to address socially responsible information technology management and when those actions will occur.

The development of better applications that require less staff to maintain and operate, the creation of better protection for digital properties, and the production of more energy-efficient out-of-the-box technology and components is in progress and ongoing. Technology manufacturers are moving at a steady pace in achieving these goals. However, these goals occupy third or maybe even fourth place compared with efforts to gain market share and maintain profits.

The critical need for more secure systems is slowly progressing. Since the September 11, 2001, terrorist attacks, the information technology sector has come under pressure from governments, consumer groups, and large end-user organizations to improve security. There has been considerable rhetoric about social responsibility and product liability.

However, the shrink-wrap software industry and the off-the-shelf computer manufacturers have been in the same mode since the early 1980s. The main goal is to get an expensive product to market as fast as possible. These goals run counter to the need for secure systems for two reasons. First, secure information technology products take longer to develop and bring to market. Second, secure information technology products will cost more to produce and will be more expensive for the end user to purchase.

When it comes to producing less expensive out-of-the-box technology and components that may contribute to reduce the digital divide, progress is also slow. In addition, the demand for more secure products will likely slow the decline in technology product prices. This, in turn, will prolong the existence of the digital divide.

13.2 ISO 14001 and the future of information technology

One of the most important environmental developments affecting business is the new standard for environmental management, ISO 14001. This standard is being increasingly adopted or considered by many companies worldwide, with considerable activity in major sectors such as the motor and electronics industries. ISO 14001 is a standard that influences both the environmental impact of manufacturing processes and the environmental impact of the product being manufactured. A major goal of ISO 14001 is to produce products that have reduced environmental impact.

ISO 14001 is an accredited international standard for environmental management systems. It was launched in September 1996 as the main standard within the ISO 14000 series of environmental standards. Key features are as follows:

- It is a voluntary standard overseen, like quality and other standards, through national standards organizations.

- Certification applies to a site or an identifiably managed organization.

- Third-party certification assessment is by accredited commercial certification bodies.

- Maintaining certification requires periodic (six-month or annual) surveillance assessments.

- An ISO 14001 system consists of the generic environmental management system with an emphasis on regulatory compliance and commitment to continuous improvement of environmental performance.

- It has some similarities to ISO 9000 and may cross-reference to or employ elements of existing quality or safety systems. However, it requires a distinct system for environmental management and specific elements of an environmental management system (EMS) (e.g., an environmental policy, evaluation of environmental effects and aspects, identification of environmental regulations).

The standard requires the inclusion within the system of significant aspects that the organization can control or influence. These can include materials or purchased product sourcing, product use, and disposal. Accordingly life-cycle effects relating to product design decisions need to be identified and, where they are considered significant and technically and economically feasible, objectives and targets need to be set for improved performance. The key elements of ISO 14001 relating to an EMS are as follows:

- Senior management commitment to improved environmental performance

- A company policy statement that communicates this commitment

- A summary or register of the environmental effects or aspects of the company with supporting information or data (air emissions; waste water discharges; use of energy, water, and other natural resources)

- A summary of relevant regulations with a process for keeping abreast of new regulatory requirements.

- Objectives, targets, and programs for improvement in relation to effects and aspects defined as significant

- Defined environmental responsibilities for all managers and others influencing environmental performance

- Appropriate levels of awareness and training to fulfill responsibilities

- Formal documented procedures and work instructions for controlling or improving performance or avoiding deterioration; also, mechanisms for prompt corrective action.

When applying ISO 14001 the concept of eco-design should be considered in the broadest sense of design decision making, not just the technical design process. Success requires a multifunctional, integrated team approach to help ensure effective links between management systems, organizational functions and business, product designs, and manufacturing processes.

13.3   Forces that drive change

We have come beyond the point where technologists drive information technology. There are now many social, political, and economic forces that drive changes in how information technology will be developed and how information technology will be used in the future. I have analyzed the progression of these forces of change for over a decade and have made presentations around the world about how these forces will impact the Internet and the definition of social responsibility for information technology. The 2002 analysis of the ten forces of change include:

- The global response. The impact and the use of the Internet have been discussed at the highest level of government and policy making around the world. The global nature of the Internet has come into conflict with local laws that govern content and commerce. Many countries, including France, China, and Saudi Arabia, are leading a backlash against openness as they attempt to control the World Wide Web.

- Growing linguistic, cultural, and physical diversity. Internet use will increase around the world, across cultures, and span a wider range of educational and economic strata. The U.S. federal government, for example, is now starting to address the usability of information technology for people with physical limitations.

- The evolution of privacy as a social and legal demand. On the Internet, privacy can be easily compromised and is bought and sold on a daily basis. Social, political, and legal pressures are mounting because of the cross-border nature of the Internet and thousands of pending laws in countries around the world.

- The process of defining and controlling access. The digital divide; Internet access in public facilities, libraries, schools; and the personal use of the Internet in the workplace, as well as the use of wireless

Internet devices in classroom settings, are now boardroom and town hall issues. Religious groups and national governments also want to control access to the Internet. The concept of access is constantly being redefined.

- The inevitability of taxation of Internet commerce. Taxation will come to Internet commerce in full force because national, regional, and local governments want revenue. International, intrastate, and local tax laws need to be addressed.

- The pattern of cyber law and disorder. Military, industrial, and commercial infrastructures have been the target of thousands of random attacks, and organized attacks are inevitable. The military and telecommunications firms are preparing, but e-commerce companies remain highly vulnerable. The use of the Internet to support criminal activity is a natural evolution in criminal behavior. Law enforcement agencies around the world face the challenge of investigating, prosecuting, and combating crime, and they need help from service providers.

- The realization of strategic turmoil. Strategic direction (how to best use the Internet) for business, entrepreneurs, government, nonprofit organizations, and Web developers will remain a moving target. Technologies and consumer response will continue to evolve. The best strategy of today can turn into a liability overnight. The most radical experiment can quickly become a standard strategy and just as quickly devolve into mediocrity.

- The conflict between bands, channels, platforms, and formats. What is the Internet: modems, DSL, cable connections, ITV, wireless, voice, images, or all of the above? Development demands and creative approaches will burst open, making the Web guru of the middle 1990s a dinosaur.

- The crowded Web from the user's perspective. Whether you are surfing or seeking, the Web is a mess. Search engines are a pain, and their usability has sharply declined. A search term often yields over 100,000 pages of results. What sites do people visit? The ones they know! And how do they know the ones they know?

- The crowded Web from the purveyor's perspective. The population of companies on the Web will continue to grow, and competition in all niches will increase. Investors in Internet companies will put more pressure on developers to create unique and more marketable applications and services.

Table 13.3   *How the Forces of Change Impact Socially Responsible Information Technology Management*

Principle	The Impact of the Ten Forces of Change
Appropriately staff IT departments	Strategic turmoil and the conflict between bands, channels, platforms, and formats require more highly qualified IT staff to meet the needs of organizations.
Fairly compensate IT workers	
Adequately train computer users	Growing linguistic, cultural, and physical diversity increases the need for better training and accessibility to computing.
Provide ergonomic user environments	Not applicable
Maintain secure and virus-free computer systems	Patterns of cyber law and disorder, and the process of defining and controlling access accentuates the requirement for more secure systems.
Safeguard the privacy of information	The evolution of privacy as a social and legal demand requires more attention be given to privacy protection.
Ethically manage intellectual property	The global response, both negative and positive illustrates the need for local solutions to global problems caused by information technology.
Utilize energy-efficient technology	Not applicable
Properly recycle used computer equipment	Not applicable
Support efforts to reduce the digital divide	Growing linguistic, cultural, and physical diversity increases and the crowded Web illustrate the need to reduce the digital divide for individual, social, and economic, growth.

Each of these forces of change helps to illustrate why one or more of the principles of socially responsible information technology management is important to address. Principle three—adequately train computer users—is influenced by growing linguistic, cultural, and physical diversity, which drives the need for better training and accessibility to computing.

Principle five—maintain secure and virus-free computer systems—is more important because of the patterns of cyber law and disorder. Table

13.3 shows how the forces of change impact and drive the need for socially responsible information technology management.

13.4   The impact of major events

Computer Economics has studied the economic impact of virus attacks on information systems around the world for several years. In 2000 this impact amounted to $17.1 billion. Economic impact is measured by the costs to clean viruses from networks, servers, and client systems; the costs to restore lost or damaged files; and the lost productivity of workers caused by system outages and downtime.

The "Love Bug" attacks, including the more than 40 variants of the virus that rampaged through systems worldwide in May 2000, caused the largest impact in 2000 and in history (so far). Many variants of the "Love Bug" were still hitting systems at the end of 2000. Computer Economics estimated that the economic impact of the "Love Bug" was $8.7 billion. There was considerable debate about this analysis. While Lloyds of London estimated that the economic impact of the "Love Bug" was $15 billion, others remained skeptical as to how analysts can establish such impact numbers.

Regardless of the debate over the amount of impact, the "Love Bug" attacks drove up the awareness for the need for virus protection on computers. The attacks also illustrated the increased vulnerability that Internet connectivity has created for the wired world. With each virus attack and with each new worm or virus design. public awareness increases. When the "Love Bug," "Nimda," or "Code Red" ate their way through an organization's computers, information technology managers had far less difficulty convincing those who fund their efforts to spend money for virus protection.

Cyber crime, fraud, and the use of computers in criminal activities are on the rise. This has prompted considerable government action. In the fall of 2001, in an agreement that more than doubles global spending to combat cyber crime, Computer Sciences Corporation won a task-order contract to support the Department of Defense (DoD) Computer Investigations Training Program (DCITP). The eight-year contract, awarded by the General Services Administration's Federal Systems Integration and Management Center, is valued at more than $86 million if all options are exercised.

Under the contract, Computer Sciences Corporation will assist the DoD in researching, developing, and delivering state-of-the-art computer investigation training courses for military law enforcement professionals. Courses will cover computer search and seizure, computer intrusions, and forensic computer media analysis to support the prosecution of criminal activities and execution of counterintelligence actions.

Under the contract, approximately 35 Computer Sciences Corporation computer investigators and forensics specialists, computer security specialists, and information technology (IT) training professionals will work at the DCITP's state-of-the-art training facility located in Linthicum, Maryland. The DCITP provides computer investigation training to law enforcement individuals and DoD elements that must ensure that information systems are secure from unauthorized use, counterintelligence, and criminal and fraudulent activities.

13.5   Major events on the horizon

In my book entitled *Information Warfare: How to Survive Cyber Attacks*, I discuss the emergence and evolution of cyber warfare and cyber terrorism. Many agree with this prediction and are preparing now for the future.

The landfills of the world are being piled high with technology waste, and the computer recycling cottage industry in China is causing considerable pollution. These trends show that the proper recycling of information technology is critical.

Future events that drive home the need for socially responsible information technology management are easily predictable. But predictions do not always prompt social action. On the other hand, once bitten (it sometimes takes two or three times) societies do respond. This is fortunate in some ways. It is better to respond late than never to respond.

How long it will take to achieve socially responsible information technology management is not predictable. However, the need for socially responsible information technology management is undeniable at this point. Hopefully the events that prompt action will not take an extremely high human toll.

Index